# The Writer's Eye

**ALSO PUBLISHED BY BLOOMSBURY**

*The Bloomsbury Introduction to Creative Writing*, Tara Mokhtari
*The Geek's Guide to the Writing Life*, Stephanie Vanderslice

# The Writer's Eye

## Observation and Inspiration for Creative Writers

Amy E. Weldon

BLOOMSBURY ACADEMIC
LONDON • NEW YORK • OXFORD • NEW DELHI • SYDNEY

BLOOMSBURY ACADEMIC
Bloomsbury Publishing Plc
50 Bedford Square, London, WC1B 3DP, UK

BLOOMSBURY, BLOOMSBURY ACADEMIC and the Diana logo are trademarks of
Bloomsbury Publishing Plc

First published in Great Britain 2018

Cover design: Hugh Cowling

A catalogue record for this book is available from the British Library.

Library of Congress Cataloging-in-Publication Data
Names: Weldon, Amy, author.
Title: The writer's eye : observation and inspiration forcreative writers /
Amy Weldon.
Description: London ; New York : Bloomsbury Academic, 2018. |
Includes bibliographical references and index.
Identifiers: LCCN 2017056559 (print) | LCCN 2018013945 (ebook) |
ISBN 9781350025325 (ePUB) | ISBN 9781350025332 (ePDF) | ISBN 9781350025301
(pbk. : alk.paper)
Subjects: LCSH: Authorship. | Creative writing.
Classification: LCC PN145 (ebook) | LCC PN145 .W3775 2018 (print) |
DDC 808.02–dc23
LC record available at https://lccn.loc.gov/2017056559

ISBN:   HB:     978-1-3500-2531-8
            PB:     978-1-3500-2530-1
            ePDF:  978-1-3500-2533-2
            eBook : 978-1-3500-2532-5

Typeset by Integra Software Services Pvt. Ltd.
Printed and bound in Great Britain

To find out more about our authors and books visit www.bloomsbury.com
and sign up for our newsletters.

*For my father*

# Contents

# List of Figures

# Acknowledgments

## Thanks to:

My students: current, former, and future.

David Avital, Clara Herberg, and Mark Richardson of Bloomsbury.

Patrick Hicks, Jerry Johnson, Molly Kelley, and Nick-Mike Hentges.

For illustrations: Michael Bartels and Daniel Bruins (http://dcbruins. weebly.com/).

For cheerful, prompt artful-edit assistance: the staff of Luther College Document Center.

For support and celebration: Kristine Dalaker Kraabel, Peggy Weldon, Rachel and David Faldet, Todd and Heather Pedlar, Robert and Victoria Christman, Steve and Krista Holland, and Kate Rattenborg.

Editors, colleagues, friends: Joe Wilkins, Keith Lesmeister, Sonya Chung, Taylor Brorby, Chip Blake, Scott Gast, Diana Owen, Camille Dungy, and Benjamin Percy.

Teachers, mentors, and workshop leaders: Marianne Gingher, Judy Troy, Jeremy Downes, Jerry Brown, Barry Hannah, Elizabeth Spencer, Jeanne Moskal, Erika Lindemann, Beverly Taylor, Rebecca Solnit, Colson Whitehead, Craig Childs, Scott Russell Sanders, and Megan Mayhew Bergman.

## Permissions Acknowledgments

For permission to reprint a passage from Mollie Panter-Downes's *London War Notes*, thanks to Lydia Fellgett of Persephone Books, which reprints neglected fiction and nonfiction by mid-twentieth-century (mostly) women writers: www.persephonebooks.co.uk.

For permission to reprint a passage from Norman Lewis's *Naples '44*, thanks to Barnaby Rogerson of Eland Books, which is dedicated to keeping the best travel writing alive: www.travelbooks.co.uk.

# A Note on Examples and Anecdotes

All examples of un-cited prose are written by me to illustrate craft issues as I've seen them in my work or others' work. Students' identifying details have been changed, and "Beth" is a composite character.

To fellow writing teachers: Please don't reproduce or circulate material from this book without crediting it and me. Thanks.

# Introduction:
# Something to Say
# and a Voice to Say It In

In her classic essay *A Room of One's Own* (1929), the English novelist Virginia Woolf conducts a thought-experiment: Imagine Shakespeare had a sister named Judith. She was as talented as her brother, maybe more. But in sixteenth-century England, she couldn't follow him to the theaters on the banks of the Thames, clutching her quill, her ink, and her knife. Even though the Protestant Reformation had made literacy desirable, in order to read Scripture and teach it to your children, many women were still illiterate.[1] Furthermore, a woman who wanted to express herself intellectually was viewed as a freak. In 1763, scholar and lexicographer Samuel Johnson would remark, "a woman's preaching is like a dog's walking on his hinder legs. It is not done well; but you are surprised to find it done at all."[2]

So deep was the belief that a woman's uterus warped her mind that the American writer Charlotte Perkins Gilman, suffering in 1885 from what we'd now call postpartum depression, was "treated" by a doctor who ordered her to "rest" in her room without books, pen, or paper. That experience inspired her short story "The Yellow Wall-paper" (1892), in which enforced confinement drives a woman insane. Woolf's story of Judith Shakespeare points in the same direction. "When," Woolf writes,

> one reads of a witch being ducked, of a woman possessed by devils, of a wise woman selling herbs, or even of a very remarkable man who had a mother, then I think we are on the track of a lost novelist, a suppressed poet, of some mute and inglorious Jane Austen, some Emily Bronte who dashed her brains out on the moor or mopped and mowed about the highways crazed with the torture that her gift had put her to.[3]

This story stirs a very old fear, found in a million injunctions to *seize the day* and *make the most of life*—if you have a gift, you must express it, or it, and you, may be lost. Elsewhere in *A Room of One's Own* Woolf describes the fear "of that one gift which it was death to hide—a small one but dear to the possessor—perishing and with it, myself, my soul."[4] Later, in her autobiography *Dust Tracks on a Road* (1942), African-American novelist Zora Neale Hurston (who was born near my own east Alabama town) names a similar longing: "the force from somewhere in Space which commands you to write in the first place gives you no choice," she writes. "There is no agony like bearing an untold story inside you."[5]

Many of us know how "bearing an untold story" feels. But how do we begin to tell it? Longing pulls us forward; uncertainty drives us back. The challenge is real, especially since varied and cunning obstacles keep us from the page. Maybe it's hard to rearrange the day to make room for writing: not for nothing did Woolf state that "a woman must have money and a room of her own if she is to write fiction."[6] Maybe we're working and caretaking and plain worn out. Maybe we're beset with what novelist Anne Lamott calls "mouse voices," those reproachful whispers inside our heads: *You're not good enough to be a writer!*[7] Maybe (let's be honest) we just don't do the work. Maybe we believe a very old myth: real writers can just sit down and let the words gush out, always in the perfect order on their very first try. School may have left you with the notion that *truly* smart people *always* use perfect grammar and spelling, but if you can't remember when *i* goes after *e*, you might as well hang it up. You may have been led to believe that "real writers" don't look or sound like you, with your skin, your hair, or the particular pitch of your voice and shape of your body out in the world.

Unfortunately, literary history is full of great writers overlooked in their own time (and sometimes in ours) because they don't resemble some vaguely imagined norm: white, straight, college-educated, almost always male. There's nothing wrong with being any of those things, but they aren't preconditions for writing. In her 1928 essay "How It Feels to Be Colored Me," Zora Neale Hurston wondered, with sarcastic mock-innocence, "How *can* any deny themselves the pleasure of my company! It's beyond me."[8] But she wasn't always taken seriously as the artist she was; in *Their Eyes Were Watching God* (1937), Janie Crawford's grandmother complains that "the black woman is the mule of the world," ground under the twin wheels of gender and race.[9] As I write, in 2017, the literary world—although still not perfect—is more widely representative than it's ever been, from the novels of African and African-American authors Yaa Gyasi, Colson Whitehead, and

Paul Beatty to the poetry of Camille Dungy and Ross Gay to the work of Maggie Nelson and Jillian Weise, which redraw the body's boundaries of gender, sexuality, and ability. Similarly, writing pedagogy has progressed from the days when "learning to write" meant *only* diagramming sentences and writing imitations of Famous Writers in Your Anthology. But the ghosts of class, race, education, and other should-bes are still walking among us, and can be tough to deal with.

Hardest for all of us, I think, is taking yourself seriously, believing that you have something to say that is worth developing a voice to say it in. Here, the advice of the poet and essayist Adrienne Rich (1929–2012) is inspiring. Speaking to the all-female graduating class of Douglass College in 1977, Rich urged the new graduates to take themselves seriously by "taking responsibility toward yourselves" although "our upbringing as women has so often told us that this should come second to our relationships and responsibilities to other people." But the young woman—like the writer of *any* station in life—mustn't sell herself short by failing to challenge herself and engage with the world:

> Responsibility to yourself means refusing to let others do your thinking, talking, and naming for you; it means learning to respect and use your own brains and instincts; hence, grappling with hard work. ... It means that you refuse to sell your talents and aspirations short, simply to avoid conflict and confrontation. And this, in turn, means resisting the forces in society which say that women should be nice, play safe, have low professional expectations, drown in love and forget about work, live through others, and stay in the places assigned to us. It means that we insist on a life of meaningful work, insist that work be as meaningful as love and friendship in our lives. It means, therefore, the courage to be "different"; not to be continuously available to others when we need time for ourselves and our work; to be able to demand of others—parents, friends, roommates, teachers, lovers, husbands, children—that they respect our sense of purpose and our integrity as persons.[10]

Self-respect means insisting to ourselves and others that our work and the good habits we want to build have value. Insisting on your own value sometimes means *being demanding, having too-high standards, being a bitch*, or other such grumblings from people who resent that you've halted their expansion into your space. (How sad for them.) But even when you seem to be the only one who thinks so, developing good habits—*mine is a body worth caring for, mine is a life worth spending well*—is a matter of self-respect. "The difference between a life lived actively, and a life of passive drifting and dispersal of energies," Rich concludes, "is an immense difference. Once we begin to feel committed to our lives, responsible to ourselves, we can never again be satisfied with the old, passive way."[11]

Claiming a version of Rich's "life lived actively" is crucial for all of us, and it starts inside our own heads. It starts with believing one big thing: despite the "mouse voices" of self-doubt, obligation, and distraction, you *do* have something to say. Your own life *is* worth showing up for and worth heightening through the practice of writing and the attentiveness it cultivates. You have a responsibility to use your writing wisely and constructively, but you also have valuable testimony to offer from the place where your particular consciousness meets the world.

However, claiming yourself as a writer gets real when you start to manage your own attention and time. Of course, there are jobs (and laundry) to do, children to feed, homework to finish, all the rest of it. But at the risk of sounding oblivious, I'll suggest that often we make ourselves "busier" than we actually are to avoid the emotions and desires swirling within us—including the desire to write—because "busyness" provides a sense of security that evaporates when we're alone and able to choose what we will do next. "What is it about silence that we're afraid of?" asks the Buddhist teacher Shugen Sensei. "Is it the silence itself? Or is it the absence of the 'me' that is known through sound?" This question rocks my world. How often have I summoned up just such a version of a "me that is known through sound," filling a space with talk or a trip to the vending machine or a scroll through the phone? How often do we reach for labels to prop ourselves up in others' eyes? *I am a successful small business owner. I am a high achiever. I have a thousand followers on Twitter.* Yet eventually everyone has to answer the following question: Who am I when my external label doesn't fit me anymore? Who am I when I retire? Who am I when my children grow up and move away? What am I really intellectually interested in once my high school credentialing fever abates and I'm asked to choose a college major? Who am I when nobody is watching?

As existentially terrifying as these questions are, they're worth asking yourself. If you avoid them, they'll run you like a sheepdog runs sheep, straight into ever-more-financially-and/or-emotionally-costly avoidance strategies—new car, not-quite-right relationship, social media addiction, helicopter parenting. How often do we channel-surf or turn to social media (three hours gone, just like that!) or membership in one more on-campus club (*ahem*, my dear students) to numb the anxiety and ennui that come with being a person in the world? (The Nobel Prize–winning fiction writer Alice Munro has confessed to housecleaning as a procrastination technique, which makes me feel better about doing it myself.) How often do we turn on the television rather than open the notebook? How often do we choose to distract ourselves when we could choose otherwise? When I ask these questions of my own life, I hear Adrienne Rich's voice, inflected with my native Alabama: *come on, honey, take yourself seriously.* Don't pawn off your own patiently waiting attention, what the poet Mary Oliver calls your "one wild and precious life," with "entertainment" and busyness you cling to to avoid looking into the silence. We owe it to ourselves to wake up and stay awake. This means paying attention to what's really happening in our own lives, day to day. Yes, it's hard. So is being an artist. So is being a reasonably aware person in any time and place. Welcome to it.

The difficulty of all of this is heightened by the fact that we live in a world of more skillfully tailored distractions than ever, which feed our egos without "improving" our lives nearly as much as they claim. Of course, I'm talking about electronic media. Bored? Check your smartphone. Emotion roaming inside you, looking for some outlet? Hop over to Amazon and see what it thinks you "might also like" depending on what you bought last time. Write a text, receive a text, dispel silence with noise. Ours is a world in which it's easy to tune out while telling ourselves we are "staying connected." Tailored by precise algorithms to anticipate our choices, sell us products based on them, and wedge itself into any previously unclaimed sliver of time, electronic media will plop itself front and center in our lives, claiming all our attention if we let it. And when we let it, we fall into the same downward spiral as lapsed exercisers—we don't read hard things (or try to write) so we can't so we don't so we can't. Inertia becomes easier. Like Melville's Bartleby, eventually we prefer not to.

Our new social normal is one of *continuous partial attention*—surrounded by televisions, laptops, and smartphones, we tell ourselves that our multitasking has no consequences, but we're actually losing the capacity to focus on and complete, with our best attention, one task at a time. Resisting this norm is possible, but it's hard. "You have to go to considerable trouble to live differently from the way the world wants you to live," novelist Harry Crews observed:

> That's what I've discovered about writing. The world doesn't want you to do a damn thing. If you wait till you got time to write a novel or time to write a story or time to read the hundred thousands of books you should have already read—if you wait for the time, you'll never do it. 'Cause there ain't no time; world don't want you to do that. World wants you to go to the zoo and eat cotton candy, preferably seven days a week.[12]

If you want to write in the twenty-first century, electronic media is one more current in the river of self-distraction against which you must swim. Its effects on your attention may be harder to resist, or even to *see*, the younger you are. The more recently you were born, the more likely you are to have grown up with the whole complex of computers, smartphones, and the Internet as *normal*. Unfortunately, if this is the case, you're also more likely to have experienced what child-reading experts call *linguistic impoverishment*, since "content" on the screens that dominate our homes and lives isn't known for its verbal nuance, and the feeling that your brain is never quite fully available for your own use, always half-listening for the next incoming-message alert. "It would be a shame," writes journalist Edward Tenner of Google, "if brilliant technology were to end up threatening the kind of intellect that produced it."[13] *Use it or lose it:* this is true of muscles, brains, and attention spans.

However, the good news is this: there is a way forward. More than twenty years of teaching and thirty-plus years of writing have shown me that writing is about establishing habits. And the habit that underlies them all is *noticing*. Learning to write starts with learning to pay attention to the world around you, even though just about everything in our lives makes this more difficult than it needs to be. Developing habits of noticing, and writing down what you notice, can be the first step away from anxieties and doubts and toward your ultimate goal as a writer: *discovering something to say and a voice to say it in*. It can accustom you to silence and uncertainty, so words of your own—not just other people's voices or consumer clichés—can bloom in that internal space. Novelist Sonya Chung says that "the difference between a writer and someone who 'wants to be a writer' is a high tolerance for uncertainty."[14] You may not know where you are going when you start to write (most writers don't, and they're okay with that). You may not know whether your words will ever amount to anything. But you're willing to try and to keep trying. And if you're at least somewhat tolerant of uncertainty, and willing to keep trying anyway, you will be a writer. You will be walking that path.

I say "walking that path" because "being a writer" isn't a place you aim for and then reach, once and for all, like a fortieth birthday. It's more like any spiritual or personal path—you may achieve goals, sure, but *being a writer* is less a matter of checking off milestones than of *doing* the writing over and over. If you've just written your first exercise in your notebook— congratulations! You're a writer and you're walking that path, just as I am, just as Margaret Atwood and Toni Morrison and Kazuo Ishiguro and Chimamanda Ngozi Adichie and Kim Stanley Robinson and Robert

Macfarlane and Hilary Mantel and Anthony Doerr are, right now. The difference between the beginning writer and the published writer is not a swat on the head with the inspiration stick—it's *mileage*. Margaret Atwood (for instance) has been walking the writerly path, doing the work and then doing the work again, for a long time. She's traveled farther along that path because over time she's done the work, refined her craft, and accumulated the experience to know how to keep herself going, how to develop new projects and push them along, and how to get around inevitable roadblocks. She's accumulated the mileage because she's put in the time. Margaret Atwood is far along on a writing path. You may be closer to the beginning. But you are both on the *same* path.

A writing teacher's job is to help you move along that path even further, navigating around obstacles as they arise. This book is designed to be your companion as you go. I'm going to walk you through processes of thinking and doing that build on one another, with observation of and experience in the living world as the common element. I'll be talking about different kinds of prose writing—fiction, nonfiction, and academic writing—because as I practice and teach them all, I find they have many craft realities in common. (Everything in your life changes for the better when you stop thinking of "writing for school" as a different beast than "creative writing" and develop a clear, sensory voice that can bend in both directions.) I'll also be analyzing good writing to help you see how it works: as the title of Francine Prose's book indicates, *Reading Like a Writer* is basic to *being* a writer. While reading this book in order is best, you can skip around or go back and review if you want to. Please do try the exercises as you go.

Ultimately, how you walk the writing path is up to you. Ask yourself: why do you want to write, anyway? Here are some possible reasons: Taking yourself seriously. Taking your memories seriously. Preserving what shouldn't be forgotten. Heightening your vision—to many writers, writing itself makes life, and the world, more real. Communing with the living and the dead. Discovering what you love and what you'll do to protect it. Being alone in your mind's own garden of silence. Communing with other writers and artists, even if you'll never meet them. "Know that there is beauty in specificity," film director Ava DuVernay said in her commencement speech to the UCLA School of Theatre, Film, and Television in June 2017. "What is your voice? What do you want to say?"

You may have grown up reading *Little House on the Prairie* (or watching the TV series on cable reruns), but you may not know that its author, Laura Ingalls Wilder (1867–1957), started writing the *Little House* books in her sixties. First, she gathered a stack of paper tablets and wrote on them—in pencil—an autobiography called "Pioneer Girl," covering her life from ages two to eighteen. Together, Laura and her daughter Rose worked to develop the material from that rough draft. The first of the *Little House* books, *Little House in the Big Woods,* appeared in 1932, when Laura was sixty-five.[15] Her story introduces several themes I'll return to throughout this book: just getting started, in your own voice, with what you want to say—whether it's with a number two pencil or a laptop—is the first step. Your writing project doesn't have to end with that initial draft; you can polish and rearrange it from the inside out to help it achieve its fullest potential. If you speak from your heart and consider the needs of your readers, you can find those readers, in your lifetime and beyond. And it's never too late to begin.

# 1

# Writing and the World Beyond Your Head

Let's get started where writing starts—in the place where our consciousness meets the world, where we experience the friction of daily experience, memory, learning, conversation, and perception, and where our thoughts flow out as the world flows in, like nutrients through the permeable membrane of a cell. A student asks a question that resurrects a memory I'd forgotten; a fox dashes across the road in front of me; picking sour cherries from my tree makes my fingers sticky; graffiti on a Los Angeles sidewalk advises *Protect Yo Heart*; a flash of wings announces a bluejay on the power line outside the window. I'm always living in a place where what's *me* meets and mingles with what's *not me*, and this process begins as soon as I open my eyes in the morning.

I imagine this place as an estuarial zone at the border of our minds and bodies, like the tidal marshes where river meets ocean, like the Chesapeake Bay or Lake Ponchartrain. "Edge zones" like estuaries, or the places where meadows meet forests, are zones of great richness, nurturing plants, animals, and insects that may be found nowhere else. In political theory, the social and mental space where people come together to talk or work together is the *polis*, a kind of edge zone of public life. We can enter this zone whenever we let ourselves encounter someone or something that is *not* ourselves— even an apparently insignificant or ordinary thing—without shutting our attention off and turning away. Noticing your surroundings becomes a way of being in the world that builds upon itself the more you do it, waking you up and keeping you awake as you pass through the world: "So feeling comes in aid/Of feeling," wrote William Wordsworth (of whom more later) in *The Prelude*, "and diversity of strength/Attends us, if but once we have been strong."[1]

# Beth and the bird's nest

Let me tell you a story to show you what I mean. Like most beginning writers I teach, the college student I'll call Beth was worried about how she would "get ideas for stories." Driven by the myths I mentioned earlier, Beth believed that perfect first drafts sprang from the writer's brain like the goddess Athena from the head of Zeus. So if she couldn't generate a perfect idea in her own head right away, there must be something wrong with *her*. One day, I took Beth and her classmates outside and asked them to walk around for fifteen minutes (with notebook and pen) and observe, then write at least one paragraph in which their characters interacted with something *they* had just seen. Beth approached me at the end of class, her eyes shining. "I found a bird's nest!" she exclaimed. "In the little spruce tree by the library. I've walked past it a hundred times and never knew it was there!" The paragraph she wrote—focused only that little woven cup of grass and twig and a single paper drinking-straw wrapper, tucked against the shaggy trunk of that spruce tree—was precise and lovely in a way her writing hadn't been before. In that moment, she wasn't just laboring to invent something from scratch—she was using the real world as a springboard to her invention, fitting her language to something outside herself that she had used her own senses to experience and then describe.

Our writing is transformed and invigorated when we see *writing* as a process of *being in ongoing relationship with the world beyond our own heads*, and when we see language as the estuarial zone in which our own perceptions, the needs of our readers, and the realities of the external world mingle richly to create something new. "Writing" isn't only *in here*, in your own head—it's *out there*, in images, actions, and sense impressions waiting to be set to words. When we wake up and look around, we are preparing ourselves to write before we ever lift a pen.

# The world beyond your head: A philosophical introduction

Philosopher Matthew Crawford uses the phrase *the world beyond your head* as the name for the whole ecosystem of creatures-and-things-not-ourselves that we encounter as we move through life. We become better people when we feel a sense of responsibility to them and let them teach us humility by acknowledging our limits.[2] In his book *The World Beyond Your Head: On Becoming an Individual in an Age of Distraction* (2015), Crawford argues that the electronic overstimulation of the twenty-first century is creating a "crisis of attention" that is raising "the question of whether one can maintain a coherent self," meaning "a self that is able to act according to settled purposes and ongoing projects, rather than flitting about."[3] A mental landscape dominated by electronic media can disembody us, trapping us inside our own heads as we seek the next distraction, distancing us from our senses and what they can tell us about our surroundings. We can swim against that tide of distraction and redirect our attention by rooting ourselves in the physical world. "The Latin root of our English word 'attention,' is *tenere*," Crawford writes, "to stretch or make tense. External objects provide an attachment point for the mind; they can pull us out of ourselves."[4]

One way to experience this, Crawford writes, is to practice a craft—a process of making or working that asks us to be responsible to the physical world. In his first book, *Shop Class as Soulcraft: An Inquiry into the Value of Work* (2009), Crawford described his own journey from working at a white-collar job he'd been taught, as a PhD in political philosophy, to think suitable. Yet he found himself unhappy and bored until he returned to his first love: engines. Now, as the owner of a motorcycle repair shop in

Virginia, Crawford argues that human beings need to enter into systems of relationships, cause-and-effect, and actions in the physical world in order to feel active and fulfilled. In *The World Beyond Your Head*, Crawford concludes that "to be in conversation with a tradition" and with the realities of what does and doesn't, has and hasn't, worked over time "is a kind of rationality; a mode of thinking that helps us get at the truth about things."[5] There's dignity and worth in fixing things, and in following processes that other hands and minds have refined before you came along. Working with our hands may settle our minds, counteract narcissism, and teach us humility and resilience.

While romanticizing labor can be too easy—"it's really hard," said one farm-kid student of mine, "and I came to college because I have other goals for my life"—lots of us are turning back toward the rewards of working with our hands in our otherwise disembodied age, especially where it can save fossil fuels. Writer Paul Kingsnorth uses a scythe to mow his own property and teaches others to do the same. "Using a scythe properly is a meditation," he writes,

> your body in tune with the tool, your tool in tune with the land. You concentrate without thinking, you follow the lay of the ground with the face of your blade, you are aware of the keenness of its edge, you can hear the birds, see things moving through the grass ahead of you. Everything is connected to everything else, and if it isn't, it doesn't work.[6]

In her memoir *The Dirty Life*, Kristin Kimball describes the first year of her Essex Farm in upstate New York, which she and her husband Mark power with draft-horse teams and solar panels. "I was fundamentally happier, I found, with my focus on the ground," she writes. "For the first time, I could clearly see the connection between my actions and their consequences. I knew why I was doing what I was doing, and I believed in it."[7] A student volunteer at the Standing Rock encampment and pipeline protest site in the winter of 2016 told me and others about how good it felt to carry supplies from one end of the camp to the other: with no social media chatter in his head and a clear task before him—a rarity in so many of our lives—he was alone with action and consequence, doing work and doing good. One former student of mine has become a blacksmith, and talking to him about his work is a pleasure not only because I get to learn words like *scale* and *swage block* but because I can see how shaping his craft has shaped his sense of spirit and purpose in life. Kristen Kimball muses that maybe it is "in the realm of TiVo and cubicles, of take-out food and central air, in that country where discomfort has nearly disappeared" that we are deprived—"deprived of the pleasure of desire, of effort and difficulty and meaningful accomplishment."[8] Even in our disembodying age, I see this desire for "meaningful accomplishment" and actually *doing*—not just phone-thumbing or task-box-checking—in my students, and myself.

Therefore, if you've spent more time doing things with your hands than writing, don't fear—you may actually be well-placed to write good prose. Homegrown American mystic and environmentalist Henry David Thoreau (1817–1862) reflected in his journal that labor makes us better writers by giving us something to write about and by focusing our style on verbs. "I have often been astonished at the force and precision of style to which busy laboring men, unpracticed in writing, easily attain when they are required to make the effort," he writes. "The scholar not unfrequently envies the propriety and emphasis with which the farmer calls to his team, and confesses that if the lingo were written it would surpass his labored sentences."[9] Novelist Larry Brown shows this effect at work in his memoir *On Fire* (1994), about his days as a firefighter in Oxford, Mississippi:

> You learn early to go in low, that heat and smoke rise into the ceiling, that cooler air is near the floor. You learn to button your collar tightly around your neck, to pull the gauntlets of your gloves up over the cuffs of your coat, that embers can go anywhere skin is exposed. You learn that you are only human flesh, not Superman, and that you can burn like a candle.
>
> You try to go easy on the air that's inside the tank on your back, try to be calm and not overly exert yourself, try and save some of your strength. You learn about exhaustion and giving it all you've got, then having to reach back and pull up some more. Suck it up and go.
>
> You learn eventually not to let your legs tremble when you're pressing hard on the gas or the diesel pedal, when you're driving into something that's unknown.[10]

Clarity, directness, sensory language: this is good prose, linking physical experience with language, and needing no "big words" to achieve its effect.

Our bodies and brains are built to think through and even take pleasure in our work every day. "The boundary of our cognitive processes," Crawford writes, "cannot be cleanly drawn at the outer surface of our skulls, or indeed of our bodies more generally. They are, in a sense, distributed in the world that we act in."[11] When we make the minute and often unconscious adjustments necessary to slice an apple with a knife that's a little too dull or catch a Frisbee on a windy day, we're thinking in the estuarial zone between body and physical world, using long-learned, near-instinctive knowledge to bow to how our bodies actually function in that world. Even as we act upon it, the world shapes us too. In the words of Shakespeare's Sonnet 111, our "nature is subdued / To what it works in, like the dyer's hand." This lovely simile evokes the sixteenth-century process of fabric making, which would permanently stain the "dyer's hand." As a teacher, I carry a chalk callus on the inside of my right middle finger. My late father, a surgeon, covertly and near-unconsciously assessed others for visible signs of illness. Both of us, as Alabama farm people, scanned the ground for snakes as we walked—a habit that follows me from city pavements to my own back yard. What and how we pay attention to shape our bodies, our minds, even our souls. "The greatest thing a human soul ever does in this world," wrote the Victorian critic John Ruskin, "is to see something, and tell what it saw in a plain way. Hundreds of people can talk for one who can think, but thousands can think for one who can see. To see clearly is poetry, prophecy, and religion—all in one."

Therefore, paying attention, and working against the forces of habit that can dull it, is a matter of survival. *I'm so busy*, we might protest. *I can't pay attention to every little thing. Noticing, and training myself to notice, takes a kind of time I don't have.* Yet noticing is part of being a writer, and it's part of being awake and alive during your one life on earth. In E. M. Forster's *Howards End* (1910), Margaret Schlegel notices an "obtuseness" in her prosperous new husband:

> There was one quality in Henry for which she was never prepared, however much she reminded herself of it: his obtuseness. He simply did not notice things … he never noticed the lights and shades that exist in the greyest conversation, the finger-posts, the milestones, the collisions, the illimitable views. Once she scolded him about it.
>
> He was puzzled, but replied with a laugh, "My motto is Concentrate. I've no intention of frittering away my strength on that sort of thing."
>
> "It isn't frittering away your strength," she protested. "It's enlarging the space in which you may be strong."[12]

To that I'd add that it's also reclaiming at least some of your strength for your own use. No matter how much our world of Facebook and climate control and automation may insulate us from it, we're still humans, in human bodies, in the physical world. As such, we've accumulated a vast library of sensory knowledge that is both highly particular to us *and* sensorily recognizable to other human bodies in other places and times—settling a sleeping baby's weight in our arms, climbing a gate, balancing weight of crutches and cast, closing our eyes and basking in the sun. Sense memories live in us, including in forms of language that recur in literature and culture throughout time. Therefore, to be a writer, you don't really need special equipment or vocabulary. You need your own human body and its sense memories developed over time by engaging the world beyond your head. A pen is *alkalami* in the Hausa language, *pene* in Maori, *stilolaps* in Albanian, *penna* in Italian. But when your character uncaps her favorite blue pen and settles it against the callus on her right fourth finger and touches it to the paper in front of her, readers in all those languages will recognize, in their own bodies, just how that feels. Therefore, writers speak to readers in *the common language of the senses*—the language all humans share.

# William Wordsworth: Everyday ecstasies and spots of time

All this talk about our bodies interacting with the world sounds obvious until you think about how deeply our everyday lives—and our myths of "writing"—encourage us to deny it. First, there's the ordinary pressure of habit and routine, which blinds us to familiar experiences and sensations. We stop noticing how we drive to work each morning; we half-listen to what the radio is saying; we leave our travel mugs all over campus because we weren't paying attention to where we set them down. Compounding this is the electronic distraction now layered over every other action in our day through the smartphones in our hands. A world constantly preaching *convenience* and *multitasking* as the greatest possible human goods ignores the costs of those things: a creeping numbness, a sleepwalking blank in our minds, continuous partial attention. Yet in letting our lives, moment to moment, be defined as *plain old routine*, we're conspiring in our own self-forgetfulness, being numbed to the presence of our own irreplaceable lives on this earth as they pass by. Call me a romantic, but it's the truth: one life, in one body, on this one earth, is all we get.

Think about a child hunkering on a streambank, reaching for a shiny rock. "Why do you want to pick that up?" an oblivious adult asks. "It's just an ordinary thing." Yet as an avid rock-picker-upper-in-creeks (then and now), I can testify that to that child, it's not just a rock. She sees something in its particular shine that escapes the adult's habit-glazed sight. In capturing the object, she's hoping to capture that moment of delight when her own perception leapt beyond herself, illuminating and encompassing the world beyond. *Oh, look at that!* That moment is ecstasy, literally *ek-stasis*, being drawn outside the self. Ordinary things do have this power, if we can train ourselves not to ignore it.

This is an impulse the English poet William Wordsworth (1770–1850), godfather of Romanticism, knew well. If you only know Wordsworth's greatest hits—like "I wandered lonely as a cloud," in which the speaker encounters "a crowd, / A host, of golden daffodils"—you might be forgiven for dismissing him as a twee old man in a twee old dream of Nature with a capital N, interested only in what's pretty. But Wordsworth's real subject is the complex and often unpretty relationship between the mind and the world. Is what we think we see really there, or is our own mind only telling us (in the positive and negative senses of this word) stories? Does the natural world contain some meaning that can sustain our imaginations and spirits, if we look for it closely enough? Or is that only wishful thinking?

Wordsworth would have cheered the creek-rock-picking child, because his own experiences showed him what that child knows: if maintained within ourselves, such memories of contact with things-not-ourselves and the sharp wonder or even fear they bring can provide us what, in "Lines Written Above Tintern Abbey," he calls "life and food/for future years," sources of inner nourishment and refreshment that will never fade.[13] In his autobiographical poem *The Prelude*, he calls such moments "spots of time," memories that renew our minds whenever we think of them.

> There are in our existence spots of time,
> Which with distinct preeminence retain
> A renovating virtue, whence, depressed
> By false opinion and contentious thought,
> Or aught of heavier or more deadly weight
> In trivial occupations and the round
> Of ordinary intercourse, our minds
> Are nourished and invisibly repaired—[14]

"Such moments," Wordsworth continues, "worthy of all gratitude/Are scattered everywhere, taking their date/From our first childhood," and "in our childhood even/Perhaps are most conspicuous."[15]

Yet these "spots of time" aren't only sweet; emotions of dread, confusion, doubt, or a sense of smallness against nature's larger power (what was called, in this period, a sense of the "sublime") can stamp them into our memories. Around age six, Wordsworth rides his pony past the site of a hanging, where the murderer's name is still cut into the grass and kept fresh "by superstition of the neighborhood." As a young man rowing in a stolen boat at night, he's surprised by the "horizon's bound, a huge peak, black and huge" rearing up in front of him, striking him with oppression and fear that lingers for days: "huge and mighty forms, that do not live/Like living men," he writes, "moved slowly through the mind/By day, and were a trouble to my dreams."[16] As a thirteen-year-old, he huddles on a rocky ridge in a storm; ten days later, his father dies. Inner and outer turmoil meet in a mental image that adult Wordsworth returns to to give his grief a name:

> And, afterwards, the wind and sleety rain,
> And all the business of the elements,
> The single sheep, and the one blasted tree,
> And the bleak music of that old stone wall,
> The noise of wood and water, and the mist …
> All these were kindred spectacles and sounds to which
> I oft repaired, and thence would drink,
> As at a fountain, and on winter nights,
> Down to this very time, when storm and rain
> Beat on my roof, or, haply, at noon-day,
> While in a grove I walk, whose lofty trees,
> Laden with summer's thickest foliage, rock
> In a strong wind, some working of the spirit,
> Some inward agitations thence are brought,
> Whate'er their office, whether to beguile
> Thoughts over busy in the course they took,
> Or animate an hour of vacant ease.[17]

Contact with the natural world—bigger and stronger than us—can stretch us into new shapes as we wrestle with what it makes us feel. Nature becomes a language in which we can explain ourselves to ourselves, often wordlessly. Oliver Wendell Holmes wrote that "a mind, once stretched by a new idea, never regains its original dimensions." Moments like Wordsworth's spots of time, in which we become permeable to the world, stretch our souls into shapes they retain forever afterwards. Writers live on these moments, mining them for images (which I'll discuss in Chapter 3) and emotional resonances. Significantly, for Wordsworth, childhood is where they start, since, for him, childhood is a time of heightened perceptions, when everything seems "appareled in celestial light" with "the glory and the freshness of a dream."[18] (Flannery O'Connor put a more sardonic spin on this: "The fact is that anybody who has survived his childhood has enough information about life to last him the rest of his days.")[19]

Those heightened perceptions perhaps explain why childhood is such rich ground for writers, as critic and novelist Mary McCarthy describes: "For most writers-in-exile—e.g., Joyce, Nabokov, the internal exile Pasternak—recollections of childhood are a literary food source and have been hoarded, squirrel-wise, against the winter, and it does not appear to matter whether the childhood was happy, like Nabokov's, or dingy, like Joyce's."[20]

But Wordsworth was onto something: starting in childhood, our lives as people in the world, experiencing and observing it, give us the emotional and sensory materials of writing, including the concreteness our language needs to communicate with others. We learn to write about the world by living in it, getting out of our own minds and houses and little rooms. "Come forth into the light of things," Wordsworth invites, "let nature be your teacher."[21]

As I mentioned, *ecstasy* literally means being opened to emotion by something outside yourself. Going through the world attentively means opening yourself to its possibility: a monarch butterfly landing on the milkweed beside the path, a night moth fumbling in the white lily whose fragrance thickens the dusk. Such moments enchant us, and they knit us deeper into a sense of connection to the world that shapes the way we use language and the way we see our relationships with readers. They bring you out of yourself, and keep you heading in that direction. When you're trying to fit your language to a thing you want to help readers see and experience as you do, you work hard to get out of yourself in good ways—writing becomes less about "see how smart I am" than "come stand beside me while I show you this." Therefore, both observing and writing become ecstatic. We move out of our small selves into the world. "I stand in awe of my body, this matter to which I am bound," wrote Thoreau, climbing Maine's Mount Katahdin (Ktaadn) in 1846. "Daily to be shown matter, to come in contact with it,—rocks, trees, wind on our cheeks! the *solid* earth! the *actual* world! the *common sense! Contact! Contact! Who* are we? *where* are we?"[22]

# Writing and language:
# It's not (only) about you

What I've been describing here is the basic orientation to the world on which my whole practice of writing is based: be present in the moment as it is, and pay attention to it. Let that present reality shape your language and its implicit contract with readers. And let it draw you out of your own mind, assumptions, and ego, at least a little. Avoiding or shortchanging reality can leave us stuck in the belief that writing is only about self-expression, only about the writer's "ideas," and, therefore, it can leave us seesawing back and forth between perfectionism and a particularly annoying kind of narcissism gently countered by astrophysicist Neil deGrasse Tyson: "The universe is under no obligation to make sense to you."[23] And the individual self is not the center of that universe, no matter how loudly it insists that it is.

Language communicates best with other humans when it is rooted in sensory detail and experience. The one thing we share with all other humans in all times and places is a human body, and, therefore, speaking to readers in the *common language of our human senses* can collapse distances of space and time. Even in little two-dimensional shapes on a page, we can travel to Dickens' London, the battlefield where Antigone sifts sand over her brother's corpse, Macbeth's castle with the martin-nests in the walls, or the Maryland shore on which an enslaved boy named Frederick Douglass sits, watching sailboats move on out of sight. Writing lives beyond its writers because of this connection through the body to people we'll never meet. To do its best work, language must be responsible to some common realities and common readerly needs—most of which are rooted in the natural world, our bodies, and our brains.

Even though writers need the world so much, the myth of "inspiration" as a completely interior process persists. Movies have more than a little to do with this: think of "Shakespeare in Love," in which Joseph Fiennes finds his words uncorked by passion and *Romeo and Juliet* is born. (The truth, of course, looks more like "Barton Fink," in which John Turturro huddles before his typewriter until the pinup girl on his calendar starts talking to him.) But believing writing is only about interior "inspiration" will trap you inside your own head, in panic, neurosis, self-absorption, or all three. With typical humor, Anne Lamott reminds us in *Bird by Bird* how false such myths of writerly inspiration can be: "Very few writers really know what they're doing until they've done it," she writes. "They do not type a few stiff warm-up sentences and then find themselves bounding along like huskies across the snow."[24]

Perfectionism is real, and rooted in a lesson women in particular learn early on: we must be "correct" in all our endeavors and never, ever make a mess. Such perfectionism, as Anne Lamott writes, acts as "the voice of the oppressor" in more ways than one, teaching us that unless we get it right on our very first try, we shouldn't try at all.[25] It grips lots of writers in worries about correctness and neatness: anxiety about grammar and the desire to produce perfect first drafts. Jean, a sixty-something member of my community writing class, confessed that she had a stack of gorgeous journals she was afraid to use. She pulled a beautiful leatherbound book from her bag and opened it. On the first page, two handwritten sentences tapered into blankness. "And I've got more at home just like it," she said. "I start writing and I just seize up, because I start worrying that my words are wrong, and maybe my grammar is wrong, and ... I just can't keep going."[26]

This fear of "correctness" isn't limited to one generation. In the first college class I taught as a graduate student, a young woman was frozen before the blank page; eventually she told me that a high school teacher had written in red ink at the top of her paper, "Doo-Doo!" next to a giant grade of D. Another young woman came to my office near tears because she couldn't get started on her paper. "It just seems like such a big task," she fretted, "you have to get the introduction right, and then that has to set up all the rest of the argument, and .... " Wait, I said. You know that you *can* write your introduction last, don't you? Nobody writes a first draft perfectly start to finish. *Nobody.* (I wrote first drafts of this book's chapters out of order, too.) When she heard these words, the student's face brightened. "You mean I can write the introduction *last*?" she said. "Sure can," I said. Nobody but you has to see how the draft gets put together, unless you choose to show it to them. The student literally skipped out of my office. In two days, she'd finished her whole draft.

Therefore, for writers, and for anyone trapped in our own anxious heads, the world *beyond* our heads can help us get out of them. We need contact with the world around us to put our own loud anxieties and egos into perspective: talking to a friend, taking a walk, building or fixing or making something can loosen the airless grip of anxiety by enlarging our perspective on reality. We need the natural world in particular at many levels: medical, psychological, creative, and mythic. In my Fall 2016 alumni newsletter from the University of North Carolina, I spot an article about the award-winning "WonderSphere" at the North Carolina Botanical Gardens, "a sealed mobile chamber that enables hospitalized, immune-compromised children to touch nature without risk of infection." (In the picture, a small girl, her head hairless and pink, cups her blue-gloved hands around a plant, her smile radiant.) More than one study has shown that hospital patients who can see natural light and green space through their windows recover faster than those who can't. Nature's effect on us is imaginative and literary, too. "The human spirit needs language, shimmering and liquid," the essayist Jay Griffiths writes. "I couldn't call language 'shimmering' without knowledge of the natural world, light on water … Language needs the natural world, each word has real 'roots'."[27] Recalling Ralph Waldo Emerson's famous remark that "language is fossil poetry," Griffiths writes that "if you've never found a fossil, held it in your real hand, given it to your real friend, you cannot treasure Emerson's remark," because you will have no way to match internal and external realities through the experience of a word: "we are animated," Griffiths concludes, "by the tutelary genius of language."[28] People need real things to do and a real world to do them in in order to live, and write, as our fullest human selves.

Poet Dean Young echoes this view: "Before we became obligated to our minds," he writes,

> we were obligated to the world, its bodied conception and celebration and morning. Our poems are what the gods couldn't make without going through us. We were answering back, not making codes, not manipulating literary devices, but offering thanks and accusation, mimicries of fundamental mysteries, the simplicities of urges that are always with us in the language of the creature, experience, weather. Our poetry is our haunting and adventure.[29]

Young suggests that art must be animated by "a conviction that arises from the closely observed and considered world itself," a conviction which can prompt "truth in language arising from the active impulse of emotion."[30] Nature can keep us honest by reminding us of something beyond ourselves: wind and sun on skin, the sound of creaturely feet in grass or wings in air. Think about the verbs that water gives us—*flow, ripple, rush, trickle*—and how richly they describe human realities, too: when thoughts or speech *flow* or *trickle* forth, we have a precise sense of their fluidity, shapeliness, and speed. Perhaps, in a reversal of the Genesis story, it's the natural, embodied world that created our human language and systems of naming—not the other way around. Perhaps the world named Adam and Eve by calling forth from them the speech they would use first to describe the wonders all around, then to turn back upon themselves, into the hearts that would be clouded and troubled sooner than they knew.

What we love to read still shows us that we love the world. Consider J. R. R. Tolkein's *The Hobbit* (1937). A medievalist of staggering erudition, Tolkein knew, from epics like *Beowulf*, what psychologist Maryanne Wolf calls "the language of books"—a set of grand storytelling gestures ("in those days," "once upon a time") that usually don't "appear in spoken language."[31] Yet he always domesticates that lofty fantasy with concrete detail. From its setting (Bilbo Baggins's warm burrow) to the fluent, confiding narrative voice ("It does not do to leave a live dragon out of your calculations, if you live near him")[32] to the expertly judged similes (riding an empty barrel in a river current, Bilbo finds, is "like trying to ride, without bridle or stirrups, a round-bellied pony that was always thinking of rolling on the grass"),[33] *The Hobbit* is lit not only by Tolkein's intellect but also by his commonsensical, earthbound writerly eye. Here's the sleeping dragon Smaug:

> There he lay, a vast red-golden dragon, fast asleep; a thrumming came from his jaws and nostrils, and wisps of smoke, but his fires were low in slumber. Beneath him, under all his limbs and his huge coiled tail, and about him on all sides stretching away across the unseen floors, lay countless piles of precious things, gold wrought and unwrought, gems and jewels, and silver red-stained in the ruddy light.
>
> Smaug lay, with wings folded like an immeasurable bat, turned partly on one side, so that the hobbit could see his underparts and his long pale belly crusted with gems and fragments of gold from his long lying on his costly bed. Behind him where the walls were nearest could dimly be seen coats of mail, helms and axes, swords and spears hanging; and there in rows stood great jars and vessels filled with a wealth that could not be guessed.[34]

For me, the detail that snaps this creature into life is that "long pale belly, crusted with gems and fragments of gold" just like a snake picks up dirt and straw from the ground. That detail anchors the potentially windy fantasy language ("a wealth that could not be guessed," "immeasurable") in the truth of the world as seen, making the dragon's cave feel not just invented but observed.

Helen Macdonald's *H Is for Hawk*, which won the Samuel Johnson Prize for nonfiction writing in 2014, also shows that readers seek contact with the natural world. Here, from the book's second page, is a short introduction to goshawks:

> Have you ever seen a hawk catch a bird in your back garden? I've not, but I know it's happened. I've found evidence. Out on the patio flagstones, sometimes, tiny fragments: a little, insect-like songbird leg, with a foot clenched tight where the sinews have pulled it; or—even more gruesomely—a disarticulated beak, a house-sparrow beak top, or bottom, a little conical bead of blushed gunmetal, slightly translucent, with a few faint maxillary feathers adhering to it. But maybe you have: maybe you've glanced out of the window and seen there, on the lawn, a bloody great hawk murdering a pigeon, or a blackbird, or a magpie, and it looks the hugest, most impressive piece of wildness you've ever seen, like someone's tipped a snow leopard into your kitchen and you find it eating the cat.[35]

Macdonald's task is a hard one: how can you convince readers to sign on for a book about killer birds while reassuring us we're not just in for grisly authenticity-porn? I think the answer lies in her engaging writerly voice and in her well-judged balance of detail and deliberate vagueness ("bloody great hawk" is the same kind of good vagueness as Leonard Michaels's use of the word "thing" to describe the Pacific Ocean; see Exercise 5 in Chapter 4). The precisely described songbird leg and beak open the scene, and our interest, wider. While acknowledging our initial suburban-minded discomfort ("gruesomely"), she doesn't let us off the hook: we look closer at the little scraps, eventually reorienting our vision to see as the hawk trainer or naturalist sees ("blushed gunmetal," "maxillary feathers"). And in the process, Macdonald trains us to follow the book's overarching thesis: beyond the visible surface of the world lies mystery. Just as the ancient Greeks and Romans read the entrails of birds (a process called haruspication) for auguries of the gods' favor or fury, Macdonald studies the signs of goshawk hunger for its marvelous, fleeting presence. "Looking for goshawks is like looking for grace," she writes, "it comes, but not often, and you don't get to say when or how."[36] The international success of *H Is for Hawk*, along with the continuing popularity of environmental writing, tells me we're still looking for grace through the natural world.

# Trust the details, trust the reader

All this means that as a writer you have to trust language to do its work, carrying the world from one human body to another. Language needn't be "fancy" to be effective. Like a good jacket, it should be fitted to what it's describing—not too baggy, not too tight, adding a little neatening and flair of its own but taking its shape from the body underneath. William Wordsworth wrote about this in 1800: "a language arising out of repeated experience and regular feelings," he writes, "is a more permanent and far more philosophical language than that which is frequently substituted for it by Poets."[37] In 1854, Thoreau seconded him: "Anything living," he wrote, "is easily and naturally expressed in popular language."[38] Almost a century later, novelist and essayist George Orwell opined, in "Why I Write" (1946), that "good prose should be like a windowpane"—your words should be so well-fitted to what they're describing that your reader shouldn't really notice your authorial presence at all.[39] Even if you don't go that far, good writing is about working toward a vision of a world beyond your own head that serves it, not just you, in the words you choose.

It's pretty easy to tell when someone's writing just to show off. But more often, we struggle along in vague, oversized words because our emotions feel too big to fit into smaller ones, or we fear that the reader just won't get what we're talking about otherwise. But in constantly straining after "big words," we start to feel uncomfortably stretched, like we're straining to reach a bowl in a high kitchen cabinet. Furthermore, we start to feel stuck in our own heads, bedeviled by a hunch that these words really *aren't* getting our meaning across after all. If we relax and look closer, we can see that the writer-and-reader relationship moves in two directions. You give readers clues and trust them to build mental pictures based on *the common language of the senses*. As we launch into talking about how to get words on the page, here's one big thing to remember: Readers can't do the mental work you're asking us to do unless you're giving us the sensory information we need. And in order to do this, you don't have to strain: ordinary, physically rooted language can work just fine.

# Language principle #1: Sensory vs. editorial

"Nothing is more ephemeral than words," the editor Norman Cousins wrote. "Moving them from the mind of a writer to the mind of a reader is one of the most elusive and difficult undertakings ever to challenge the human intelligence."[40] In this task, writers are helped by a general rule: *sensory, specific* language moves more effectively into the reader's mind than language that is *editorial*. By "sensory and specific," I mean based in the five senses of sight, touch, smell, sound, and taste, sharpened by your habits of attention and contact with the world, evoking the cool wind bending the grass, the thick short fur of the cat's throat, dishwater-puckered fingertips, or the tang of the first strawberries. Editorial language wants the reader to accept the writer's *judgment* of something without giving the reader any of the sensory information on which that judgment is based, and it shows up most often in adjectives and adverbs: *beautiful, horrible, thrillingly, meaningfully*. It hands down an opinion from inside the writer's own mind while hiding her reasoning—or, we might also say, being vague. Here's an example:

*The beautiful sunset over the lovely lake made her happy as she thought about all the wonderful things she had been blessed with in life and how much she loved her family, even if it was hard to tell them so sometimes.*

This writer has a point and wants us all to know it—and while we can get a general sense of a positive feeling, we still feel like we're standing outside her idea, straining to look in. It's natural to want your writing to convey your feelings. But here, the writer inserts herself between us and the scene, handing down judgments ("beautiful," "lovely," "wonderful") at which she's already arrived rather than giving us the materials we need to get there on our own. The Russian writer Anton Chekhov told the then-apprentice writer Maxim Gorky that because of his overwriting (and editorial language), he was "like a spectator in the theater who expresses his delight with so little restraint that he prevents himself and others from listening."[41] For me, this writer's editorial language has just that effect; her enthusiastic voice is loud in my ear, but I'm not being given the information I need—even just a detail or two—to build the picture in my own mind. Ever heard that writing axiom "show, don't tell?" This is what it means.

Because this sentence gives us very little to *picture* in our minds, it isn't doing writing's most important work. Dramatist David Mamet has said that particularly at moments of high drama, you should write *only what a camera could record*—sights and sounds, such as actions, gestures, and speech. That test works in reverse, too. What would this sentence give a camera to record? Well, there's a generic "she" (Who? How old?) looking at a lake (From a boat? From a dock? From a chair? Sitting down? Standing up?). But what color is the sunset? Are there trees? Is anything happening out on that lake to prompt "happiness" in our generic "she?" If we do have a picture, it's probably because we're doing the work ourselves, hauling in our own painted backdrops of sunsets we've known. But all the other content is *feeling*, which neither a camera nor the reader can see.

Vagueness is tempting for a couple reasons. First, it's easy. (See *cliché*, Chapter 2.) Sometimes students protest that a vague description is "more relatable" because "it lets people bring their own feelings to the situation." At this point, other students counter, "But you're the writer—it's your job to take me somewhere and show me something I *don't* already feel." Think about it this way: editorial language tells us how to feel, and people usually don't like that. You can tell us a hundred times the sunset is "beautiful," but we won't believe it until we see the pink and gold streaks of cloud, that soft evening light, for ourselves.

And is language that's so vague and editorial *actually* more "relatable?" *Do* precision and specificity keep readers from identifying themselves with what they see? Let's take a look at Marie Howe's poem "Hurry," from her 2008 collection *The Kingdom of Ordinary Time*[42]:

> We stop at the dry cleaners and the grocery store
> and the gas station and the green market and
> Hurry up honey, I say, hurry hurry,
> as she runs along two or three steps behind me
> her blue jacket unzipped and her socks rolled down.
>
> Where do I want her to hurry to? To her grave?
> To mine? Where one day she might stand all grown?
>
> Today, when all the errands are finally done, I say to her,
> Honey I'm sorry I keep saying Hurry—
> you walk ahead of me. You be the mother.
>
> And, Hurry up, she says, over her shoulder, looking
> back at me, laughing. Hurry up now darling, she says,
> hurry, hurry, taking the house keys from my hands.

Sure, the speaker makes a big leap ("To her grave? To mine?"). She's tackling some heavy issues here—growth, aging, the bittersweet transfer of authority from parent to child. But she never uses any of those words. She stages people in a place, doing things we can picture, and tailors the words to fit them, just one or two syllables apiece. (Even "finally" and "grocery," the only three-syllable words I can spot, are ordinary; no special vocabulary skills needed.) Yet we get her point anyway, don't we? This is the paradox of specificity: precise detail is *more*, not less, "relatable" to the reader, because it invites us into your world by giving us the information we need to do the mental work by which we can imagine it. That mental work is what makes the writing feel "relatable" to us by involving us as readers, inviting us into the world on the page.

Let's look at a prose example from the English writer Mollie Panter-Downes (1906–1997), who wrote a series of short "Letters from London" for *The New Yorker* during the Second World War. This is August 30, 1940, a week after German bombs began falling on central London:

> By midweek, the work of reconstruction was already going ahead. Men were running up scaffolding around the damaged buildings, hurrying to and fro, like ants in a heap which someone had just kicked apart. What had been an ill wind for many people had blown good to the glaziers, from whose vans, backed

against the pavement, hundreds of square feet of glass were being lifted out of straw packing. The danger from falling glass and odd bits of masonry was still considerable, and police barricaded the surrounding streets to anyone who couldn't show a pass or prove legitimate business there. Opposite St. Giles, the church where Milton is buried, the front had been blown out of a dark and Dickensian little eating house, and two men in bartenders' aprons sat together discussing events among the broken mahogany hatracks and scattered spittoons. A notice tacked up outside announced business as usual. Around the corner, in Aldersgate, a sign in front of a delicatessen shop which had suffered the same fate proclaimed cheerfully, "We are wide open." It was doing a good trade among customers who did not seem to be moved by the fact that they could leave by the conventional door or through the space where the window had been.

At St. Giles, a bomb had fallen slap on the sandbags protecting a stained-glass window, blowing a hole in the wall and toppling Milton off his plinth outside. On the vacant plinth were still inscribed Milton's own curiously appropriate lines: "O Spirit … what in me is dark illumine, what is low raise and support."[43]

Many writers would have filled this space with anxious, are-you-getting-this words like *resilience, tragedy, history, human spirit*; Panter-Downes, who observed scenes like this all over London, fills it with detail that makes us feel all those abstractions without needing to name them. Unfussily layering English history and colloquial speech ("it's an ill wind that blows nobody good," Dickens, and Milton) and well-chosen detail, she makes readers believe what she obviously believes herself: London has survived many things, and it will survive the war, too.

Where do you get that detail to include in your writing? By paying attention to the world around you, which gives you enough of a sense memory to imagine or remember the thing you're writing about, "acting it out" in your own head to get the words right. What facial expression or physical gesture expresses the feeling you sense in a character? What would a person in this situation actually say? What's the smell of rain rushing toward you over the field? What color *is* a sky at sunset? What sound does new snow make when you step on it? Asking these questions keeps you always turning back to reality, in language and in imagination, and that process gives the world on the page color and shape in your reader's minds.

How do you act out a scene in your own head? Through a process I call *enfleshing* an image by drawing on your sense memories. I summon up a mental picture of what I am describing, then fit words to that, going back and forth between the words on the page and my mental picture until I am satisfied with my sentences (at least for now). If I don't know enough yet about my character or situation, I might do research or other kinds of writing exercises (more about that later). Sometimes, if I am looking for the right verb, I'll even get out of my chair and act out what my character's doing: saunter? Stride? Leap? Always, enfleshing involves trying to get clearer about what I do and don't yet know. Expand your experience—even if it's only your imaginative experience—and you can expand the clarity and specificity of the language in which you write about it.

The sneaky truth about editorial language (and life) is that it's usually easier to have judgments about something than to perceive it as it is. *That's beautiful! That's important!* These things feel good and authoritative for us to *say*, but they leave readers unsatisfied, asking *why?* "But real writers use big words!" you may protest. Not so: real writers take account of what their readers need to *picture* things. Also, readers can tell when you're hiding a lack of knowledge under big words. We'll feel tricked if you are, in George Orwell's words, "trying to give an appearance of solidity to pure wind."[44]

Editor Susan Bell tells a story in her book *The Artful Edit* that illustrates this idea. When F. Scott Fitzgerald was working on what would become *The Great Gatsby*, his editor, Maxwell Perkins, read his drafts and sent critiques— including that he couldn't tell what Jay Gatsby looked like. "Among a set of characters marvelously palpable and vital—I would know Tom Buchanan if I met him on the street, and would avoid him—Gatsby is somewhat vague," Perkins wrote. "The reader's eyes can never quite focus upon him, his outlines are dim."[45] At first, Fitzgerald argued that, in Bell's words, "a vague Gatsby was a mythic one; to make him too clear would make him too human and unheroic: no longer a God."[46] Eventually, though, Fitzgerald admitted to Perkins, "I myself didn't know what Gatsby looked like or was engaged in & you felt it."[47] To sharpen his own sense of Gatsby's appearance and history, Fitzgerald went back to a real-life inspiration for the character—his onetime neighbor, convicted white-collar criminal Edward Fuller—and had his wife Zelda "draw pictures [of Gatsby] until her fingers ached."[48] After this research, Fitzgerald could sharpen his description of Gatsby to the line we know: "His tanned skin was drawn attractively tight on his face and his short hair looked as though it were trimmed every day."[49] Having freed himself imaginatively by increasing the range of his knowledge, Fitzgerald could select the details that bring Gatsby to life: crisp, athletic, a little tense. "If a character feels muddy and we cannot make her clear," Bell writes, "we could go to a museum, open an art book, look at postcards, or sketch until we find a face that fits her" and "might do the same to envision a landscape."[50] It's usually when we haven't done the work to enflesh the image that we strain to stretch a thin canvas of abstractions over empty space.

Let's go back to that sentence about the sunset. How would it look if we trusted the simple language of the senses, enfleshed the picture in our heads, and revised accordingly?

**Original:**
*The beautiful sunset over the lovely lake made her happy as she thought about all the wonderful things she had been blessed with in life and how much she loved her family, even if it was hard to tell them so sometimes.*

**Revised:**
*She sat cross-legged on the dock as the sun went down, lighting the sky pink and gold. Out on the lake, her sons were rowing toward her. She waved at them, smiling, although they were too far away to see her face.*

Interestingly, each of these passages has the same number of words (42), but the second is using those words to create a picture *and* the feelings associated with it, fulfilling a motto for prose revision we'll see again in Chapter 4: "More ideas per square inch." Trust your reader—and trust yourself—to see what is there. Respond to the world beyond your head by writing what you see, and then your readers can see it too.

# Writing principle #1: Just get started (and make a mess)

So how does actual *writing* get started? Meet the writer's best tool beside a pen: a notebook, small enough to carry wherever you go. By "notebook," I really mean "any writing surface which can receive words." Some of my students use smartphone notes; although I've done this myself in a pinch, a paper notebook and pen better respect the privacy of mind and page, and cognitive research has shown that handwriting on paper produces richer thoughts than typing.[51] Anne Lamott, as she describes in *Bird by Bird*, uses index cards. The habit of writing things down will, over time, shorten the distance between your words and the things you see. It's weird, but I've found it true: knowing your observations have a place to go, getting in the habit of noticing and writing down, will make your brain give you more of them. By contrast, ignoring them can make them fade and disappear. "Look sharply after your thoughts," advised Ralph Waldo Emerson in his journal in 1872. "They come unlooked for, like a new bird seen on your trees, and, if you turn to your usual task, disappear; and you shall never find that perception again; never, I say—but perhaps years, ages, and I know not what events and worlds may lie between you and its return!"[52]

What do you write in your notebook? Scraps, bits and bobs, pieces of drafts, whatever you want. Over time, a notebook becomes a record of what you think and feel in a way nothing else can, because it keeps pace with your life as it happens. "Of all strange and unaccountable things," mused Thoreau in 1841, "this journalizing is the strangest:"

> If I make a huge effort to expose my innermost and richest wares to light, my counter seems cluttered with the meanest homemade stuffs; but after months or years I may discover the wealth of India, and whatever rarity is brought overland from Cathay, in that confused heap, and what perhaps seemed a festoon of dried apple or pumpkin will prove a string of Brazilian diamonds, or pearls from Coromandel.[53]

Just like images and scenes add up to a book (see Chapter 3), what you write down on an ordinary day can be unexpectedly valuable, even beautiful, when you look back at it later on.

The novelist and nonfiction writer Peter Matthiessen (1927–2014) used his notebooks to record observations while traveling, then draft them into paragraphs: "Peter traveled with universal notebooks, taking notes on the right-hand pages, leaving the left blank until he used them for his first run at usable copy—usually in the evening after a day of reporting," writes Mathiessen's friend and editor Terry McDonell.[54] The notebook may not always be consciously connected to projects in progress, but it is always part of some ongoing dialogue with ourselves. Joan Didion describes this in her essay "On Keeping A Notebook" (1966): "[H]owever dutifully we record what we see around us, the common denominator of all we see is always ... the implacable 'I.' ... we are talking about something private, about bits of the mind's string too short to use, an indiscriminate and erratic assemblage with meaning only for its maker."[55] But a notebook also leads us into magpie-like engagement with the world, picking up scraps and saving them to train our eyes, our minds, our sense of delight. In "Why I Write," Orwell says, "So long as I remain alive and well I shall continue to feel strongly about prose style, to love the surface of the earth, and to take a pleasure in solid objects and scraps of useless information."[56] That's my notebook manifesto. For me, journals are longer narrative reflections and notebooks are dispatches from the moment, stuffed in pocket or bag, jotted, spilled on. "How do you keep track of things you've put down?" students ask me. I can only say that having written the detail down increases the likelihood that it will come back to me when I am writing it. Case in point: once I was writing an essay and remembered the German word *Geschichtsmudigkeit*, a weariness of history, which I had read in a magazine at an airport and jotted down. A quick notebook-dig later, I had the word (and the spelling) again.

It's also fun to just flip through and see what I've totally forgotten. In Knoxville, Tennessee, up the hill from the river Cormac McCarthy evokes in *Suttree* (1979), a woman sits on a square of cardboard on a street corner, slowly combing her long blonde hair. Looking up through a half-open window shutter on a narrow street in Florence, Italy, I catch a glimpse of high ceiling frescoed with leaves and vines, hear a snatch of laughter and voices I can't quite understand. An oak tree tosses leaves into my lap as I sit in the grass with my students, talking about *Frankenstein*. A green poker chip glows amid the pennies (and one bored, bright orange goldfish) in a Los Angeles city fountain. A skinny Alabama boy, gentle and delighted, lifts a gray and brown rat snake from the grass, lets it flow from hand to hand, then sets it down. A girl in a halter top and shorts pads barefoot down the sidewalk of my little town in July, grinning as a thunderstorm begins, then slows down to prolong the rain on her skin. That same rain, bouncing off a metal roof, makes a fuzzy halo. A fat little bird lands on a reed in a watery slough, then, when it feels the reed's tip bending toward the water, inches backwards toward the root to correct the balance. Noticing life keeps it from feeling unlived. Writing doesn't happen in those grand imagined moments when you sit down at age eighty to Look Back Over Your Life. It happens just as you live—in jots and scribbles and assembled moments, day by day and year by year, right now.

And I do mean *jots and scribbles*. For a journal and/or notebook to be really useful, it has to be really yours, meaning no one else knows or, God forbid, evaluates what's in it unless you choose to show them. In his classic novel *Nineteen Eighty-four* (1949), George Orwell gives a name to that constellation of thoughts and memories unfolding moment to moment inside our heads, which no one else can see: "ownlife." We need some space of privacy and dignity to be ourselves, to think our own thoughts and to grow into artists. This is why dictatorships like Orwell's Ingsoc control citizens by setting up surveillance "telescreens," abolishing written communication, and destroying records of the past. (Orwell's hero, Winston Smith, begins his rebellion by writing on paper in a journal, with a pen.) I shudder when a teacher says she takes up students' notebooks to grade them. (If students aren't choosing to live like artists, that's their problem.) In 2015, my student writers decided for themselves that Instagram couldn't serve as a notebook, because social media is for public consumption. The students know—and I agree—that a notebook needs to be messy, angry, sappy, random, weird, and, above all, private. If you want your notebook to help you connect with the page, you have to feel free there: to make a mess, to be alone and judgment-free, to write down things that aren't perfect and might not ever be.

# Nuts and bolts: Gathering tools, managing energy

Now let's talk specifics: notebook? Lines? Pencil or pen? Trust your own preferences, although it's good to avoid getting overattached to one tool. I use pen for everything—black or blue rollerball ink with a fluid and hefty line. For my journal, I like black softcovered Pentalic sketchbooks about the size of a standard sheet of paper. For my notebook, I like red Moleskine Cahiers, a little smaller than a standard page but still portable. In both cases, I like blank pages—no lines—and soft covers so I can fold them backwards. The important thing is that your notebooks be comfortable for you to write in, to improvise with, to mess up, and to do with what you want. I urge paper and pen. It breaks us out of our cycles of electronic reward, and the cognitive science is in: pen on paper by hand is better for thought. "But I can type faster," you may protest. Trust me: your relationship with writing will improve, permanently, when you connect with the page by hand.

This is also where you may be wondering, "Do I have to write every day?" Well, anything gets easier the more we do it. The *less* we do something—traveling, exercising, connecting to a blank page—the more daunting it seems. So, yes, you have to write—if not every day, then near it—if you want to give yourself the chance to develop the habit and to keep that space open for writing in your head and in your life. But there are different ways to organize it. At the Tin House Summer Writers Workshop in 2008, my teacher, the award-winning novelist Colson Whitehead, told my workshop group about his writing habits. At that time, he set himself an eight-page-per-week quota; if he reached it before the end of the week, then he'd met his deadline, but if he hadn't, then he knew he needed to double down on his efforts to meet his goal.

Hearing Whitehead talk about this was really instructive. First, he knew himself and his preferences well enough to design a system for himself that would let him produce his best work. Second, he had fixed a larger goal in his sights: completing a manuscript of a certain number of pages in a certain period of time. (This speaks to another good principle: "one year from now, what will you wish you had done now?") Third, he had broken down that larger goal into a series of concrete, manageable steps. In my own writing life, I need breaks and variety—I usually move among two or three projects at once, some long, some short, some fiction, some nonfiction—and between those projects and others and general notebook and journal writing, I connect with the page at least five or six days out of every seven. Writing needs to be a regular part of your life if you want to go anywhere with it.

Think about exercising or playing sports, with which writing has a *lot* in common. If you're used to running, you can go out and do your thing with no problem. But if I—who am *not* a runner—go out and try to run four miles without stopping, I've taken on a challenge that's bigger than what I'm used to, and it's going to hurt. I think that's why people so often try to write once in a while but give up in frustration, intimidation, or some combination of the two. If writing is only an occasional thing for you, you'll probably find it harder to connect with the page and develop as a writer over time than you would if you were giving yourself regular opportunities to grow. For better or worse, anything gets easier the more you do it.

In developing writing practices, I prefer the phrase *managing energy* to *managing time*. Rather than seeing a day as a container with fixed borders—a certain number of hours—into which you fit as many activities as possible, go back to your own physical rhythms. What time of day is your mind clearest? When do you feel a slump? What do you *want* to have done by, say, the end of a week, and what do you *have* to have done? What stresses you out more *not* to have done it *than* to do it? You have a finite amount of energy and focus, so see if you can save your "best energy times" for writing, the thing you really want to use that energy on. Other things (like the laundry) can fit in around the edges. Sometimes they can be reassigned to other members of the household. Sometimes, if you are tired of the energy-draining stress and noise they produce—social media, yet another extracurricular activity, the constant blare of the television—they can simply be cut out. Remember the question from earlier in this chapter: is it the silence I am afraid of, or the absence of the "me" that is known through sound? Can I give myself the opportunity to discover who I am when no one is watching?

Of course, this life is going to include a lot of variables. We go through illness, a death in the family, childbirth or adoption, divorce, job change or loss, so many other things. Even without such obvious milestones, our patterns of energy may change. In college and graduate school, I was a classic night owl, scribbling the opening scene of what I grandiosely called "my first novel" at 4 a.m. when I was supposed to be studying for the media law final exam I had at 10. (Luckily my media law professor, still a mentor of mine, was interested in hearing this explanation for my mediocre performance.) Now, in my forties, I find that mornings are my time of best and clearest-minded focus, before other obligations and endless varieties of adult noise rush in to fill the gap. When I'm working the way I want to work, I'm getting up first thing in the morning (5 a.m. during the school year) to make coffee and get right down to writing. Crucially, I don't let myself succumb to the impulse to wash breakfast dishes and make the bed until *after* I've written at least a couple of pages. Tidying and chore-ing—and I definitely include checking email in this category—siphons off my best energy and focus if I let myself think, "First, I'll just start this load of laundry … " Nuh-uh. Just say no and turn to the page instead. I've learned this the hard way. And after the focus of writing, doing laundry feels like a break.

# Words on the page: A place to start

To start filling their notebooks, poet Marie Howe gives her students the same exercise I do: make lists of things you observe. Just make lists. Ten things you saw, heard, smelled, tasted, or touched in the last week. Three things you saw on the way to work this morning. Five pieces of advice you've gotten. Seven objects in your bag right now. This is a quick way to make a mess and get words on the page. It also helps you notice your own state of mind. One adult student of mine stared at her page, then shook her head. "I've been a bad Buddhist this week," she joked. "I can't remember a thing. Have I *really* been such a sleepwalker?"

And when I say *random things*, I mean it. In my introductory creative writing classes, we do this exercise together at the beginning of the semester. Each student makes a list, then writes one item from that list on the board for everyone to see. Here are some samples:

Cloth-covered buttons on an old purple coat
The German word *Geschichtsmudigkeit*, "a weariness of history"

A man's plastic Adidas flip-flop washed up in a storm drain
Sticky chocolate patches on the sidewalk outside the Whippy Dip (our local
    ice-cream stand)
Bees burrowing into purple sage blossoms behind Olin Hall
The squeaky *crimp crimp* sound of new snow underfoot
Hollow body of a double bass; you put your arms around it to play
The smell of grandparents' house: old quilts and Sunday pot roast
Limestone rock with a snail-shell fossil stuck inside
Suddenly he throws his head back and laughs
Music overheard from a passing car, trailing after it in the air
On the bus, a twentysomething woman with long braids and a toddler in her
    arms; both leaning against the window, asleep

# Exhausting the place: Georges Perec in Paris

The French filmmaker and writer Georges Perec (1936–1982) made lists to make discoveries—might some unconscious order emerge? Might you see your own preoccupations in a way you didn't before? Might you generate images too odd to come upon any other way? Or might you simply let chance take over and see what happens? At least three of his books are primarily lists: *I Remember* (1978, a list of cultural associations and objects from his generation and place), *La Boutique Obscure: 124 Dreams* (1973, which is exactly what it sounds like), and *An Attempt at Exhausting a Place in Paris* (1975). This small book is forty-five pages of lists, made when Perec spends three days sitting around the Place Saint-Sulpice in Paris, observing and writing down everything that catches his eye.[57] Here's a typical passage (the numbers are buses):

> It is 1:35 p.m. Groups, in gusts. A 63. The apple-green 2CV [a small Citroën sedan] is now parked almost at the corner of rue Ferou, on the other side of the square. A 70. An 87. An 86.
>
> Three taxis at the taxi stand. A 96. A 63. A bike courier. Deliverymen delivering beverages. An 86. A little girl with a schoolbag on her shoulders.
>
> Wholesale potatoes. A lady taking three children to school (two of them have long red hats with pom-poms.)
>
> There is an undertaker's van in front of the church.
>
> A 96 goes by.
>
> People are gathering in front of the church (for a funeral procession?)

An 87. A 70. A 63.
Rue Bonaparte, a cement mixer, orange.
A basset hound. A man with a bow tie. An 86.
The wind is making the leaves on the trees move.
A 70.[58]

Sometimes Perec makes lists of things by categories, like "outline of an inventory of some strictly visible things," including letters on signs and uniform jackets, "stone," "a cloud of pigeons that suddenly swoops down on the central plaza, between the church and fountain," and "lettuce (curly endive?) partially emerging from a shopping bag."[59] Other times he records people: "a little boy wearing an English school cap; he crosses, making sure that he steps only on the stripes of the crosswalk."[60] Once, he muses on the randomness of randomness: "the buses pass by because they have to pass by, but nothing requires a car to back up, or a man to have a bag marker with a big 'M' of Monoprix, or a car to be blue or apple green, or a customer to order a coffee instead of a beer …. "[61] Sometimes he asks questions: "why are two nuns more interesting than two other passerby?"[62] Although he doesn't stray too far from the list format, he follows his line of thought wherever it goes, receiving whatever the place he's in chooses to give.

The work of writing begins with observation of and connection to the world around you, which feeds a concrete, observational intelligence that will animate your words. It's fueled by an enthusiasm for the world around you and for observing detail—geeking out, scribbling words, making a mess. Writing starts up in your head, not just on the page. And it starts with writing something *on* that page, where you are, right now. Trust the details and the words to take you where you want to go.

# Exercises

All these exercises are designed to help you develop habits of observation, then try to fit language to what you see. Give them a try, and don't worry if it feels weird at first to be doing this. Any new thing feels a little strange until you get used to it.

*Sharpen your senses (and memories): Make lists*
1) List ten sensory, specific things that you observed while going to work, while taking a walk, while riding your bike, in the last week or month … .

2) Make lists of particular tools or technologies associated with some particular person, place, or time (the heavy channel-changing dial on the black-and-white TV, my grandmother's rotary phone, the eggbeater with its worn wooden knob, cassette mixtapes labeled in my undergraduate handwriting with sticky cheap blue pens, the heady, dry, faintly chemical smell of new library books, the purple-inked copies coming out of the mimeograph machine in the principal's office, the old red Massey-Ferguson tractor … ).

3) Write about a person or place by writing down lists of flowers, plants, trees, animals, insects, or other natural features associated with that person or place. Circle one of those and describe it in more detail, focusing on that plant or natural feature. What features speak to you of that person or place? Why?

4) Write down your dreams as soon as you wake up. Keeping a pen and paper beside your bed increases your chances that you *will* remember your dreams.

5) "Exhaust a place," like Georges Perec: Find a place you can sit unobtrusively for at least an hour and write down everything you see. (I like this for its ability to build presence and attention without any agenda—you literally *are* just writing what you see.) Set your list aside and look at it after some time has passed. What do you notice? This may be particularly useful while traveling, as it can get you past the anxiety of feeling as if you have to write something deep and original. Try making lists by category: colors, sounds, letters, means of locomotion or movement, animals, smells …. Push yourself for sensory detail, not editorial language.

6) In your memory, open the door or lid of a space remembered from childhood and belonging to an adult relative—refrigerator, barn, jewelry box, cabinet, toolbox, pickup truck, dresser drawer, a pot on a stove—and write about what's inside.

*Sharpen your language: Write what you see (sensory vs. editorial)*

7) Describe something you observed recently with one of your five senses in words limited only to those five senses and preferably one syllable each (something can be *green, rough, sharp,* or *sour,* but not *beautiful, amazing, hideous,* etc.)

8) Write down something you heard someone say, exactly as they said it. Include in your dialogue the physical gesture they were making at the time, like so: "DIALOGUE," s/he said. S/he GESTURED. "DIALOGUE."

**Examples:**

"Let's go," she said, jingling the keys in her hand. "We're going to be late."

"That ought to do it," he said. With a heave, he slammed the truck tailgate and tossed the shovel on top. "Enough compost to fill the whole tomato bed."

9) Take a walk outdoors, without music, by yourself, and observe what is inside and outside your head. Describe at least one thing you saw and one thing you thought.

10) Write a description of an animal using only details a camera could record.

**NOT:** "The fox looked at me as if to say hello … " or "The fox, so wild and free, so innocent, looked at me inquiringly …." This language is (a) inserting human ego and interpretation where they don't belong and (b) annoyingly editorial. I love a line from Thoreau's journal of January 1841, describing a fox in the snow: "He ran as though there were not a bone in his back."[63]

**INSTEAD:** "The fox paused on the yellow center line of the road and looked at me. Its eyes were bright golden brown, its fur a rusty mix of red and gray. From over the hill, the rumble of car tires approached. The fox lowered its tail and trotted into the high grass and purple flowering vetch at the edge of the asphalt."

## Make a mess

"Wreck this journal," as author Keri Smith says. (Remember Jean in my adult writing class, the one who kept getting two lines into her beautiful blank journal and stalling out? She scribbled all over one page, her grin getting wider and wider, in front of all the rest of us as we cheered her on. Jean wrote happily in all her journals after that.) Tape things to pages scrapbook-style, spill things, make fingerprints. Draw pictures. Interrupt yourself to complain, loudly [in brackets], about something going on in the background while you are writing a semi-coherent narrative about something else. Use different-colored inks or different kinds of pen. Get another person's handwriting on the page, if only for a line or two. Pick it up and write for five minutes, right now. Write in it without looking back for six months. For a year. (I think not looking back too often helps you get more deeply and unselfconsciously into journals. Write it down, leave it, and keep going.)

### Connect with the page: Fill the space

11) Write in your notebook for ten to fifteen minutes without stopping, following the line of thought wherever it goes. This is an old standby, endlessly adaptable and always interesting. I like it because it teaches you that you can connect to the page without an agenda and without seeking "perfection."

12) Begin an entry with one or more of the following:

Today I am remembering …
> There was a time when …
> It makes me smile to remember …
> I get really pissed off when …
> I don't know how I feel about …
> When I taste [name], I think about …
> Suddenly I looked up and saw …
> A Wordsworthian "spot of time" for me is …

### Circle the most interesting thing

Variations of this activity are endlessly useful. This is the basic one: When you have a certain critical mass of writing (at least two pages is good), go back through it and, without thinking too much about it, circle the most interesting thing. What "interesting" means is up to you. Another way to say this is, "what has the most energy." Don't overthink. Then write that "most interesting thing" at the top of a new page and start writing again from there. (You can repeat this process several times, drilling down into your material with a new "most interesting thing" in each set of pages.)

# 2

# Fighting the Brain, Writing the Brain: Neuroscience for Writers

Like many middle-aged people, I sit—a lot. My best intentions and that scary fact that "sitting is the new smoking"—it wrecks your life expectancy, cardiovascular health, and mood—push me to do better. Away from the office, I bike, walk, and garden. A couple of years ago, I made places to stand in my campus office and my home writing room, and I'm inspired by *New Yorker* writer Susan Orlean's description of her walking desk, a platform with a low-power treadmill underneath.[1] (Winston Churchill had a standing desk too.) But when you have books to write and read and papers to grade, you're going to spend a lot of time at a desk, one way or another. And—true confession time—you aren't always going to do the responsible thing and stand up. *I'm so busy,* your interior voice whines. *I'm tired! I work so hard! I focus better when I'm sitting. I'll go for a walk when I finish this. And I'll definitely take the stairs to even things out.*

Except that when you're standing on the ground floor of your building, staring up six flights of stairs to where your office is, toting your books and papers and bag and a handful of mail, it's easy to let the excuses swarm in, steer you toward the elevator, and lift your finger helplessly, zombie-like, to the call button. *I'm carrying too much. I don't have time. I work so hard.* Et cetera. Sometimes you can guilt yourself into heading for the stairs with thoughts of step-counters or what you ate for lunch or plain old personal shame. But more often what began as a one-time exception soon becomes a habit, even when you don't have much (or anything) to carry. Taking the stairs—as I said earlier about writing—becomes harder and more intimidating the less often you do it, even when you know better. "Habits," says the proverb, "are cobwebs at first, chains at last."

Of course, *you* really means *me* in all of the above. And I'm telling you (the real you) this story (which I *am* writing standing up) to illustrate what I've learned about life and writing: habit roots itself in us at a level below simple laziness, deep in the places the brain uses to comfort itself and make sense of its world. Our brain seeks comfort, familiarity, and routine even though difficulty and challenge are what make it grow and what sent our species in new evolutionary directions. To borrow the biological truism, although challenging any organism is essential to its survival, the organism itself prefers comfort—and this starts at the level of the brain, including the way we learn and recognize language on the printed page. Getting the words on the page in the right order is made harder by habits we don't even know we have: we learn them as we're learning language itself, and they spring from the actions of the brain's own built-in meaning-making features, which operate at a level too subtle, and too familiar, for us to recognize. Avoiding cliché is hard because, at one level, cliché is what the brain itself prefers.

I'm not a neuroscientist; although I once thought I'd become a neurosurgeon, I'm really only an enthusiastic amateur medical science and medical history reader. I don't believe biology can explain everything about human life, although it helps. But I've learned enough to change the way my students and I think about writing and revising. Now I believe that these processes and many craft sayings—avoid cliché, describe things in fresh, specific language, bring an image to life in your reader's mind—

become much less mysterious if you have some basic understanding of how language and brain interact. Let's call what we're about to do *Neuroscience for Writers*. We'll be thinking about how the brain creates meaning (and sentences) from little black shapes like this on the page. Mostly, we'll be learning about habits we don't even know we have in order to examine the writing process and turn it inside out, with the freshest surface of our attention and word-precision facing into the world.

# Recognizing, not reading

What if I told you you weren't really reading these words, you were recognizing them and letting your brain supply the meaning? Even before you actually get to the end of this zebra? Wait. *Zebra*? Isn't that word supposed to be *sentence*? Yes, it is—and that little startled swerve you just felt is your brain waking up from habits it's been learning ever since you learned to read.

First, let's think about why brains love habit. At the center of the brain live a pair of little almond-shaped bodies called the amygdala, which are responsible for processing and storing emotions—especially those that cluster around startling or fearful things. That jolt of adrenaline that comes with something new or scary wakes us up and imprints that thing into memory via the amygdala, but it also takes attention. And attention takes calories, which any organism wants to conserve, not expend. Therefore, the brain has other areas (like the frontal lobe, center of reflection and judgment, which is the last to fully develop) and systems of habit to help itself calm down and save energy while still processing all the information we receive and carrying on a dazzling amount of self-reorganization on the fly. The more often we do something, the less it registers as new and startling and the less it's likely to remain in memory as a distinct event. The brain wants to save its spikes of adrenaline and attention for new things (which may be dangers) so it lumps familiar things together to save storage space. The reflective, assimilating, judging powers of the frontal lobe, which hits its stride in our thirties, assist this process by helping us connect past events to present ones: *calm down*, it whispers, *you were stressed out before and you survived, so you'll probably be all right this time too.* We live always amid the brain's paradox: while malleable and self-engineering, it's also eager to form networks of habit to save its energy.

This energy-saving tendency of the brain helps us learn to read by recognizing shapes and patterns, then generalizing—especially as we read more and our pool of data gets larger—about those patterns we see on the page. We read by recognizing the shapes of words and stringing them together with other word shapes that we've learned make sense in that context ("sentence" does, "zebra" doesn't). We learn to put together units of words and decipher those units as words on their own: "ant" becomes "chant" becomes "enchantment."[2] Even more amazingly, we read in the midst of our eyes' constant tiny jumps, or saccades, around the page— "three or four times per second," writes Alberto Manguel in *A History of Reading*, "at a speed of about 200 degrees per second."[3] Yet the brain still manages to put shapes together to help us recognize meaning: "as the networks of cells responsible for recognizing letters and letter patterns learn to 'fire together,'" writes Maryanne Wolf, "they create representations of their visual information that are far more rapidly retrieved."[4] Here's an example:

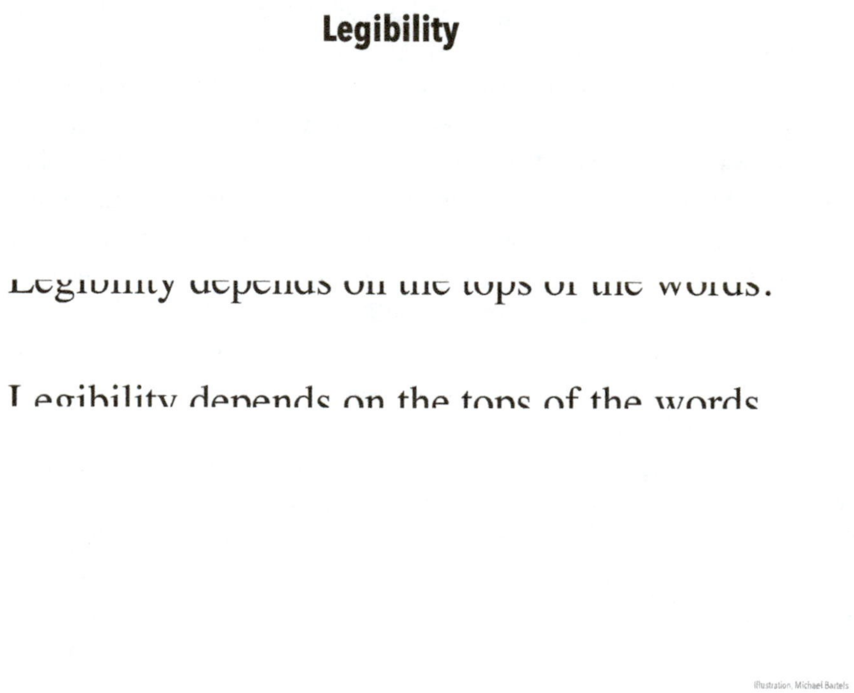

## Legibility

Legibility depends on the tops of the words.

Legibility depends on the tops of the words

**Figure 2.1** "Legibility depends on the tops of the words"—illustration by Michael Bartels.

If you guessed that this sentence reads "Legibility depends on the tops of the words," you're right.[5] We depend on words' shapes to recognize them, and therefore to recognize their meaning. Because of this, we can usually also read and understand words whose letters have been scrambled, as long as their general shape is the same as the word we know. Take this famous letter to the magazine *New Scientist* from Graham Rawlinson of Aldershot, Hampshire, on May 29, 1999[6]:

> You report that reversing 50-millisecond segments of recorded sound does not greatly affect listeners' ability to understand speech (In Brief, 1 May, p 27).
>
> This reminds me of my PhD at Nottingham University (1976), which showed that randomising letters in the middle of words had little or no effect on the ability of skilled readers to understand the text. Indeed one rapid reader noticed only four or five errors in an A4 [standard] page of muddled text.
>
> This is easy to denmtrasote. In a puiltacibon of New Scnieitst you could ramdinose all the letetrs, keipeng the first two and last two the same, and reibadailty would hadrly be aftcfeed. My ansaylis did not come to much beucase the thoery at the time was for shape and senqeuce retigcionon. Saberi's work sugsegts we may have some pofrweul palrlael prsooscers at work.
>
> The resaon for this is suerly that idnetiyfing coentnt by paarllel prseocsing speeds up regnicoiton. We only need the first and last two letetrs to spot chganes in meniang.
>
> This was not easy to type!

The third and fourth paragraphs show that we can make sense of scrambled words as long as the first letter, the last letter, and the word's general shape are the same as the originals.

We read by familiarity, and the more familiar with language we are, the faster and more habitually we read. This is why it's so hard to spot typos in our own writing, and why editing your work is easier if you've stepped away from it for a while. This is also why reading your work aloud is so helpful in proofreading, since the ear is less forgiving than the eye. As you reread your manuscript silently, your brain is filling in what it "knows" you meant to write as well as what it "knows" is the word's right shape, and the ideas behind the words are familiar to you because you thought of them, so you have to peer through three layers of your brain's own meaning-making functions to evaluate what you have actually written. We may register the scrambled words in Graham Rawlinson's letter and note "that's wrong," yet our brains can still make order out of the disorder by seizing on recognizable word shapes and contexts and filling in the blanks themselves. I've come to see this process as something like Google's autocomplete—the word's general shape enters the brain and the brain fills in a meaning either confirmed or denied by the words around it, then adjusts accordingly. All this happens at lightning speed. So powerful is the brain's desire for order and meaning that it can smooth over the literal disorder of letters out of place, which shows us that meaning doesn't live in letters alone.

Graphic designers—especially typographers, or font designers—can teach us a lot about how we process words, because the shapes and cases of letters and the associations we bring to different styles of type affect the brain's meaning-making processes. "This is the most interesting thing about typography," writes designer Jason Santa Maria; "it's a chain reaction of time and place with you as the catalyst."[7] Scroll through the library of fonts in a word processing program and you can see that each signals a different personality, and, therefore, different contexts in which it's going to convey meaning best: you might type a child's birthday party invitation in Comic Sans, but you'd cast your resume in Times New Roman. Cases (uppercase or lowercase) make a difference too; TEXT IN ALL CAPITAL LETTERS is harder to read than Text In Sentence Case Like This, because ALL-CAP TEXT makes a blocky shape with few of the features, like the high tops of f's and h's and the bottom-hanging swoops of g's and p's, that we use to distinguish words from one another and from the white space around them.[8] Different cases have become associated with voice volumes, too; in online communication, typing in ALL CAPS is considered rude because it's the equivalent of shouting, and all-lowercase writing (beloved by student poets) can feel quiet, sometimes too quiet. Italics and capitalization used for emphasis—I *told* you **this** is IMPORTANT!!!—get weirdly boring; if everything is important, nothing is. Therefore, considering your words' impact on your reader begins by considering how her brain builds meaning from the shapes of letters and words.

# Defamiliarization and self-protection

As we've seen, brains are not only building meaning from the sensory world around them—they're also building habit, assembling patterns of familiarity that reassure us we don't have to pay full attention to what's in front of us because we've seen it before. Pulling into our parking space at work, for instance, we realize we have little memory of how we actually got there. Yet if we're unaware of them, these patterns of auto-completing habit—especially when they meet our use of language—can dull the edges of our art, and our lives. In his essay "Art as Technique" (1917), the Russian literary critic Victor Shklovsky (1893–1984) described how this phenomenon begins:

> If we start to examine the general laws of perception, we see that as perception becomes habitual, it becomes automatic. Thus, for example, all our habits retreat into the area of the unconsciously automatic; if one remembers the sensations of holding a pen or of speaking in a foreign language for the first time and compares that with his feeling of performing the action for the ten thousandth time, he will agree with us … .[9]

Therefore, habituated by routine, we stop seeing what's in front of us: "we do not see [objects] in their entirety," Shklovsky writes, "but rather recognize them by their main characteristics," just as we have seen the brain doing with letters and words earlier in this chapter. "We see the object," Shklovsky continues, "as though it were enveloped in a sack. We know what it is by configuration, but we see only its silhouette."[10] Shklovsky quotes a passage from the great novelist Leo Tolstoy's diary (March 1, 1897) to show this process in action:

> I was cleaning a room [Tolstoy writes] and, meandering about, approached the divan and couldn't remember whether or not I had dusted it. Since such movements are habitual and unconscious, I could not remember and felt that it was impossible to remember … If some conscious person had been watching, then the fact could be established. If, however, no one was looking, or looking on unconsciously, if the whole complex lives of many people go on unconsciously, then such lives are as if they had never been.[11]

This is why it's important to wake up and pay attention to your own life as it passes by: if you don't, then it's as if you had never lived your life at all. "Habitualization," Shklovsky declares, "devours works, clothes, furniture, one's wife, and the fear of war."[12] Excitement wears off the purchase of that new pair of shoes, you drop onto the couch at the end of the day without quite seeing it, magazines blare about Ten Ways to Keep Your Marriage Exciting. The cure, of course, is the heightened attentiveness that art springs from and fosters in return: "art exists that one may recover the sensation of life," Shklovsky writes, "it exists to make one feel things, to make the stone stony. The purpose of art is to impart the sensation of things as they are perceived and not as they are known."[13] What's the difference? Look around you right now at the familiar room in which you may be reading these words. Known. Now get out of your chair, lie down on the floor, and look again, noticing the odd shapes of the undersides of tables and chairs, the altered pitch of the angles where walls meet ceiling, the steep upward curves of the tree branches beyond the window. Perceived. This is what art is for: removing the veil of habit from our perceptions, over and over again, so we can actually behold what is in front of us rather than sleepwalk through the world. Shklovsky writes that "the technique of art is to make objects 'unfamiliar,' to make forms difficult, to increase the difficulty and length of perception, because the process of perception is an aesthetic end in itself and must be prolonged"; it's up to us to keep the freshness of renewed vision from wearing off.[14] This takes a continual effort at self-renewal from the writer and from her readers, but there are ways we can use our words to achieve it.

# Brain-quickeners: Sensory language and motion

In his delightful book *What We See When We Read*, Peter Mendelsund, known for his book jacket designs, explores how our eyes move around the page to gather meaning and bring it to life in our imaginations. "Words are like arrows," he writes, "they *are* something, and they also point *toward* something."[15] The process of reading involves being channeled across and down the page by the habitual direction of words and sentences—in English, "forward" is from left to right and top to bottom—but even as we hurtle along in the direction the words are pointing, we are also being directed back into ourselves, into thickets of memories and associations the writer can invoke but not predict. "To read is: to look *through*; to look *past*," he writes, "though also, to look, myopically, hopefully, *toward* …. There is very little looking at."[16]

When we read, looking at and then quickly beyond words, we are seizing on their recognized shapes and then using those shapes to build our own mental structures of memories, images, and thoughts. "Words are effective," Mendelsund writes, "not because of what they carry in them, but for their latent potential to unlock the accumulated experience of the reader. Words 'contain' meanings, but, more important, words potentiate meaning."[17] As an example, he offers the word *river*:

> *River*, the word, contains within it all rivers, which flow like tributaries into it. And this word contains not only all rivers, but more important all *my* rivers:

every accessible experience of every river I've seen, swum in, fished, heard, heard *about*, felt directly or been affected by in any other manner …. . I read the word *river* and, with or without context, I'll dip beneath its surface. (I'm a child wading in the moil and suck, my feet cut on a river's rock-bottom; or the gray river just out the window, now, just to my right, over the trees of the park—spackled with ice. Or—the almost seismic eroticism of a memory from my teens—of the shift of a skirt on a girl in spring, on a quai by an arabesque of a river, in a foreign city …. )

This is a word's dormant power, brimming with pertinence. So little is needed from the author, when you think of it.

(We are already flooded by river water, and only need the author to tap this reservoir.)[18]

As we've seen in Chapter 1, this is exactly why sensory and specific language "potentiates meaning" in a reader's mind—it unleashes a flood of individual associations, stored in our bodies and senses, that invest your words with significance and visual detail that only we can supply. Readers want to be cocreators, with the writer, of the world on the page, and specific, sensory words make that possible by releasing those associations into our minds. They also create effects more powerful than even the best writers can manage on their own, since no writer could know and deliberately invoke all the associations *river* has for Mendelsund, or any one of us. "Reading is a neuronally and intellectually circuitous act," writes Maryanne Wolf, "enriched as much by the unpredictable indirections of a reader's inferences and thoughts, as by the direct message to the eye from the text."[19]

Knowing about language's "circuitous" qualities helps a writer choose which word she really needs. For me, the editorial adjective *beautiful* just potentiates a blur of positive feeling and a scattershot flash of images and sounds: the pink and gold lilies from my June garden, Kathleen Battle singing "Batti, batti," from Mozart's *Don Giovanni*, the serene face of Luca Signorelli's Renaissance angel. But it doesn't steer me decisively in any of those directions. *River* will also produce a cluster of pictures in your reader's head, but, alongside other sensory, specific words, it will channel (so to speak) that emotional energy and mental work in a direction that flows alongside yours, helping us accompany you rather than meander off on our own. As we've mentioned, readers want to be taken up and carried along by a reading experience; we're willing to cocreate a world on a page, but we need the constant subtle assistance of sensory, specific language—which rewards us by immersing us in a satisfying reading experience—to help us do that.

Let's see what one great writer does with one great river—Charles Dickens on the Thames, in Ch. 1 of *Our Mutual Friend* (1865). Gaffer Hexam and his daughter Lizzie are floating between Southwark Bridge and London Bridge, looking for bodies to fish from the current:

> Wheresoever the strong tide met with an impediment, his gaze paused for an instant. At every mooring-chain and rope, at every stationary boat or barge that split the current into a broad-arrowhead, at the offsets from the piers of Southwark Bridge, at the paddles of the river steamboats as they beat the filthy water, at the floating logs of timber lashed together lying off certain wharves, his shining eyes darted a hungry look. After a darkening hour or so, suddenly the rudder-lines tightened in his hold, and he steered hard towards the Surrey shore.[20]

Dickens shows us the Thames' human landscape—boats, logs, bridge abutments—through Gaffer Hexam's eyes as his "hungry look" darts over the water, but he also shows us that water in motion as Gaffer sees it, with particular focus on every place the current breaks over what could be a body.

Asking readers to imagine motion in particular ways—as we imagine the flickering, lantern-lit current breaking around objects—can literally animate those pictures in our minds. *In Dreaming by the Book,* aesthetic philosopher Elaine Scarry investigates how writers create sensory images (including sights, smells, sounds, and tastes), although a writer's medium ("monotonous small black marks on a white page"), unlike theater, film, painting, or music, doesn't actually give us things to see and hear. "The question is," she writes, "by what miracle is a writer able to incite us to bring forth mental images that resemble in their quality not our own daydreaming but our own (much more freely practiced) perceptual acts?"[21] Analyzing the work of Marcel Proust, Homer, Gustave Flaubert, and Emily Bronte, among others, Scarry argues that this is because writers layer moving things and still things together in a way that makes them both easier for our brains to picture, so that those images are stored in our heads the same way our own memories are. In the following passage, Marcel Proust is describing a room overlooking the sea:

> [The room] which I found myself occupying had set against the walls, on three sides of it, a series of low book-cases with glass fronts, in which ... was reflected this or that section of the ever-changing view of the sea, so that the walls were lined with a frieze of sea-scales, interrupted only by the polished mahogany of the actual shelves.[22]

We may be able to imagine glass-fronted bookcases sitting still in a room, but the whole image quickens to life once a thin, transparent, moving layer of a second image is laid on top of that initial solid one. The same effect is true for shadows blowing across grass, firelight flickering on skin, or even armor or cloth sliding over a living body (as in Homer.) As I'll discuss in Chapter 3, this effect can help you usher your reader across the bridge from her mental world into yours; writers often employ this effect when "the fiction is especially fragile," or "the story is still in its very early pages," since it helps our imaginations solidify the fictional world and move deeper into it.[23] "By the peculiar gravitational rules of the imagination," Scarry writes, "two or more images that are each independently weightless can nevertheless confer weight on one another."[24] In *Wuthering Heights* (1847), Emily Bronte asks us to imagine hands clenching, seizing, or tearing, "acquaint[ing] us with our own ability to make the images move by having us picture a hand that acts on them."[25] This sparks the sense memories and cause-and-effect relationships our bodies have learned and our brains have stored, since we have seen and felt our own hands at work. It takes advantage of the way our brains learn by mimicking: our *mirror neurons,* just as the name describes, are activated when we see someone doing something and then do that thing ourselves. Therefore, setting your images in motion, or layering one type of motion over another, may make them literally easier for readers to imagine, sidestreaming one type of action with another so that both enter our brains at once. The whole process leads to a sense of quickening—that rich and wonderful word—in our brains, as our picture-making ability stirs and our attention brightens and sharpens. The right pictures, when they come to life inside our minds, quicken our whole brains too.

# Drawing to defamiliarize

Pictures can help us sneak up on our brains and surprise them when we try to draw the scene or object we're writing about: this is a great exercise for writers, although you might immediately protest, "But I can't draw!" Relax—the kind of drawing I'm talking about is for information-gathering purposes, not representational ones. And like all the other exercises I offer, it's going to happen in your notebook where no one else has to see.

Trying to draw something, even if—perhaps particularly if—you don't have much experience with it can jostle your vision and shake loose habitual ways of seeing. As the Victorian critic John Ruskin (1819–1900) wrote, drawing tunes up our attention in many ways:

> Let two persons go out for a walk; the one a good sketcher, the other having no taste of the kind. Let them go down a green lane. There will be a great difference in the scene as perceived by the two individuals. The one will see a lane and trees; he will perceive the trees to be green, though he will think nothing about it; he will see that the sun shines, and that it has a cheerful effect; and that's all! But what will the sketcher see? His eye is accustomed to search into the cause of beauty, and penetrate the minutest parts of loveliness. He looks up, and observes how the showery and subdivided sunshine comes sprinkled down among the gleaming leaves overhead, till the air is filled with the emerald light. He will see here and there a bough emerging from the veil of leaves, he will see the jewel brightness of the emerald moss and the variegated and fantastic lichens, white and blue, purple and red, all mellowed and mingled into a single garment of beauty. Then come the cavernous trunks and the twisted roots that grasp with their snake-like coils at the steep bank, whose turfy slope is inlaid with flowers of a thousand dyes. Is not this worth seeing? Yet if you are not a sketcher you will pass along the green lane and when you come home again, have nothing to say or to think about it, but that you went down such and such a lane.[26]

We process the world a little differently through our eyes if we also process it through our hands, with the craft of drawing (and language, too). As Alain de Botton notes, "Drawing brutally shows up our previous blindness to the true appearance of things."[27] Therefore, giving drawing a try can sharpen your general habits of observation. It can also hone your writing in particular ways. When students are developing their initial images (see Chapter 3) into stories or poems, I often ask them to draw the incident, place, or object they are trying to write about. A quick and messy sketch is fine, as it is in freewriting; don't overthink it, since, as I mentioned, representational accuracy or "good drawing" is not the point. Rather, drawing will clarify your mental picture of a scene (where exactly are the characters standing relative to one another?). It will give you information about what you don't yet know: what is hard to draw because it's not clear in your mind's eye? It will help you focus on what details are particularly interesting to you, or, in other words, where the energy of this image really is. What did you draw first? (That can be a signal of how you're thinking about this image, or what you find important; if you're drawing your childhood kitchen, did you start with the table or the stove, or neither?) What part of the drawing do you keep going back to and adding to—what's getting more attention or less attention? Has drawing reminded you of some feature of this object that you had otherwise forgotten? Do you find yourself focusing on or including something you hadn't thought would be in the drawing when you started? In developing fiction and nonfiction projects of my own, drawing has helped me explore these questions and more.

# Universals: Reading across space and time

When we look at the stories humans have told over time, we can see patterns of language use that suggest human brains may work in similar ways everywhere. Literary scholar Patrick Colm Hogan calls these patterns "literary universals." He suggests that some "universal" features of literature might be allusion ("used to enhance the aesthetic effect of a new work by invoking in the reader associations with a prior work"),[28] alliteration and rhyme (word sounds that echo one another in a meaning-producing, sensorily pleasing way), metaphor and symbolism (features of the natural world, for instance, standing in for human emotions), and even poetic structures ("standard line lengths for poetry in a wide range of traditions," Hogan writes, "tend to fall between five and nine words," perhaps because that length is easier for those composing or reciting poetry to remember and for listeners to hear[29]). Just to take one example, the five-to-nine-word rule above is supported by poetry in Chinese, Dinka, Basotho, Hawaiian, and ancient "Babylonian creation poems," as well as by twenty-line samples from Chaucer's *Canterbury Tales*, Milton's *Paradise Lost*, the *Odyssey*, and the *Aeneid*. Certain plots may also recur, like the "romantic tragicomedy … in which lovers are separated, typically by death, and in which there is often the suggestion of literal or metaphorical reunion after death."[30] This describes the Ramayana (100 BCE), fifteenth-century and eighteenth-century Japanese plays, Arabic and Persian tales, and Shakespeare's *The Winter's Tale*.[31] The tenth-century Indian theorist Abhinavagupta wrote that "we 'savor' poetry" and "Persons aesthetically sensitive, indeed, read and taste many times over the same poem"—just as Victor Shklovsky wrote, a millennium later, that "the process of perception is an aesthetic end in itself and must be prolonged."[32] Two different language systems, ancient Sumerian and Chinese, have been found to contain "secret women's dialects," with specialized script and vocabulary only women knew or wrote; the Sumerian system was called Emesal, or "the fine tongue," and the last speaker of *nu shu* ("female writing") died in 2004 at the age of ninety-six.[33]

You can see this sort of universal patterning at work in mythology, too, which lays down in our heads what I call the old bones of story. It's there, somewhere in our hearts and our heads: that shape to which we respond when it rises and walks in those first words, *once upon a time*. Creation stories from Gilgamesh to Genesis to Native American Ojibway stories feature earth-destroying floods from which humans and animals must rebuild. The West African medieval epic of Sundiata features a misfit boy who, with some supernatural assistance, grows into a powerful warrior king—kind of Britain's King Arthur or Moses in the Book of Exodus or *Luke* Skywalker in the Star Wars franchise. As Joseph Campbell writes in *The Hero with a Thousand Faces* (1949), "It would not be too much to say that myth is the secret opening through which the inexhaustible energies of the cosmos pour into human cultural manifestation. Religions, philosophies, arts, the social forms of primitive and historic man, prime discoveries in science and technology, the very dreams that blister sleep, boil up from the basic, magic ring of myth."[34]

The history of reading and writing suggests another universal at work— our trust in physical objects or marks on physical objects to transmit meaning over time. As described in Maryanne Wolf's *Proust and the Squid: The Story and Science of the Reading Brain*, humans have invested many different objects—turtle shells, clay tablets, paper in all its forms—with meaning we hope the marks on those objects will preserve.[35] Sometimes the object itself is the language: for the ancient Incans, quipus, "ancient dyed fibers and twine shaped into patterns with extremely intricate systems of knots and attachments," may have represented not only an abacus-like counting tool but "an undeciphered Incan written language system," in the same way that "each knot in the Jewish tallith, or shawl, does."[36] Sometimes the marks on a particular surface are important: to ask the gods questions, an ancient Chinese person could have consulted an "oracle bone," a turtle shell or cow's shoulder bone. The user would write a question on the surface, then apply a hot poker until the surface cracked in patterns that might have appeared to be the gods' own writing, responding to that question.[37] In *A History of Reading*, Alberto Manguel describes "two small clay tablets of vaguely rectangular shape … found in Tell Brak, Syria, dating from the fourth millennium BC"; each has a figure of an animal that may be a sheep or goat and a "small indentation near the top" that may be the number ten. Therefore, each little tablet means "ten goats." "By the mere fact of looking at these tablets," Manguel writes, "we have prolonged a memory from the beginnings of our time, preserved a thought long after the thinker has stopped thinking, and made ourselves participants in an act of creation that remains open for as long as the incised images are seen, deciphered, read."[38] Even as meaning may be tantalizingly elusive, the presence of the tactile world, perennially used by humans to think with, can remain close, ushering us into a space of paradox in which it's fascinating to linger. For instance, *boustrophedon*, Greek for "the turning around of the ox," is the name for the pattern of Egyptian and other early writing, in which the reader's eye progresses from left to right, drops down to the next line, then proceeds back across the page from right to left—just like an oxen plowing a field.[39] The Egyptian "hieroglyphic sign for 'house,'" Maryanne Wolf writes, "looks a lot like a house seen from above—as the gods were thought to see it."[40] Patterns of written and spoken language across place and time reinforce a human reality: since we're embodied beings, we think of things we can't see in terms of those we can.

Although we might fear that the term "universal" would flatten cultural difference, Patrick Hogan argues that a proper study of literary universals can enrich our understanding of our common humanity and its variations in time and place. For instance, to understand how allusion works in ancient Indian literature, you have to know enough about ancient Indian culture to recognize the allusions in the first place, and you have to know enough about other cultures to have an informed basis for comparison. Therefore, studying "universals" can enable us to celebrate the dazzling range of human variety and to see more deeply into human commonalities. The universal inflected by the local: this seems to me a good way to think about what a human culture is. Perhaps this can lead to what the philosopher Kwame Anthony Appiah has called *cosmopolitanism*, being rooted in your own place while also being curious about and appreciative of others. This is a healthy way to live in a shared and diverse world: knowledgeable about your own history, responsible to your particular place but curious to learn about others, expanding your sense of your own life's meaning and of what it means to be a human being on Earth.

At the end of his book *Millennium*—a survey of how Western civilization has changed over the past thousand years—historian Ian Mortimer offers some thoughts on things that endure:

> And at the end of it all, I find myself wondering what hasn't changed over the last thousand years, and what won't change over the next. At first, those questions seem vast, and overwhelming. But then I think about them

again. I picture a troubadour singing in the shadows of a hall fire. I imagine thousands of people walking beneath the overhanging eaves of narrow streets to see Shakespeare's plays. I hear the shouts of drunken farm workers in the candlelit gloom of a seventeenth-century inn as Jan Steen studies their ruddy faces, preparing to paint them. The simplicity of the answer makes me smile. What doesn't change is that we find so many things in life worthwhile—love, beauty, children, the comfort of friends, telling jokes, the joy of eating and drinking together, storytelling, wit, laughter, music, the sound of the sea, the warmth of the sun, looking at the Moon and stars, singing and dancing ... .

What won't change? Everything that allows us to lose ourselves in the moment.

Everything that is worth dreaming about.

Everything that is without price.[41]

Human beings seek meaning, and we seek artists as companions in that search. That's one universal that will never change.

# Humans vs. cliché: Good writing can save the world

If there's one thing that dims the great human light of language, it's probably that dreaded writing-class word: *cliché*. As we've seen, brains love habit, and therefore brains also love predigested little units of language (*in the final analysis, he was always there for her, it is what it is, every cloud has a silver lining, yada yada yada*) that signal predigested little units of habitual thought we can blurt forth without really thinking about them. In fact, the word *cliché* comes from the French for *clicked*, the sound that a unit of movable type— letters used so often it was quicker to keep them together—made as it dropped into its slot in the printer's machine. In "Politics and the English Language," Orwell complains that clichéd phrases are "tacked together like the sections of a prefabricated hen-house" to compose too many political speeches.[42] Writers experience this tendency from the other end—when we reach out for a word or image, we may put our hand on a cliché, something we've heard or seen so many times (particularly on TV) that it's stopped meaning much of anything. (Characters raise one eyebrow to signal wry bemusement, take off hats to reveal hair tumbling down, or wake to a ringing alarm clock as a story begins.) "This invasion of one's mind by ready-made phrases," wrote Orwell, "can only be prevented if one is constantly on guard against them, and every such phrase anesthetizes a portion of one's brain."[43] Cliché can include habits of thinking and speaking as well as phrases or characterization gestures or the mental shrug with which we write off a person with an assumption or a familiar phrase. We're all guilty of this at one time or another. But to understand why cliché matters as more than just a word for an editor to scribble in the margin of your story, I'm going to talk about politics and philosophy, because both these fields can speak to what threatens humanity—including cliché.[44] Like Orwell in "Why I Write," I use "political" in "the widest possible sense," meaning a "desire to push the world in a certain direction, to alter other people's idea of the kind of society that they should strive after"—a society that respects the dignity of human and nonhuman beings.[45]

I illustrate cliché in class with an exercise called "The Two Weddings." First, students write a short description of a wedding using as many clichés as they can. *It was their special day, the happiest day of their lives. The bride had never been more beautiful. They swore to love one another forever. The weather was perfect, and the families were so proud as they stood on the church steps throwing rice. The ring bearers were adorable.* Students can seldom get beyond one paragraph before complaining, "This is so boring!" And rightly so. Things get more interesting when I ask them to write a second wedding description, using non-clichéd details that get some human complexity into the picture. Right away, their pens start scratching; smiles creep across their faces. I stop them around ten or fifteen minutes. "So," I offer, "read me what you've got." The scenes are vivid, funny, sometimes heartbreaking: a groom and a groom and two tense families; tantrum-throwing ring bearers in their satin Lord Fauntleroy shorts; hiking sandals peeking under the hem of a wedding dress; a bride in a wheelchair, adjusting her veil on her hairless scalp and smiling. Each story contains a phrase or image of a wedding I've never heard before. And by the time they've read their scenes aloud, each student can see that emotion inheres in the quirky, particular details of real life like water in a sponge. Trust your detail, and your specific, sensory language, and your reader to sense the emotion it bears.

Like that Saul Steinberg sketch of the man drawing himself,[46] specific words expressing our thoughts can write better thoughts—and better selves—into being. Enfleshing a real, complex situation in our minds keeps us from succumbing to cliché on the page and in real life, which means that it keeps us morally and artistically responsible to reality. In his essay "Politics and the English Language" (1946), George Orwell wrote that politicians use so many clichés because they want to hide their real goals from their audiences and even from themselves. "In our time," he writes, political speech and writing are largely the defense of the indefensible. Things like the continuance of British rule in India, the Russian purges and deportations, the dropping of the atom bombs on Japan, can indeed be defended, but only by arguments which are too brutal for most people to face, and which do not square with the professed aims of political parties. Thus political language has to consist largely of euphemism, question-begging and sheer cloudy vagueness … .Such phraseology is needed if one wants to name things without calling up mental pictures of them.[47]

Because "the great enemy of clear language is insincerity," Orwell writes, we can become better writers by thinking better about what we actually mean to say—and that starts with enfleshing an image honestly and clearly in our heads: "What is above all needed is to let the meaning choose the word," Orwell advises, "and not the other way about … . Probably it is better to put off using words as long as possible and get one's meaning as clear as one can through pictures or sensations. Afterwards one can choose—not simply accept—the phrases that will best cover the meaning, and then switch round and decide what impression one's words are likely to make on another person."[48] *Choose, not simply accept*—what a great way to avoid cliché.

Like Orwell, the political philosopher Hannah Arendt (1906–1975) believed that cliché comes from moral blindness. In 1961, Adolf Eichmann, Hitler's Minister of Jewish Affairs (basically, the organizer of the trains running to the death camps), was captured in Argentina and brought to trial in Jerusalem; Arendt's account of the trial for *The New Yorker* became her book *Eichmann in Jerusalem* (1963). At one point, Eichmann was asked, essentially, whether he really could have been unaware that his plans would lead to the deaths of millions of people. He replied with a German proverb—a cliché—that translates roughly as "Nothing's as hot as when it's being cooked." Friends who know Germany well have told me this means, "Things often look more extreme in the planning process than they turn out to be in reality." To Arendt, Eichmann's clichés were significant. "Whether writing his memoirs in Argentina or in Jerusalem, whether speaking to the police examiner or to the court, what he said was always the same, expressed in the same words," she writes.

> The longer one listened to him, the more obvious it became that his inability to speak was closely connected with an inability to think, namely, to think from the standpoint of somebody else. No communication was possible with him, not because he lied, but because he was surrounded by the most reliable of all safeguards against the words and the presence of others, and hence against reality as such.[49]

That "reliable safeguard" was his own obliviousness, or—in a very important word for Arendt—his *thoughtlessness*, or his "inability to think from the standpoint of someone else." To varying degrees, Arendt suggest, this thoughtlessness can be present in any of us if we aren't paying attention to what we're saying and doing and what will happen in other people's lives as a result. Therefore, avoiding cliché isn't just an artistic goal but a moral and political one, since it asks us to pay attention to and be responsible to the reality in front of us, not to our assumptions or stereotypes about it.

When the periscope of cliché surfaces in a culture, you can bet there's a submarine of thoughtlessness underneath, even when someone doesn't mean to do wrong. Take the example of James Patterson, a commercial-fiction author and a one-man literary industry who not only writes many books himself but also employs other writers to churn out books that are packaged and sold under his name.[50] Critics and readers may dismiss Patterson's work as "just light reading" or "fluff," but what does that judgment actually mean? Where does it come from? Look at the first paragraph of *Suzanne's Diary for Nicholas* (2001):

> Katie Wilkinson sat in warm bathwater in the weird but wonderful old-fashioned porcelain tub in her New York apartment. The apartment exuded "old" and "worn" in ways that practitioners of shabby chic couldn't begin to imagine. Katie's Persian cat, Guinevere, looking like a favorite gray wool sweater, was perched on the sink. Her black Labrador, Merlin, sat in the doorway leading to the bedroom. They watched Katie as if they were afraid for her.[51]

Reading this together, students and I stumbled over each sentence. How does an apartment "exude 'old' and 'worn?'" What is "shabby chic," and how do you "practice" it? How does a cat look like a favorite sweater? What is so "weird" and/or "wonderful" about an old porcelain tub? The fundamental problem is the prose itself: readers can't see what the author's describing because he doesn't seem to be taking the time to imagine it clearly and "see" it in his own mind first. Readers are offered a series of clichés—shorthand characterization gestures, editorial adjectives, brand-focused (and therefore instantly dated) descriptors, and analogies that collapse at the first nudge toward real meaning.

"Start with the tub," I said. "Picture an old porcelain tub in your mind. Now describe it." Immediately, students blurted vivid sensory words (*clawfoot, white porcelain worn down to the gray iron underneath, scuffed, deep, chipped*) that contrasted with Patterson's editorial language (*weird, wonderful*). Next, the animals. Aside from the puzzle of how an animal looks "afraid for" a person, how could a cat look like a sweater? "When I think of a sweater," one student volunteered, "I think of rough, scratchy, knit. With cables up the front. Rough, not furry and soft. A flat thing." Right: a mismatch of textures and shapes punctures the simile from inside. And what about the verb for what the cat is doing? "Let's perch, everybody," I suggested, and we all sat up straight on the edges of our chairs. "Now do what a sweater does when you toss it down on the sink." Immediately, we all sagged sideways. "What's this verb?" I asked. *Slump*, students said. *Sag, drape, slouch*. Right.

This prose is meant to be read just like you'd watch television—perhaps even at the same time—accepting superficial imagery without asking what these words in this order actually mean. You don't have to pay attention to this book; in fact, you might get more pleasure from it if you don't. The logic of prose like this is the logic of cliche—reach for the closest phrase and slap it into place without bothering to see whether it fits—and the logic of consumerism, since to envision this world, you have to import hazy pictures from commercials and movies. "Shabby chic," for instance, was a decorating trend branded into a line of slipcovers and shower curtains sold at Target around the time this book came out. The writer John Gardner famously described good fiction as creating "a vivid and continuous dream" that unfolds in the reader's mind.[52] The dream this prose (and this first paragraph is typical) offers us is the same one television does: we are all part of a great genial tribe of people roughly like ourselves, aspiring to significant lives by buying the products we see on the screen. In that dream, we're created by what we buy and what is sold to us in the media we consume, not by what we feel or imagine from inside our own heads. And we're all half-asleep, with at least one eye on a screen—a reality in too many "average" American homes, where screens outnumber books and demand our attention during homework, dinner, and leisure time.

Now for the hard part: as elitist as my objections sound, I think the real social sin here is the lack of attentiveness to and respect for readers that cliché-based writing like this shows. Who is Patterson's imagined audience? First, *Suzanne's Diary for Nicholas* is part of a specifically designated women's-fiction product line within the Patterson empire, and its cursive lettering and landscape-painting cover strike recognizable women's-fiction branding chords. Later on in the chapter, Patterson overdefines New York neighborhoods as a real New Yorker would never do: "Trips to NoLita (North of Little Italy) and Williamsburg (the new SoHo.)" In combination with the "weird, wonderful" bathtub and "New York apartment" (studio? walkup? prewar six-room?), this combination of under- and overexplanation suggests, in one student's words, "that he's writing for people who've never been to New York but always wanted to go." Right. "But let me ask y'all this," I say. "I'm a woman from rural Alabama, living in rural Iowa. I've dreamed about going to New York City. Some of y'all feel the same way, right?" Students nod. "So do you feel James Patterson's speaking to you?" No, students say, because the language isn't showing us New York as New Yorkers understand it and as we'd understand it too, given well-imagined detail. (Compare this novel with Garth Risk Hallberg's *City on Fire*, Jonathan Lethem's *Motherless Brooklyn*, or Tom Wolfe's *The Bonfire of the Vanities* and see the difference.) And here we confront that great truth of writing and of politics, articulated by the anticolonial theorist Frantz Fanon in 1969: "You can explain anything to the people provided you really want them to understand."[53] Language used carelessly can show that a writer doesn't really care if we understand or not—or that he doesn't really believe that if he gives us his best and most precise words, we will follow.

So here's another question: why do so many people buy books like this? To be sure, they give pleasure to readers for a variety of reasons, and I'm not knocking those readers, or the author, as people. But commercial cliché lowers the intellectual capacity of a whole society by lowering our expectations for more artistically satisfying fare and our ability to enjoy it—and, over time, our visions of what a book should be. On and off the page, we start to prefer cliché because it's "easier," which makes us easy prey for politicians and other public figures who find our credulity very profitable. "It's better to be reading this than to be reading nothing at all," some might say. But that's not our choice: we do have better options. How would things be different if we actually read enough to have a basis for comparison between the sweater-like cat and—say—George Orwell? How would things be different if we asked for the entertainment we deserve, and if we fashioned our expectations for our home lives and leisure time around it?

Maryanne Wolf's research on children's reading acquisition offers important insights here: linguistic deprivation—including a lack of rich, specific, and varied words that expand experience by matching names to it—can hinder children's social and emotional development, with lasting effects. "Unbeknownst to them or their families," she writes, "children who grow up in environments with few or no literacy experiences are already playing catch-up when they enter kindergarten and the primary grades," not only in terms of "numbers of words" but also "concepts" and "syntactic forms"—as well as the intangible emotional education reading brings, helping children learn to "infer," to "predict," and to understand, through characters, "what other people feel."[54] One study shows that "by five years of age, some children from impoverished-language environments have heard 32 million fewer words spoken to them than the average middle-class child."[55] Essentially, children learning to read have two thousand days to capitalize on the brain's prime language-learning period, and during that 2,000 days, "not a word, a concept, or a social routine is wasted."[56] Children who are "talked to, read to, and listened to" will thrive in their language acquisition, but, Wolf notes, "the reality in many families (some economically disadvantaged, some not) means that too little time will be given to even these three basic elements before a child reaches the age of five."[57] Ultimately, early deficits in language acquisition will lead to social, intellectual, and even economic deficits later in life, described by scholar Keith Stanovich with the Biblical analogy "Matthew effects": to paraphrase the moral of the Parable of the Talents in Matthew 25, the (word-) "rich" will get "richer" and the (word-) "poor" will get "poorer."[58]

I'm no sociologist, but when I look around I see the twin currents of cliché and technology making all our homes—not just those labeled as "disadvantaged"—into "impoverished-language environments," replicating social and economic injustices that affect us all more than we think. I've known working-class parents who took their children to the library every week and upper-middle-class parents whose bookless homes gleam with sixty-inch televisions, talking refrigerators, and blue-haloed Alexa cylinders in the kitchen. Like low-quality, starchy food, the nutrient-deprived language of cliché is marketed to us as a substitute for the more nourishing words and ideas we dimly sense we should be looking for, if only we weren't so distracted and tired and unsure of what else to read and diverted by what's streaming past on the Internet all the time. It's possible to ask for something better, just as it's possible to seek out organic food and turn off screens. But the knowledge, critical-thinking ability, money, and general cultural wherewithal needed to make those choices aren't evenly distributed, and are sometimes actively withheld, in our society. Look how many food deserts—areas without access to supermarkets, farmer's markets, and other sources of healthy food—are located in inner cities and rural areas. Look at where funding for public schools is lowest: in those same areas. Access to nutrition for body and brain are linked. Like empty-calorie foods, empty-calorie words are cheap to produce, profitable to sell, and easy to pass off as the real thing to consumers (and voters) who have been taught to accept fake as substitute for real and to be content, in every area of our lives, with just a little less than we need and deserve. Income and educational level are only part of the story, because when I look around I see all of us—no matter whether we went to school or have high-paying jobs—asked to be consumers rather than critical thinkers, TV viewers rather than readers, wallets rather than thinking minds. That's insulting, unfair, and immoral.

Resistance to cliché is political in the best way—it asks for honesty, clarity, and responsibility to reality in the language we use so that we may be more responsible to one another as human beings. Making the effort to sharpen the picture of what we're really talking about, then fit language to that honestly and precisely, tunes up our mental muscles and our appetite for truth—and that can make not just better writers and readers but a better world.

# Technology and writers: Thank me for this?

Last semester, I tried a little experiment with my students: auto-complete poetry. "Take out your smartphones," I said (with affectionate snarkiness, they marveled at this rarity), "and start a text or email using only the words that pop up in the suggestion windows underneath. Just keep hitting different words until it's time to stop." Trying it right now, I get this: "Thanks so much for your support to this great game and I love you so much please follow me and thank you for everything you do thank me for this." We found this funny but deeply unnerving: amid the cliché and pleasantry, each message took some odd swerve, some *cri de coeur* that didn't feel only algorithmic, and that colored everything around it. After we read them aloud, we fell silent and stared at each other, wide-eyed and freaked out. Is this my smartphone talking to me? Is this a whisper from some ghost in the machine? Where, exactly, should I put a punctuation mark to divide "thank you for everything you do thank me for this"—is it gratitude or command?

Unlike found poetry or erasures—as seen in Annie Dillard's *Mornings Like This* (1995) and Nick Flynn's *The Captain Asks for a Show of Hands* (2013)—the smartphone poem, like those racist chatbots that hit the news every so often, has bootstrapped itself up from human scraps into some realm that isn't human anymore, layering bits of our language to make a voice and a face like the Beowulf-poet invokes the layers of bone in a warrior's chest. In aggregating our choices, our clicks, and our patterns of behavior—then selling those to advertisers for profit—the Internet is reducing us to mathematical patterns and those patterns to profits in a way that will weird you out further the longer you stare into its apparently innocent heart. *Thank you for everything you do. For everything you do, thank me. You do thank me for this.*

I wrote about this in my book *The Hands-On Life* so will only rehearse the main points here. First, technology's effects on us aren't socially or cognitively neutral; we think we're on top of our multitasking, but we're being conditioned to think in 140 characters or the moments between incoming-message dings. (Our bodies are conditioned too; slumped in the posture that deepens depression, inactive and thrombosed, avoiding eye contact, we're sad without quite knowing why.) If we're not old enough to know a before and after the Internet—I was a sophomore in college when I learned to use email, and in graduate school when Friendster, my first experience with social media, came along—it's easy to accept its effects as normal. Second, technology is using us, not the other way around; read Nicholas Carr's *The Shallows: What The Internet Is Doing to Our Brains* (2010), Jacob Silverman's *Terms of Service: Social Media and the Price of Constant Connection* (2015) and Tim Wu's *The Attention Merchants: The Epic Scramble to Get Inside Our Heads* (2016) for fascinating and frightening views of how attention-capture, advertising, and personal data sale on the Internet really work. Third, it's reshaping us in its own image so we're more "efficient" (that favorite technocentrist, antihumanist word) processors of its values and goals. We become its means to its end, without ever having been given the chance for fully informed consent. And that should worry us. Writing in the *London Review of Books* about Facebook—prime example of all these tendencies—John Lanchester concludes,

> I am scared of Facebook. The company's ambition, its ruthlessness, and its lack of a moral compass scare me. It goes back to that moment of its creation, Zuckerberg at his keyboard after a few drinks creating a website to compare people's appearance, not for any real reason other than that he was able to do it. That's the crucial thing about Facebook, the main thing which isn't understood about its motivation: it does things because it can.[59]

This is why I argue that the essential logic of technology is a totalitarian one, as Hannah Arendt and George Orwell identify that term: with the proper engineering, all things are possible, all obstacles removable, in the pursuit of power and profit for their own sakes.

Therefore—and I'll say more about this in Chapter 6—writers need to think very carefully about how we use technology and why, even though we're told ad nauseam that constant social media availability is fun and professionally necessary. Sure, I'll probably put notifications on Facebook when this book comes out, and friends from grad school, writers' conferences, and so many other places all over the world can learn about it and send their good wishes, which will be fun. I know some great writers who are on Facebook all the time. But, Lanchester writes, "there is a lot of research showing that Facebook makes people feel like shit."[60] (For real: especially in young people, Facebook use is correlated with depression.) I'm using Facebook less and less these days, myself, because I find that it dispels the energy writing and thinking take. It scatters the words that need to gather inside me and work themselves out in secret for a while. It holds its user in a sort of breathless crouch, awaiting its every word rather than producing words of your own away from its "friends"-focused gaze: what will *they* think of *me*? It fashions you into its obedient creature. And at that prospect, a certain Alabama mulishness speaks up in my blood: *hell, no.* To chirpy tech-despotism and the whole great ocean of greed on which it floats, resistance is honorable—particularly for writers, whose work and privilege it is to resist the constant subtle bullshit-wards coercions of cliché. If we don't, nobody else will.

Language—particularly on the printed page—can hold the line for truth and human dignity in ways no other medium can, or will. For instance, as Tim Wu describes in *The Attention Merchants,* television, built and driven by advertising, has never been as responsible as we think. In the 1950s, the CBS television network featured a news show called "See It Now," starring veteran journalist Edward R. Murrow, who had honed his craft as a radio reporter from the front lines of the Second World War and famously defied demagogue Senator Joseph McCarthy.[61] Yet as "I Love Lucy," "The Ed Sullivan Show," westerns like "Gunsmoke," and the then-new format of game shows captured high ratings and advertising profits, corporate sponsors took notice. In 1955, "See It Now"'s corporate sponsor, Alcoa, "dropped" the show, requesting from CBS chairman William Paley "something different, 'perhaps fictional, or like the Ed Sullivan program.'"[62] Paley duly transformed "See It Now" into an "occasional special," then "sold the now vacant slot to the Liggett & Myers tobacco company, which wanted to run a quiz show called 'Do You Trust Your Wife?'"[63] "In 1958," Wu writes, "See It Now was canceled for good."[64] But Murrow had seen the writing on the wall. Speaking to the Radio and Television News Directors Association in October 1958, he "deliver[ed] his lament," Wu relates, "for what he felt had befallen television over the decade," saying:

> Television in the main insulates us from the realities of the world in which we live. If this state of affairs continues, we may alter an advertising slogan to read: LOOK NOW, PAY LATER, for surely we shall pay for using this most powerful instrument of communication to insulate the citizenry from the hard and demanding realities which must be faced if we are to survive ... [T]here is a great and perhaps decisive battle to be fought against ignorance, intolerance, and indifference.[65]

Sixty years later, television still scrambles toward the lowest common denominator of human life—reality shows, sonorous clichés, fake "wins," and trivia. Even as viewers are cutting the cable cord and seeking refuge in good long-form drama (more about this in Chapter 3), broadcast overlords still aren't getting the message, because neither are we: humans still give ourselves over a little too easily to spectacle and show without asking what's underneath. And what Murrow called the "battle ... against ignorance, intolerance, and indifference" rages on.

As our wilderness shrinks and corporations grab at every aspect of our world to remake it in their own image, I see ordinary people being offered screen-based "fun" as a substitute for larger meaning—and that makes me furious and sad. "We're a culture of hungry ghosts," said writer Paul Kingsnorth. "We've dissociated desires from appetite and walk through the world, eating it."[66] We're so sadly willing to accept the diminished versions of ourselves that our own big brains have engineered—Twitter-chatter, shouting pundits who would make Edward R. Murrow weep, and advertising papering every available surface, from the bottoms of TSA airport security bins to the backs of students' report cards.[67] As Adrienne Rich advised those graduates in 1977, we deserve to take ourselves more seriously, and to ask for something more than what we've got. Art is where that happens. And artists—writers, us—are the people who speak those inconvenient words to others, but, first, to ourselves. It all starts with lifting the veil of habit over our faces and choosing—really choosing—how and where to direct our attention in the only life on Earth we will ever have.

# Exercises

1) Pick some random thing outside the window and write without intention or self-censoring for ten minutes. Let one idea lead to another. Circle most interesting thing, put it at the top of the page, and begin with something else.
2) Pick a cliché, then reinhabit it, as with my "Two Weddings" exercise. It can also be fun to write a story that literalizes a familiar phrase, like "trying to kill two birds with one stone," particularly if it's a bit magical or nonrealistic (see the next chapter).
3) What am I? Defamiliarize a familiar object in sensory language.

   **Example:** I'm a sticky clump of brown-edged paper with thicker paper for its roof and floor. One edge is covered with gold words that promise something inside. What am I? An old hardcover book (which I am looking at as I write.)

4) Draw the thing you are looking at, then the thing you are trying to describe in your own work. Remember, you're not producing a work of art—you are using drawing to investigate that thing. Where you have more lines and more detail, there you have more creative or emotional energy—and that's significant.
5) Write a static description that you then animate as we watch (something goes from still to moving):

   **Example:** In my garden, sunflowers stretch their wide faces to the sky. A wind passes over them and they sway, bowing and shaking their heads.

6) "Potentiate" memories in yourself and unlock associations by writing about a powerful sensory word: *river, tree, soil, blood, stone*.
7) Pick up a best-selling book and analyze what the author's doing on the page. What are the actual effects of its language on you? What can you learn?
8) Take a technology fast for twenty-four hours, or longer. Walk without headphones. What do you notice?

# 3

# Building a World on the Page

Perhaps you've seen the Steven Spielberg film *Indiana Jones and the Last Crusade* (1989). Adventurous archaeologist Jones (Harrison Ford), accompanied by his father Henry (Sean Connery), is hunting for the Holy Grail, the legendary healing cup from which Christ drank at the Last Supper. Near the end of the film, Jones and his father have reached the cave where the Grail waits on the other side of a rocky chasm. The Nazis, who want the Grail for themselves, have followed them. To force Jones to retrieve the Grail for them, they shoot his father in the stomach. And so Indiana Jones, following a clue in his father's archaeological notes, takes a leap of faith—he stands on the edge of the chasm, shuts his eyes, and steps forward into what looks like thin air. Miraculously, a bridge appears under his feet (it's been camouflaged in the surrounding stones) and he is able to cross it. The ending, of course, is a happy one.

When I talk to writing students about what they have to do for the reader in the first paragraphs of anything they write, I tell them that the reader is Indiana Jones, standing on the lip of the chasm, about to lift her foot and take a step out into the world of their writing. As clear and rich as your work is in *your* mind, your reader, still residing within the separate world of *her* mind, has never been there and knows nothing about it. She can see only the words right there on your first page. She doesn't know whether she'll like what she's about to read and want to stay with your work, or whether she'll put it down and turn away. Therefore, your words are the bridge that must appear under her feet and carry her farther into your world. As a writer, you're building what I now call the "Indiana Jones bridge" from the first page to the last. (This is true of academic papers, too, which carry a reader forward through an argument's stages and support her with evidence along the way.) Writers build an Indiana Jones bridge under our own feet by writing, too. Therefore, as we said in Chapter 2, your writing needs to take account of what readers need to understand language on the page and to make the "barrier to entry" in your first paragraphs relatively low, but it also needs to be sensory and specific enough to give your reader the means to keep imagining your world, step by step, as she walks further in.

Here's another analogy. Your novel is a swimming pool, with steps at the shallow end and a floor that slopes downward to its deepest point. Your reader is a hesitant swimmer, standing on the concrete, her toes hooked over the pool's edge. It's a July day, and the pool looks inviting. But stepping from her element (the hot, dry air) into your element (the water) is a risk. What if it's too cold? What if that shock of water on skin is too much? Your first sentences are the water she's eyeing as she makes her decision. Then they become the steps on which she sets her feet. If she likes them, she steps deeper in. Your sentences become the water that rises around her and the floor of the pool that slopes downward as she walks further in. The novel deepens around her as she gets more involved in its images, its voice, its world. She turns the page. Her feet lift off the floor of the pool. And somewhere around page three, if all goes well, she's fully immersed in the novel, floating in it, swimming along happily as the novel itself has become both the pool that contains her and the water that's buoying her up.

Right now, building that swimming pool on the page may seem an impossibly huge task. You may feel like my frustrated student in Chapter 1, frozen before her paper's looming introduction. How do you ever get *started* on a task so huge? Relax; it's not as bad as it looks. I'm going to walk you through the steps I use to build a world—one big idea first, then we'll go to ground level and work back up. Here and in the following chapters, I'll be using examples from other writers and from a novel manuscript called *Eldorado, Iowa* that I wrote a few years ago.

# Shitty first drafts: Liberation and knowledge

One big idea, learned from Anne Lamott's *Bird by Bird*, has transformed my students' and my writing processes: "shitty first drafts." "All good writers write them," Lamott says. "That's how they end up with good second drafts and terrific third drafts."[1] The shocking word is useful, since it rattles the cage of perfectionism until the door swings open. My students and I use "shitty first draft" as an affectionate term for what you get when you push yourself—expectations deliberately low—to write a draft of a project, beginning to end, as early as you can, so that you have an idea of its general shape and something to revise. As Lamott points out, you may also find something that surprises you:

> There may be something in the very last line of the very last paragraph on page six that you just love, that is so beautiful or wild that you now know what you're supposed to be writing about, more or less, or in what direction you might go—but there was no way to get to this without first getting through the first five and a half pages.[2]

An SFD, as we call a shitty first draft in my classes, lowers your anxiety; revision is challenging but better than a blank page. This is as true for me as it is for my first-year college students; when I start a project, I don't know how it will end and usually have only a vague idea of what it'll contain, so I need to build the Indiana Jones bridge for myself by writing it. SFDs aren't for everyone; some writers prefer to write in pieces, polishing each section before moving on to the next. Still others (like the short story writer Amy Hempel) spend a lot of time thinking about their work so that when they write it, it emerges all of a piece, with relatively little revision on paper. [3]But if you're a nervous writer, and/or a perfectionist, and/or someone who worries about ideas blowing away before you can get them all organized, the SFD is life-changing—you just write fast and loose, throwing in anything you're afraid you'll forget or any images that come up, doing your best to get to the end so you can look back over the whole thing and see what you've got.

Here's how the process tends to look for me. No matter what my project is—a novel, a book chapter, an essay, a short story—I push myself to write a shitty first draft of the whole thing as quickly as I can. (I announce my goal in those terms: "I'm trying to have a complete shitty first draft of this book by the end of the month.") Otherwise I'll yield to that paragraph-by-paragraph perfectionism that's great for revision but will stop me from finishing anything. (This is the culprit behind all those polished beginnings that taper off into nothing, deep in our drawers or computer files.) Following an excellent suggestion in Susan Bell's *The Artful Edit*, I back up drafts electronically but try not to print them out until I've finished them, including the drafts of books. (Trust me; it defamiliarizes your view of your project well.) When I do have a complete draft of a book, I send the file electronically to our on-campus print shop, where they print it on double-sided paper and bind it between plastic covers, creating a manuscript "book" I can tote around and mark up. These "books" are easier to read, store, and carry than stacks of loose pages, and they give the project a nice *gravitas* in my own mind.

So, your overall goal is a complete draft, with a beginning, middle, and end. But how do you get there? Once again, Anne Lamott's wisdom points the way. "Often when you sit down to write," she says, "what you have in mind is an autobiographical novel about your childhood, or a play about the immigrant experience, or a history of—oh, say—say women. But this is like trying to scale a glacier."[4] Therefore, to get started, think instead of doing what Lamott calls "short assignments," one by one. "All I have to do," she says, "is to write down as much as I can see through a one-inch picture frame."[5] Perhaps, "all I am going to do is describe the main character the very first time we meet her, when she first walks out the front door and onto the porch."[6] Bit by bit, in small pieces imaginatively enfleshed and then written one by one, the larger project is built.

For me, the idea behind Lamott's "one-inch picture frame" expresses itself slightly differently in what I call, and teach my students to call, *images*. I'll say more about images in a minute, but for now, just know that they work kind of like Anne Lamott's picture frames—they are small moments of prose or poetry, focused on something closely observed and then described. And they can be written in as few as fifteen to twenty minutes, if that's all the time you have.

# It all adds up—really!

Right now, you may be thinking, "Great, but can all those little pieces *really* add up to a whole project?" I—and many other writers—are here to tell you that they can. Flannery O'Connor wrote that "in the best stories," form and technique are "something organic, something that [grow] out of the material."[7] Novelist and short story writer Lorrie Moore has quipped that "some people think the novel is the perfect form for the busy single working mom," since "you can just go in and write a paragraph and then go away," while "stories need to be written, or at least mapped out, in a single sitting" to keep a certain energy and unity of form.[8] In an interview, George Saunders describes his realization that writing his novel *Lincoln in the Bardo* (2017) wouldn't require a fundamentally different form or process than he'd been using to write short stories:

> … I don't know if other writers do this, but there's that moment where you go, "Oh my God, I'm writing a novel. Anything goes!" And a couple of times I got in trouble because that mind-set took over. And then I would get that back in the box and say, "No, it's by the same principles as all these stories: efficiency, one section producing and then leading to another. That's it." And then I would get back on track. So it was like the more I said, "The principles don't change, but maybe the scale changes," then I could do it. It was really a comfort to know that, in art, form is a way of accommodating one's natural inclinations. If your natural inclination is to make small, concise structures, then form shows up and says, "Would you like me to help you link your small, concise structures?" And then form seems organic; it doesn't seem whimsical. It doesn't seem arbitrary. It seems organic, because it's what allows you to accommodate your strengths.[9]

As those "small, concise structures"—perhaps written by Lamott's one-inch-picture-frame method—add up, you can weave a stronger novel tapestry by threading details or images from one scene into others. Novelist Alice McDermott, in her craft essay "Only Connect," describes this process at work in E. M. Forster's novel *A Passage to India* (1924). Eager to assist and impress an Englishman, young Dr. Aziz lends him his own collar-stud, only to be mocked (out of his hearing) by another (more racist) Englishman later on: "Aziz was exquisitely dressed, from tie-pin to spats, but he had forgotten his back collar-stud, and there you have the Indian all over: inattention to detail; the fundamental slackness that reveals the race."[10] *No*, we immediately protest, *you've got it all wrong, the collar-stud is missing because he gave it to*—but the characters can't hear us. We're on one side of a wall of oblivion separating people from each other, with a lump of unfairness lodged in our throats, and, therefore, with one detail that reappears in a later place, Forster has made us *feel*, not just editorialize about, the ugly sadness of misunderstanding. That missing collar-stud becomes thematically weight-bearing and pays off for the reader. McDermott encourages her students to reread their novels in progress for this reason, so that they can tighten and brighten the weave of detail and imagery. Sometimes this process is conscious; more often it's not, not quite. McDermott quotes the great Mississippi writer Eudora Welty to explain:

> Writing a story or a novel is one way of discovering *sequence* in experience, of stumbling upon cause and effect … Connections slowly emerge. Like distant landmarks you are approaching, cause and effect begin to align themselves, draw closer together. Experiences too indefinite of outline in themselves to be recognized for themselves connect and are identified as a larger shape. And suddenly a light is thrown back, as when your train makes a curve, showing that there has been a mountain of meaning rising behind you on the way you've come, is rising there still, proven now through retrospect.[11]

"For the novelists in the middle of composing a novel," McDermott concludes, "rereading is retrospection—to revisit what has already been set down is to provide ourselves with the opportunity to glimpse that mountain of meaning rising behind."[12] Yet the most productive rereading is also that done with the kind of attention and defamiliarization I discussed in Chapter 2, "allowing ourselves, as we read," McDermott says, "to hear and see them anew."[13] Both these processes begin with writing: one short assignment, or image, onto the page at a time, building the Indiana Jones bridge under our own feet as we walk forward. And, crucially, we can make discoveries about our projects as we're writing them: a writer does *not* have to know the ending when she begins.

# Richard Price's cat: Structure and detail on film

For years I've been a fan of the crime novelist and screenwriter Richard Price, a Bronx native whose sharp-edged way with dialogue and detail has been honed by ride-alongs with the NYPD. So when I heard about his eight-episode series *The Night Of* (2016)—part of the long-form-drama renaissance for which I'll happily adjust my anti-TV stance—I couldn't wait to see it. And I wasn't disappointed. Cocreated for HBO with Steven Zaillian and set in post-9/11 New York, *The Night Of* begins as geeky college student Nasir Khan (Riz Ahmed) sneaks away in his father's cab to go to a party. One thing leads to another, and Nasir finds himself charged with a murder he didn't commit. Riveting and sobering, *The Night Of* glints with memorable, character-driven moments: Nasir's shattered mother (Poorna Jagganathan) taking a janitorial job to pay the family's bills; Michael Williams (Omar Little in David Simon's "The Wire," another Price project) as Freddy, Nasir's prison mentor; the mouthy, malaprop-y witness Trevor (J. D. Williams) who complains, "See, no good deed goes unturned." (Warning: spoiler ahead.)

You can learn a lot about writing from a film or long-form series as good as *The Night Of.* For now, let's focus on one detail, like E. M. Forster's collar-stud, that ties the series together from within: an orange and white cat. First spotted in the murder victim's living room in Episode 1, the cat approaches lawyer John Stone (John Turturro) outside her brownstone in Episode 3. Following his gaze, we register along with him that the cat was hers, and that it's homeless now. In the next scene, Stone lets the cat into the victim's kitchen and rummages in the refrigerator for milk—he's the only character who feeds the cat at any time. Now, our sympathy for pets has hooked us into the story *and* established Stone as our proxy; despite his considerable quirks, we're on his side. As Stone gets deeper into Nasir's case, he also feels more responsibility to the cat, despite the fact that he's allergic. Tension thrums around three interwoven questions: Will Nasir go free? Will Stone defend him? And what will happen to the cat?

As Nasir adjusts to life inside Rikers Island, Stone reluctantly takes the cat to the animal shelter. Near the end of Episode 3 (significantly titled, "A Dark Crate"), an attendant bears the cat away down a corridor of metal cages, rattling with barks that almost drown out the cat's plaintive *meow.* Through the scarred glass door, John Stone's face is as stunned as our own. Another innocent in jail.

From here, as we approach the series' midpoint, the stakes rise even more. Nasir's story darkens. Stone labors to save him, and the cat's story continues alongside both. Stone rescues the cat from Death Row just in time, barricading it in a spare room of his apartment with elaborate anti-allergy precautions that make us smile even as they still don't slacken the suspense. All this could be temporary. We still don't know for sure until the last minute of the last episode, a bright, sweet note in an otherwise somber ending. Just as Eudora Welty wrote, we're able to turn and look back at the mountain of meaning that has been rising behind us all this time. Novelist

Henry James advised that a writer should be someone "on whom nothing is lost." In a series like *The Night Of,* constructed with subtle but devastating skill, no detail—even a homeless cat—is wasted.

# Images: One little painting at a time

Think about a memory you've held onto for a long time, some mental picture—either still or moving—that seems saturated with meaning for you, that releases some emotion whenever you touch it and that carries vivid sensory details within itself. In my writing classes and my own writing life, I call this an *image*. Of course, an image can literally be a picture, interesting but perhaps not hugely emotional, something observed (like the barefoot girl on the street or the boy with the rat snake, from my discussion of notebooks in Chapter 1.) But just as the name indicates, an image is a picture that releases emotions into your mind and, often, seems to ask to be illustrated in words. "The fiction writer finds in time," Flannery O'Connor wrote, "that he cannot proceed at all if he cuts himself off from the sights and sounds"— namely, images—"that have developed a life of their own in his senses."[14] I think of images as working in the brain like my summer garden herbs work in water—if you gather a handful of mint and a handful of lavender hyssop, crush the leaves in your hands, and steep them in a pitcher of water, their peppermint-and-licorice-flavored oils seep outward, creating a green-gold tea that's delicious on a hot day. Images do the same thing in your mind— they release some essence of emotion and memory that never seems to fade, like Wordsworth's "spots of time." And if you can evoke them on the page, they will evoke emotion in your reader's mind, too.

Poet and memoirist Nick Flynn has described "an enduring image from my childhood, one that returns to me often, unbidden"—a watermelon vine "that somehow took root in the backseat of my grandmother's car," growing in the "mixture of sand and dirt" from beach feet and muddy shoes. The plant remained, growing and growing, watched over by Flynn as a kind of secret until, eventually, his grandmother discovered it too and they could "laugh together at the weirdness" and marvel of this object. Yet in that accidental car-borne garden, memory also takes root. "Without those images," Flynn writes, "how else can I hold her now?"

> Her voice? (like sandpaper and smoke.) Her hands? (gnarled from tending her roses.) Her roses? (in the summer they nearly swallowed her porch.) All

of these, too, are images, and all images are containers for meaning. Images hold the meaning of our lives. Without images we have no memory; they give the past shape, keep the memory. It makes sense, then, that the image is one of the poet's most reliable tools, the foundation of many poems.[15]

Because images are suffused with so much sensory information and emotion, they can spark whole essays, stories, poems, even novels. I encourage students to talk about *images that can be starting points for* a story or poem rather than *ideas for* a story or poem. "Ideas" can lead to an outline-heavy, paint-by-numbers focused approach to writing that forecloses discoveries and bores you *and* your reader; an "idea" feels dead on arrival to me in a way an image never does, because it doesn't allow for discoveries, fresh insights, and realizations as I go in the way that a starting image does.

Images can arise from something remembered, or from some source that's harder to name. My first completed novel manuscript, *Eldorado, Iowa*, started in just this way. On an unseasonably warm afternoon—the last day of October 2008—I was outside with my creative-nonfiction-writing students, on the lawn under the big cottonwood tree. They sat on the grass in small groups, reading each other's drafts, and I strolled among them, answering questions and eavesdropping. I looked down at my own feet, brushing through the yellowing grass. Suddenly—I don't know how else to describe it—I blinked and saw them transformed. In my mind's eye, I looked down at the toes of high-topped, lace-up leather boots, peeking from under a long brown skirt that bent the grass sideways as it trailed the ground and tented gently outward with every step. I had entered the body of some other woman, more than a hundred years ago, walking through the grass on a warm afternoon. And—I knew from somewhere inside that body—this woman was pregnant. What was her name? Sarah. Her name was Sarah. What year was this? Sometime in the 1870s, when the Civil War and the idea of the frontier still felt raw to living people. Where was she? Iowa. Where had she come from? Alabama. Just like me. And, like me, she gets a lot of her ideas about the world from books.

That image became the opening lines of my manuscript:

Alone, Sarah wanders out the front door and into the September sun. Her skirts brush down the sagging steps and over the grass, crushing one fallen leaf, then two. The maple sapling quivers in a sudden breeze, and she sets both hands on her belly. A quiver under the skin answers her. She has to soak in as much light as possible, before the winter comes and the sun is gone; she's storing it up for the life that will begin here in Iowa. When her baby thinks of *home*, it will think of this little town. Not the plantation. She's made sure of that.

Despite herself, her mother's voice natters in her head, approving her: *a lady, walking on her lawn.* Her lawn. That's what it would be called back home, in Alabama. Here it's really just the clear square of ground in front of the house, where the old doctor broke up the prairie sod before he died. There are no flower borders, no herringbone brick walks, no walls. Under her feet, the soil is deep and black, netted with tangled roots tamped down by buffalo. By whatever large creatures walked this corner of Iowa with their milch-cow snufflings as the glaciers melted and the grass grew tall. She imagines them lumbering into this tiny town, like Mr. Dickens's Megalosaurus waddling up Holborn Hill. Inside the row of red-leather novels on her parlor shelf, London teems, unimaginably crowded. A great city. Not like this place, this small town at the edge of the world. This place with its optimistic signpost: *Eldorado.*[16]

Once you have your image pinned to the page—where it sits there, radiating with emotion and possibility—you can start spinning it into a draft by asking questions. First, if she's pregnant, who is the baby's father? Her husband, Galen, who, I immediately knew, is a doctor. (I geek out on medical history big-time.) But why would a young doctor and his wife leave Alabama for a small town on the frontier? How had they gotten there? Who else is with them? And why *Eldorado?* I didn't have to invent an answer to that. Eldorado is the name of a tiny town in a river valley near where I live. Driving past to take students to readings at the Iowa Writers Workshop, I had seen the sign and the phrase had lodged in my head: *Eldorado, Iowa.* Now at last I could use it.

# Scenes: Images in motion

If images are small building blocks of a piece of writing, **scenes** are the next-size-larger blocks. Essentially, a scene is a section of a longer story that can function kind of like a story on its own; it has a beginning, a middle, an end, and a sense of motion and tension that rises, then subsides. It meets the classic criteria for success in any piece of writing: by the time we finish, we feel that "something's different now." Something within our own minds, the characters' lives, or both have shifted or changed, so that things aren't the same at the end as they were at the beginning.

If this idea sounds too abstract, think of how we move through dozens of scenes in our own lives, every day, simply by involving ourselves in interactions that change a situation and move it forward. We walk into a colleague's office, she says hello, we ask our question, and then our interaction moves toward some peak of action (like when we get our question answered) and ends when things are done. That's a scene. In the grocery store coffee aisle, we run into a friend who tells us about his new job; that's another scene. So are Sethe and Paul D.'s kitchen conversation in Toni Morrison's *Beloved* (discussed later in this chapter), Pip's first meeting with Miss Havisham in Charles Dickens's *Great Expectations* (1861), John Stone's moment at the animal shelter in Episode 3 of *The Night Of* (as I described it earlier), or Ernest Hemingway's short story "Hills Like White Elephants" (1927), which could be considered a single self-contained scene in its own right. Scenes work within the larger piece like the small gears and cogs in the engine that swallows Charlie Chaplin in the film *Modern Times* (1936); each gear is turning forward on its own even as it *also* assists the forward motion of the whole engine, which draws the reader in and keeps the story going.

An image can be the seed for a scene, because you can write a scene to answer questions you ask yourself about an image and to help clarify the novel's world in your own mind. Look back at all my questions about *Eldorado* above; here I had a person walking on a lawn, but I needed more information to start to build a story's world around her. To answer those questions, I wrote other scenes, and those scenes led to others; some were set in the present time of the story, others (flashbacks) in the past, as I tried to show Sarah and her husband Galen in their present life as well as what had driven them to Iowa. For instance, an early scene of Galen performing minor surgery introduced me to two other characters in the story: Norwegian immigrant brothers farming their own nearby land, who will reappear in Chapter 4 of this book. Before I knew it, I was deep in a draft, writing along piece by piece, and a sense of where the novel as a whole was going—its own particular Indiana Jones bridge—developed underneath my feet as I wrote. As the novelist E. L. Doctorow said, "writing a novel is like driving a car at night. You can see only as far as your headlights, but you can make the whole trip that way."[17] Think of writing a scene as writing a larger version of an image, or a short assignment: imagine a character in a place, set that character in motion, bring another character (or two) into the scene, let the interaction spark, follow it along and let it develop, then let the energy subside once the scene has partially or completely played itself out.

# Layering a scene: Several things at once

Writing scenes, my students and I run into a variety of issues, most of which have the same cause: we don't know enough, at enough levels, about what is happening in the scene to be able to illustrate it vividly. The writer and teacher John Gardner famously says that fiction should operate in the reader's mind like a "vivid and continuous dream." Detail is the constant low-level feed of imagery (like an IV drip) that we absorb and use in the construction of our own mental dream as we read, almost without noticing that we're doing so. If we get a wrong or insufficient detail, or even too much (which shows the presence of the anxious writer, breathing down our necks), the dream breaks and we wake up. So how to select the right details? And how do you avoid writing an airless, stagy scene where not enough is happening at once—where, for instance, two people are just standing and having a conversation, like talking heads in space? Or where you are only giving your reader description, nothing else? How can you bring to the page a believable feeling of life itself, where there is always more than one thing happening at once?

First, let's consider the layering of *time*, which becomes the layering of *significance* and *tension* in a story that gives us a sense there is *something at stake*. When we think about our own lives, we can see we are always both experiencing the present moment *and* "reading" it through the histories we carry in our heads—through all that has been going on in our lives up until that present moment. These two layers of time exist in stories, too—the first (present) layer is called the *immediate,* and the second (past) layer is called the *ongoing*. A story's (or novel's) structure grows out of a dance between them, and out of a negotiation of the pressures each layer of time is exerting on your characters. Plot, tension, and a sense of something at stake arise from how characters respond to those pressures. Therefore, to raise the tension of your story, increase the pressure your character is under, and consider the way that pressures in the present moment may be interacting with, or intensified by, pressures from within the character's history. (We'll see this at work in a scene from Toni Morrison's novel *Beloved* in a moment.) Characters' actions will feel believable if we can see those actions as believable responses to pressures that have built up on, or within, them.

Research is another way to build your picture of your fictional world; if you don't know (for instance) what a nineteenth-century locomotive looks like, then you can go and look it up. You can ask friends who know more about a subject than you. You could visit a real place and see what it's like. In *Thrill Me,* his collection of craft essays, novelist Benjamin Percy relates that when he was writing a story about a taxidermist, he went to a taxidermy shop and made notes, "stroked the polyurethane forms, clacked the glass eyeballs around in my palm, and sniffed the formaldehyde."[18] As this anecdote suggests, research for writing purposes usually happens on a need-to-know basis, at least it has for me—"need to know" being the detail or bit of information I need to move the story forward. Loading up with too much research in advance can suffocate you, although you do need a solid base of walking-around knowledge. When writing my *Eldorado, Iowa* manuscript, I didn't read everything published about women on the Iowa frontier in the 1870s, although I read enough to get a general picture, and I drew on my existing knowledge of American history. But I did look up what kind of boots my character, Sarah, might be wearing in 1876, and what her "maternity corset" (yes, she was wearing one, and yes, they did exist) would look like. When I wrote about her, I tapped into sense memories of wearing long skirts, that particular weight against my legs, that little flare in front where you kick out against them as you walk. (I even wrapped a blanket around myself and pretended it was a skirt, then observed how the cloth fell over my feet.) Too much research can bog a story down, though, weirdly separating the writer from a full imagining of the material; in a letter dated January 10, 1936, legendary editor Maxwell Perkins wrote to a writer he was rejecting: "This story still seems superimposed upon its background, and not in any real sense to grow out of it ... It is as if you had carefully gone over the local newspaper files of the eighties, made copious notes, and used this background material valiantly, with the result that much of it seems dragged in, and awkwardly handled."[19] This sounds to me like a classic historical-fiction issue—the fear of lacking authority, and the fear that readers can't be trusted to help build the fictional world. You might find, when doing research, that you have to let information drop out of the manuscript; there may not be a logical place for everything you know.

In my classes, I stage for students similar encounters with the place where experience and research meet real life—doing things on your own, by hand—and let them practice research on a need-to-know basis. The activity has several steps. First, we read this passage in Toni Morrison's *Beloved* (1987).

Sethe, a former slave, is making biscuits while telling another former slave, Paul D., who she hasn't seen since their time on the plantation, something he didn't know about abuse she suffered at the hands of the overseer and his sons.

Paul D fished in his vest for a little pouch of tobacco—concentrating on its contents and the knot of its string while Sethe led Denver into the keeping room that opened off the large room he was sitting in. He had no smoking papers, so he fiddled with the pouch and listened through the open door to Sethe quieting her daughter. When she came back she avoided his look and went straight to a small table next to the stove. Her back was to him and he could see all the hair he wanted without the distraction of her face.

"What tree on your back?"

"Huh." Sethe put a bowl on the table and reached under it for flour.

"What tree on your back? Is something growing on your back? I don't see nothing growing on your back."

"It's there all the same."

"Who told you that?"

"Whitegirl. That's what she called it. I've never seen it and never will. But that's what she said it looked like. A chokecherry tree. Trunk, branches, and even leaves. Tiny little chokecherry leaves. But that was eighteen years ago. Could have cherries too now for all I know."

Sethe took a little spit from the tip of her tongue with her forefinger. Quickly, lightly she touched the stove. Then she trailed her fingers through the flour, parting, separating small hills and ridges of it, looking for mites. Finding none, she poured soda and salt into the crease of her folded hand and tossed both into the flour. Then she reached into a can and scooped half a handful of lard. Deftly she squeezed the flour through it, then with her left hand sprinkling water, she formed the dough.

"I had milk," she said. "I was pregnant with Denver but I had milk for my baby girl. I hadn't stopped nursing her when I sent her on ahead with Howard and Buglar."

Now she rolled the dough out with a wooden pin. "Anybody could smell me long before he saw me. And when he saw me he'd see the drops of it on the front of my dress. Nothing I could do about that. All I knew was I had to get my milk to my baby girl. Nobody was going to nurse her like me. Nobody was going to get it to her fast enough, or take it away when she had enough and didn't know it. Nobody knew that she couldn't pass her air if you held her up on your shoulder, only if she was lying on my knees. Nobody knew that but me and nobody had her milk but me. I told that to the women in the wagon. Told them to put sugar water in cloth to suck from so when I got there in a few days she wouldn't have forgot me. The milk would be there and I would be there with it."

"Men don't know nothing much," said Paul D, tucking his pouch back into his vest pocket, "but they do know a suckling can't be away from its mother for long."

"Then they know what it's like to send your children off when your breasts are full."

"We was talking 'bout a tree, Sethe."

"After I left you, those boys came in there and took my milk. That's what they came in there for. Held me down and took it. I told Mrs. Garner on em. She had that lump and couldn't speak but her eyes rolled out tears. Them boys found out I told on em. Schoolteacher made one open up my back, and when it closed it made a tree. It grows there still."

"They used cowhide on you?"

"And they took my milk."

"They beat you and you was pregnant?"

"And they took my milk!"

The fat white circles of dough lined the pan in rows. Once more Sethe touched a wet forefinger to the stove. She opened the oven door and slid the pan of biscuits in. As she raised up from the heat she felt Paul D behind her and his hands under her breasts. She straightened up and knew, but could not feel, that his cheek was pressing into the branches of her chokecherry tree.[20]

This marvelous passage braids several plot threads and narrative necessities at once, making what is in fact a tricky technical scene look easy. First, as with any novel, there's the question of exposition: how to help the reader learn about a character's background? Here, it's natural for Sethe to tell Paul D., who's just arrived at her house, what he never knew about the abuses she suffered in their shared past, which have left scars like a "chokecherry tree" on her back. As she tells him, she's telling us too. Yet she isn't only standing and delivering a speech. True to her character—by necessity and inclination—she's also working to prepare food for herself and her one remaining daughter. (Of course, a busy woman is always going to be doing more than one thing at a time.) The action of making biscuits both relieves and intensifies the pressure within the scene; it gives Sethe a welcome distraction as she relives the painful memory, yet it also keeps her still in one spot as the words pile up and up. (This is where ongoing tension—the pressure of painful memory from Sethe's past history—and present tension—Paul D.'s arrival—interact, since he's asking Sethe to relive those memories, and her task requires her to stand in one place as she talks to him, so she can't evade her rising emotion, and tension rises correspondingly within the scene.) There's also the realism and conviction of well-observed detail; this is exactly how a woman would have made biscuits in this time and place: flour, lard, water, soda, salt. (I was taught a similar recipe-less biscuit-making technique as a child and use it still.) Layers of action reinforce layers of emotion, all grounding a difficult revelation in the texture of daily life. Morrison has built characters with believable emotions and speech in a believable, multilayered world of immediate action and ongoing tension, using precisely observed and physically grounded sensations. And when Paul D. embraces Sethe, it feels like a believable response to and release of the pressures Morrison has built up in the scene, at both the immediate and the ongoing levels.

After we've read and discussed this passage together, my students try the following assignment. First, write and post to our class online forum a short, factual description of something you know how to do or make by hand, involving physical actions in the world. (Someone else should be able to follow your directions and repeat the process.) Then, after a few days, log back onto the forum, read your classmates' posts, and pick an activity that interests you but that you aren't totally familiar with. Draft a scene in which your character—like Morrison's Sethe—is doing or making that thing while thinking and/or talking about something else. Conduct research as needed to fill in any gaps in your knowledge and push the scene along, but use your own sense memories too—you may be able to get farther than you think.

This exercise always produces some of students' best writing. Aside from the pleasure of learning about classmates' diverse interests—building canoes, carving wooden spoons, blowing and decorating traditional Ukrainian *pysanky* eggs, making bread, climbing a tree, gardening, saddling a horse, archery, playing a cello—this exercise gives them something to write *about,* and a way to ground what can be very difficult matters of emotion and exposition in physical action. In every case, the physical activity ends up reinforcing the mental or emotional one in the same way Sethe's biscuit making, shaping and working the dough, reinforces what Morrison elsewhere in the novel calls "the day's serious work of beating back the past."[21] It helps students learn what ongoing pressures might be driving their characters, and it helps them weave those with immediate pressures in a believable way. It also helps us cut through the technology-centeredness of our lives and relearn the importance, and the pleasure, of thinking through our bodies. Try this exercise too, by giving your character an activity you already know or one you are learning, and see what it reveals about your character and your fictional world.

# Showing what you feel:
# Detail and emotion

As we talked about in Chapter 1, it's easy to give readers a lot of vague, big words when our emotions about the story are also big and vague. Therefore, I like to use a technique borrowed from Chekhov, called "the police report." The Russian playwright and short story writer Anton Chekhov (1860–1904) was also a doctor, and you can see that medical training in the advice he gives writers: look carefully at what is in front of you and focus. This can be particularly hard when the subject matter is, itself, emotional. But—much like emergency-room physicians—we have to calm down, look carefully at what's in front of us, and get to work in concrete, sensory language, not excited editorial phrases. Even when it goes against our first instincts, *understatement* will carry emotion to readers in surprising ways. Here's Chekhov's advice to Madame M. V. Kiselev in a letter of December 3, 1886:

> You might write a sketch, "Ivan Gavrilov," or "The Wounded Doe." In the latter story, if you have not forgotten, the hunters wound the doe which looks at them like a human being, and nobody can make up his mind to kill her. This is not a bad subject, but dangerous in the sense that it is hard to escape sentimentality; you ought to write it like a protocol [**police report**], without pitying words, and begin thus—"On such and such a date, some hunters wounded a young elk in the Daraganov forest" … But if you let fall a tear or two, you will rob the subject of its austerity and of all that is worthy of attention.[22]

Sounds harsh, but imagine the smarmy alternative: "The shattering shot rang through the formerly peaceful woods as the dying doe lifted her luminous eyes pitifully toward the cruel hunters and breathed her last breath …" As *San Francisco Chronicle* movie critic Peter Stack famously wrote, "my tears stuck in their little ducts, refusing to be jerked." Here, editorial language is not helping us see the doe's death as sad—it is making the situation sentimental, and thus annoying. The writer's also brandishing her own "superior" feelings in language here, which adds another layer of sentimental fakery, or *kitsch*. As Czech novelist Milan Kundera writes in *The Unbearable Lightness of Being* (1984), "Kitsch causes two tears to flow in quick succession. The first tear says: How nice to see children running on the grass! The second tear says: How nice to be moved, together with all mankind, by children running on the grass! It is the second tear that makes kitsch kitsch."[23]

By contrast, look at two anecdotes from another letter of Chekhov's, dated January 26, 1891, when he was traveling to the island of Sakhalin, a notoriously brutal penal colony in eastern Russia. Partly he was seeking adventure (and a subject for what would become another book); partly he wanted to offer his medical services to the inmates. There's no doubt he felt strongly about the misery he saw there: "[W]e have sent *millions* of men to rot in prison," he wrote, "have destroyed them—casually without thinking, barbarously ... have depraved them, have multiplied criminals, and the blame for all this we have thrown upon the gaolers and red-nosed superintendents. Now all educated Europe knows that it is not the superintendents that are to blame, but all of us."[24] But by trusting observed detail, he lets that misery speak for itself, particularly through the children he observes:

> On the Amur steamer with me there was a prisoner in foot shackles who was going to Sakhalin for having murdered his wife. He had his six-year-old daughter with him. I noticed that whenever the father went below to the lavatory from the upper deck, his escort and his daughter followed him, and while he sat in the lavatory, his daughter and a soldier with a gun stood outside the door. When he made his way back up the ladder, his daughter clambered up behind him holding onto the shackles. At night the girl slept in a pile with the prisoners and soldiers.[25]

Significantly, without a break, he continues with another story of a child:

> I remember once attending a funeral on Sakhalin. The wife of a settler who was away in Nikolayevsk was being buried. Four *ex oficio* convict pallbearers; the paymaster and I, in the capacity of Hamlet and Horatio wandering around the cemetery; a Circassian, who had been a boarder of the deceased and came out of idle curiosity; and a woman convict who came out of pity were all standing around the newly dug grave. The woman had brought along the two children of the deceased, an infant and a four-year-old boy named Alyoshka who was wearing a woman's jacket and blue pants with bright patches on the knees. It was cold and damp, the grave had water in it, and the convicts were laughing. We were in sight of the ocean. Alyoshka peered into the grave with curiosity. He tried to wipe his chilled nose, but the jacket's long sleeves got in the way. While the grave was being filled in, I asked him, "Alyoshka, where's your mother?" He made the gesture of a landowner who has been wiped out at cards, laughed, and said, "Buried!" The convicts laughed. The Circassian turned to us and asked what he was supposed to do with the children, since he's not obliged to feed them.[26]

"It was cold and damp, the grave had water in it, and the convicts were laughing." The details radiate an enduring chill of the body and the spirit right into our brains. No amount of well-meaning sociological language about *the hardening effects of a violent environment on children* or *the suffering of innocents* or *the lonely funeral of a pitiful woman who had no friends* can reproduce that effect. The paragraph ends with the Circassian's question—rendered in indirect speech, so that it doesn't compete with the shocking, sad maturity of the gesture that the little boy has learned to get a laugh from adults. Like the girl who surely would not have accompanied her father to Russia's worst prison on a ship full of men if there were anywhere else for her to go—and who clings to him with what Chekhov need not tell us is desperation—Alyoshka and his infant sibling have now joined the orphans whose condition infuriated Chekhov so much that he tried to start a charity campaign for their benefit. Even more enduring is the testimony of what he saw.

Chekhov's police-report technique threads its way through two memoirs of twentieth-century war, with equally devastating effects. Here is poet, novelist, and memoirist Robert Graves, writing about his service in the First World War in *Good-bye to All That* (1929):

> After a meal of bread, bacon, rum, and bitter stewed tea sickly with sugar, we went through the broken trees to the east of the village and up a long trench to Battalion Headquarters. The wet and slippery trench ran through dull red clay. I had a torch with me, and saw that hundreds of field mice and frogs had fallen into the trench but found no way out. The light dazzled them, and because I could not help treading on them, I put the torch back in my pocket.[27]

Here, the gesture leaves us reeling with emotion before which Graves himself retreats, tactfully and firmly: turning off the flashlight may help frogs and mice flee his approaching feet, but it will also keep him from seeing their deaths, which he can't help causing. Graves knows, and knows that we know, that frogs and mice were not the only beings trapped in trenches where they would die.

As a British intelligence officer stationed in Italy during the Second World War, the remarkable travel writer Norman Lewis kept a journal that became his book *Naples '44: An Intelligence Officer in the Italian Labyrinth* (1978). Like Chekhov, he notices vulnerable people—particularly women. In this scene, Lewis has followed a crowd of soldiers into a public building in Naples:

> Here a row of ladies sat at intervals of about a yard with their backs to the wall. These women were dressed in their street clothes, and had the ordinary

well-washed respectable shopping and gossiping faces of working-class housewives. By the side of each woman stood a small pile of tins, and it soon became clear that it was possible to make love to any one of them in this very public place by adding another tin to the pile. The women kept absolutely still, they said nothing, and their faces were as empty of expression as graven images … There was no soliciting, no suggestion, no enticement, not even the discreetest and most accidental display of flesh. The boldest of the soldiers had pushed themselves, tins in hand, to the front, but now, faced with these matter-of-fact family-providers driven here by empty larders, they seemed to flag … There was some sheepish laughter, jokes that fell flat, and a visible tendency to slip quietly away. One soldier, a little tipsy, and egged on constantly by his friends, finally put down his tin of rations at a woman's side, unbuttoned and lowered himself on her. A perfunctory jogging of the haunches began and came quickly to an end. A moment later he was on his feet and buttoning up again. It had been something to get over as soon as possible. He might have been submitting to field punishment rather than the act of love.[28]

Here, the details, the construction of the sentences, and the verbs highlight Lewis's growing shock and sympathy. First, he shows us the women with an active, human specificity he doesn't give the soldiers. But the longer the passage goes on—as he watches the soldiers jostle and hesitate—the more passive and distancing the language becomes. The act itself is the most distant and dehumanized of all. "A perfunctory jogging of the haunches" is precise yet dissociated (one action, limited to one part of the body), and deliberately unerotic, since only necessity is driving this transaction. The author recedes from what he's witnessing and from what these women are forced to do, allowing our own horror and pity to rush in.

In her autobiography *Incidents in the Life of a Slave Girl* (1861), Harriet Jacobs heightens readers' emotions by understating detail and by knowing when to stop. Over and over, she strikes a note of ambiguity, rage, or irony at the end of a paragraph or chapter, then moves on. But that note rings through our minds, drawing us toward conclusions for which her careful details have already prepared us. As part of her escape from slavery in Edenton, North Carolina, Jacobs hid for seven years in an attic crawl space in her (free) grandmother's house, only coming down occasionally to stretch her legs, reading by the light of a peephole under the eaves. "In summer the most terrible thunder storms were acceptable," she writes, "for the rain came through the roof, and I rolled up my bed that it might cool the hot boards under it."[29]

Dark thoughts passed through my mind, as I lay there day after day. I tried to be thankful for my little cell, dismal as it was, and even to love it, as part of the price I had paid for the redemption of my children. Sometimes I thought God was a compassionate Father, who would forgive my sins for the sake of my sufferings. At other times, it seemed to me there was no justice or mercy in the divine government. I asked why the curse of slavery was permitted to exist, and why I had been so persecuted and wronged from youth upward. These things took the shape of mystery, which is to this day not so clear to my soul as I trust it will be hereafter.[30]

Here, the end of the paragraph leaves us just where Jacobs must have been: amid deep anger, pain, and enduring spiritual doubt. In denying readers easy consolation, she makes us feel her conviction that slavery is a moral evil, alienating humans from one another, from their own best selves, and from the God that white masters claim to worship. Aiming at an audience of white self-professed Christians—many of whom, in the antebellum period, quoted the Bible to justify slavery—Jacobs strands us with an uncomfortable realization: a system that causes a young woman to lose her faith is a system that cannot be defended by anything in Scripture, or by anyone who professes to believe in it.

Therefore, as all these examples show, detail and understatement are more powerful than we sometimes give them credit for. As you write and revise, remember: you can trust observed detail to carry your meaning into your reader's mind. Fact isn't only fact when, as Thoreau wrote in his journal, it serves as "the vehicle of some humanity."[31] And there's great art in knowing when to stop.

# Locating meaning: Setting and place

Designing a visible world around your characters has to do with what novelist Alice McDermott calls *consequence*: the place in which a story (or essay, or novel) is set becomes weight-bearing, and, if we are allowed to see them, the weight of a landscape's details will press on your story and characters to move them in certain directions and create particular impressions of what the story's world is like. I use the word *place* rather than *setting*, because while "setting" refers literally to the environment in which a story happens, "place" refers to a much richer brew of history, personal association, plants, animals, weather, and all the other factors that make one geographical location look and feel different from another and that create those associations in readers' minds. Place can also create or heighten pressures on your characters, since weather, social mores, and other factors can be connected with them; Jane Eyre's struggle for independence and self-respect in Charlotte Bronte's 1847 novel is heightened by the reality that women in the Victorian period were routinely denied both. A rich fictional place in which your characters move and act is created by well-chosen details which you observe carefully, then describe in language that highlights particular emotional associations, "leaning" your description in the direction you want your reader to look and capitalizing on the pressures that place exerts on its people. Above all, I think, that place has to mean something to you; something about your imagination has to find a natural home there. "The writer operates at a peculiar crossroads where time and place and eternity somehow meet," Flannery O'Connor wrote. "His problem is to find that location."[32]

The Anglo-Irish writer Elizabeth Bowen (1899–1973) wrote about many places, but particularly about the rural Irish landscape she knew as a child. In her novel *The Last September* (1929), a shabby-genteel country house comes to life in expertly defamiliarized sentences: "Exhausted by sunshine, the backs of the crimson chairs were a thin, light orange; a smell of camphor and animals drawn from skins on the floor in the glare of morning still hung like dust on the evening chill. Going through to her room at nights Lois often tripped with her toe in the jaws of a tiger; a false step at any time sent some great claw skidding over the polish."[33] Her short story "The Jungle" (written in the 1920s) begins with a characteristic note—a shiver of the gothic dread and delight that can be found on borders between things, people, or states of mind. Here, the protagonist, Rachel, an upper-middle-class girl at boarding school, pushes beyond the secure garden into a literal and figurative wilderness:

> It was full of secret dog-paths threading between enormous tussocks of bramble, underneath the brambles there were hollow places like caves; there were hawthorns one could climb for a survey and, about the middle, a clump of elders gave out a stuffy sweetish smell. It was an absolutely neglected and wild place; nobody seemed to own it, nobody came there but tramps. Tramps, whose clothes seemed to tear so much more easily than one's own, had left little fluttering tags on the bushes, some brownish newspaper one kicked away under the brambles, a decayed old boot like a fungus and tins scarlet with rust that tilted in every direction holding rain-water. Two or three of those tins, in some fit of terrible rage, had been bashed right in.[34]

Again, you see how effective knowing when to stop can be: after all the precise detail, defamiliarized just enough ("scarlet with rust"), Bowen makes us linger at the end of the paragraph on "bashed right in." Those three sharp syllables land like blows at the peak of a simmering, thrilling uneasiness that's been building all along. As sheltered Rachel sees them, "tramps" are frightening, yet also signs of the larger world's alluring, uncontrollable danger. Their garbage is rot and rust and—in its decay—reality. Eventually Rachel hunkers down in the brush and registers a strange feeling the place gives her: "She had felt a funny lurch in her imagination as she entered the Jungle, everything in it tumbled together, then shook apart again, a little altered in their relations to each other, a little changed."[35] By the end of the story, this statement has come to describe her view of the world.

When a writer sets an observed detail in a story, it can become effortlessly metaphorical by reflecting the larger social or emotional realities around it. James Baldwin's essay "Notes of a Native Son" (1955) opens by placing his tyrannical father's funeral amid the riots of 1960s Detroit and Harlem, expressions of the general racial oppression that had distorted the man's hopes and personality and that Baldwin himself, as we meet him on the page, is also struggling against. "On the morning of the 3rd of August," he writes, "we drove my father to the graveyard through a wilderness of smashed plate glass."[36] This image's placement at the end of the opening paragraph makes it quietly powerful: the space following it, and even the crunching, breaking sound of the words themselves (with three sharp blows, like Bowen's), means that readers have to let that destruction sink in. "A wilderness of smashed plate glass" is cemented in our minds from that point onward as a visual way to understand a whole world of emotional and social pain—a metaphor that grows organically from the thing Baldwin describes as he sees and understands it. In the opening paragraph of his story "Sonny's Blues" (1957), the narrator's reflection in a subway car window also tilts us into metaphor:

> I read about it in the paper, in the subway, on my way to work. I read it, and I couldn't believe it, and I read it again. Then perhaps I just stared at it, at the newsprint spelling out his name, spelling out the story. I stared at it in the swinging lights of the subway car, and in the faces and bodies of the people, and in my own face, trapped in the darkness which roared outside.[37]

In the next paragraph we learn that "he" is the narrator's brother Sonny, a gifted jazz musician who's been arrested for using heroin but whose art—rendered near the story's end, in one of the most moving passages in American literature—offers him, and us, a kind of transcendence that's difficult but real. Our respectable narrator, a teacher, feels trapped, like his students and Sonny, by cyclical poverty and racism, so Baldwin's image feels literally and symbolically true: looking up from his seat and meeting his own reflection in the glass, he feels borne through and into a dark and chaotic place. (Notice, too, that Baldwin's glass-related imagery shows Elaine Scarry's principles of aesthetic design at work, as discussed in Chapter 2, layering suggestive emotion over the physical world just as glass itself— transparent but still present—does when we look through it.)

Sometimes, a single detail of a domestic setting can tell us volumes about the person living there. In her essay "Goodbye to All That" (1967)—an ironic echo of Robert Graves—Joan Didion describes her life as a twenty-something writer in 1950s New York City, trying to make a series of empty spaces feel like home. "All I ever did to that apartment," she writes, "was hang fifty yards of yellow theatrical silk across the bedroom windows, because I had some idea that the gold light would make me feel better, but I did not bother to weight the curtains correctly and all that summer the long panels of transparent golden silk would blow out the windows and get tangled and drenched in afternoon thunderstorms."[38] (Later, she wrote that her mother had hung "gold silk organza" curtains in her childhood home: "they hung almost two stories, billowed iridescently with every breath of air, and crumbled at the touch."[39] How often, when we try to make our grown-up homes, do we recreate what our parents did?) "That was the year, my twenty-eighth," she continues, "when I was discovering that not all of the promises would be kept, that some things are in fact irrevocable and that it had counted after all, every evasion and every procrastination, every word, all of it."[40] Like the smells Didion threads throughout the essay, the yellow theatrical silk precisely enacts her younger self's way of being in the city— evanescent, impractical, lovely, temporary. (And, like James Baldwin's glass, it also meets Elaine Scarry's criteria for imagery: billowing fabric, moved by some external force against a solid wall, is easy for us to picture.)

"We see things not as they are, but as we are": this quote, attributed to everyone from the Talmud to Anais Nin, governs the writing of description too. It takes on a spiritual dimension in the work of Peter Matthiessen (1927–2014), writer, explorer, activist, and devout Buddhist, whose notebooks we've seen in Chapter 1. In 1973, Matthiessen traveled into the Himalayas—the foundational landscape of Tibetan Buddhism—with the wildlife biologist George Schaller, who was studying the Himalayan blue sheep and hoping to spot the elusive snow leopard. The book Matthiessen wrote about that trip, *The Snow Leopard* (1978), is a quest narrative that's not only about the quest but also about the path and the ongoing path of discovery, physical and spiritual. "When one pays attention to the present," Matthiessen writes, "there is great pleasure in awareness of small things."[41] This sentence embodies a central teaching of Buddhism—paying attention, even when it's not pleasurable, is spiritually necessary. Yet writing about spirituality of any kind is famously difficult; how to keep from lapsing into windy generalities or a private language of feeling? Matthiessen lets the details of the landscape and people speak from the page with the same clarity of vision his Buddhist practice has trained up in him, so that in reading, we experience the same process of journeying and seeing that he does. His descriptions of this very spirit-imbued landscape are precise, rhythmic, and alive, springing from a state of hyper-awareness that unites inner and outer realities.

> A silhouette crosses the white wastes below, a black coil dangling from its hand. It is Dawa Sherpa carrying tump line and headband, yet in this light, a something moves that is much more than Dawa. The sun is roaring, it fills to bursting each crystal of snow. I flush with feeling, moved beyond my comprehension, and once again, the warm tears freeze upon my face. These rocks and mountains, all this matter, the snow itself, the air—the earth is ringing. All is moving, full of power, full of light.[42]

Use the details to lean into the scene and let your feelings about it show themselves. Details can be the edge of the wedge to cut deeper. Why have you written this word rather than that one? Why do Elizabeth Bowen's boots and tins look sinister to young Rachel, rather than forlorn?

# Describing people: Mirrors and stereotypes

In their hilarious guidebook *How Not to Write a Novel*, Howard Mittelmark and Sandra Newman review some basic errors writers make, including *character description*. "The reader wants to know what your characters look like," they write. "But how do you get your point-of-view character to rattle off his height, weight, and skin tone? Easy! Frog-march him to the mirror! Unfortunately, this is so obviously a convention of bad fiction that it might as well read, 'Looking in the mirror, Joe saw a tall, brown-haired man, trapped in a poorly written novel.'"[43] The mirror feels particularly artificial for protagonists and first-person narrators (see Chapter 5), since, at some level, readers invest a first-person character with the details of our *own* appearance; if I'm seeing through her eyes, our unconscious logic runs, then she must look like me.

But writers take the risk because readers do need at least some idea of how a character looks. We need some visual shorthand, some hook on which to hang our image of a character as the story progresses. ("You have got to learn to paint with words," Flannery O'Connor advised an apprentice writer. "Have the old man there first so the reader can't escape him.")[44] But the key to making this work is the same as with sensory vs. editorial language in Chapter 1: give us information we need in order to form a mental picture at a time it feels relevant to us, and avoid passing a judgment on a character's appearance and then pushing the reader to agree with you. Since a sense of how our bodies are perceived by others arises, fairly or not, when we interact with the world and with other people, try to show features of a character's appearance arising or producing consequences within a meaningful context—a wrestler trying to make weight, or a tall junior high school girl who's shot up past all the boys in her class. When Character #2 walks into a room and Character #1 turns to look, that's a natural place for a short visual sketch of Character #2. Associating characters with particular objects, like items of clothing, can be useful (*ah, yes*, readers can think, *the guy in the leather jacket again*). But overall, appearance description is like research: it works best when it enters a story on a *need-to-know basis*, perhaps over time, in the same way we become aware of others' appearances, and our own. You may find that if you're showing your character in action, her gestures and words may give readers all the information we need—you may not even need to deliver a direct picture of her appearance. A description that's just dropped in ("She was a forty-year-old woman with blonde hair and large hands") can feel like a police report, and not in a good way. ("The suspect is a forty-year-old woman with blonde hair and large hands, last seen leaving the convenience store with a six-pack of Pabst Blue Ribbon …") By contrast, consider this: "Officer Constance Pratt pulled her jacket tight around her and shivered as she trudged up the hill. She'd forgotten her gloves, and her hands were turning red." Our picture of a character forms as we see her in action in her world, which should be the narration's focus.

How a writer handles a character's looks can be unintentionally revealing. Consider the classic case of the character the writer wants the reader to find physically attractive. First, there's the question of whether this is even important to *say*. You're not a Hollywood casting director; readers are capable of being interested in characters for reasons other than bicep size and waist measurement. And what does "attractive" even *mean*, anyway? Even a cursory tour of "female beauty" of the last 150 years will show you how that meaning can change. From tall and statuesque (the Gibson Girl) to skinny and boyish (the flapper) to busty siren (Marilyn Monroe) to the athletic heroines of my own childhood (Farrah Fawcett and Lynda Carter), this ideal changes all the time. And that's only the white girls.[45] African-American, Asian, Native American, Indian, and Hispanic women have been left out of standards of "beauty" in serious and shameful ways. ("And while we're on the subject," said a young woman of color in one of my creative writing classes, "can we please stop describing brown-skinned girls in terms of food? Cinnamon, mocha, chocolate?" Great idea.) Women whose bodies don't conform to particular standards of weight, age, height, shape, size, sexuality, or mobility get left out too. All this is to say that if you're reaching for a particular image of "attractiveness"—particularly white, blond, blue-eyed, young, and "perfect," which reads as cliché at this point in history—you should ask yourself why that is, and why you think your reader needs that information. If handled wrongly, your attempts to make readers see a character as attractive will come off as socially limited, prurient, or both—a little too reflective of a judgment you've reached for reasons of your own—at which (as with editorial language) we'll balk, especially if we don't share the assumptions on which your judgment is based.

By contrast, consider what happens when you get a complex, believable body with a history onto the page. Maurizio de Giovanni's Commissario Ricciardi mysteries, set in Fascist-era Naples, feature a melancholy detective whose green eyes act as a constant, unusual signal of that interiority. Walter Mosley's Easy Rawlins, an African-American detective in mid-twentieth-century Los Angeles, registers his own race when he encounters a white person who reacts to him (but in Easy's own neighborhood, brown skin, not white, is the norm.) In *The Giant, O'Brien* (1998), based on the real-life story of Charles Byrne, the eighteenth-century "Irish Giant" Hilary Mantel shows how an unusually tall man is perceived by others but also how it feels from inside his skin, as his body grows and grows and then starts to break down. Perhaps your character has an old injury that acts up (which can provide a nice source of ongoing tension or pressure), scars (which will then give the character an opportunity to tell another character, and thus the reader, how s/he got that scar), or a feature emerging because of some external circumstance ("her hair was curling since she'd run from the bus stop through the rain") or in comparison to others ("She looked around and sighed inwardly; once again, she was the tallest person in the room.") This will help your character's appearance emerge and acquire meaning in the way a real person's does, in interactions with others in the world—not as a static set of features readers are invited to judge.

# Bold, but not too bold: Nonrealism and worldbuilding

"Be bold, be bold, but not too bold"—this line from Edmund Spenser's epic *The Faerie Queene* (1596) comes to mind whenever I think of the particular challenge of nonrealistic writing (magic realism, science fiction, fantasy, dystopia, fairy tales), which is enjoying a redefinition and a renaissance. While you have to step decisively out into thin air, announcing your concept with a certain Indiana-Jones-like boldness, you also have to build the bridge under our feet with great care. The wrong detail or insufficient understanding of your alternate world's rules can be particularly fatal, but you can learn quite a bit from writers who might not seem at first to be walking a strictly fantastical path.

French author Jules Renard (1864–1910) wrote a great and unusual series of short "nature tales" (*Histoires naturelles*, 1909), illustrated with delightful line drawings by the painter Pierre Bonnard. Each "nature tale" is a short description, around 200 words, that spins a precise observation of the natural world into something part prose poem, part fable. "The Butterfly" is only one line: "This love letter, folded in two, is looking for a flowery address."[46] Here, in its entirety, is "The Toad" (translated by Douglas Parmée):

> Born out of a stone, he's living under a stone. He's building a tomb there.
>
> I often visit him, and each time I lift the stone up, I'm afraid of seeing him—and afraid he may not be there.
>
> He is there, hiding in this dry, clean, narrow den which he owns and fills, completely; he's as swollen as a miser's purse.
>
> If rain forces him to leave it, he comes toward me. A few lumpy jumps and there he is, watching me through his blowsy eyes.
>
> People are unfair: they insult him by treating him as a leper. I squat down beside him and move my human face close to his.
>
> Then I'll swallow any disgust I still feel and I'll stroke you, you toad!
>
> You have to swallow many more insults in your lifetime that make you sick.

But yesterday, I was tactless. He was oozing and fermenting, his warts had all burst.

"You poor chap!" I said. "I don't want to hurt your feelings but, heavens above, aren't you hideous?"

He opened his toothless, childish mouth and replied, with a slight English accent, "And what about yourself?"[47]

Renard teaches us that even overtly "nonrealistic" writing is rooted firmly in this world, and that responsibility to observed detail keeps the work from feeling too whimsical or unbelievable. Through sensory detail, a writer can ground us in an unreal, imagined setting to say something emotionally true. (Isn't it good for humans to feel rebuked by other beings, to which we imagine ourselves superior, as Renard's speaker is rebuked by this toad?) You can see this principle worked out on a larger scale in deliberately fantastical writing—fantasy, science fiction, dystopia, magic realism, or the ever-expanding family of literary-fiction writers that borrow from all of these—like Octavia Butler's *Kindred* (1979), Angela Carter's *The Bloody Chamber* (1979), Benjamin Percy's *The Dead Lands* (2015), George Orwell's *Nineteen Eighty-four* (1949), Ray Bradbury's *Fahrenheit 451* (1953), Gabriel Garcia Marquez's *One Hundred Years of Solitude* (1967) and "A Very Old Man With Enormous Wings" (1955), Gary Shteyngart's *Super Sad True Love Story* (2010), Jim Shepard's story "Creature from the Black Lagoon" (2004), Ben Winters's *Underground Airlines* (2016), Margaret Atwood's *The Handmaid's Tale* (1985), and so many more. For now, I want to focus on a short story and two novels that show us the place where emotional truth and nonrealism meet.

The first is Lesley Nneka Arimah's "Who Will Greet You at Home," from her collection *What It Means When a Man Falls from the Sky* (2017). From the first paragraph, it teaches us how to read it on its own terms:

The yarn baby lasted a good month, emitting dry, cotton-soft gurgles and pooping little balls of lint, before Ogechi snagged its thigh on a nail and it unraveled as she continued walking, mistaking the little huffs for the beginnings of hunger, not the cries of an infant being undone. By the time she noticed, it was too late, the leg a tangle of fiber, and she pulled the string the rest of the way to end it, rather than have the infant grow up maimed. If she was to mother a child, to mute and subdue and fold away parts of herself, the child had to be perfect.[48]

My twenty-ish-year-old students were captivated by the fairy-tale oddity: right away, we've been transported to a world where a woman can make a living, pooping baby out of yarn. Forty-ish me stared, rapt, into the lights and shadows of that last sentence—"mother a child, to mute and subdue and fold away parts of herself"—and the complex emotions it points to, especially in the twin echoes those long graceful sentences make as they land: *maimed, perfect.* All of us happily succumbed to the concrete, assured writerly voice. *Okay, we're in!* we assented. *Now tell us how it works!*

And the second paragraph delivers, deepening what we know about this world's rules and Ogechi's relationship to them:

> Yarn had been a foolish choice, she knew, the stuff for women of leisure, who could cradle wool in the comfort of their own cars and in secure houses devoid of loose nails. Not for an assistant hairdresser who took danfo to work if she had money, walked if she didn't, and lived in an "apartment" that amounted to a room she could clear in three large steps. Women like her had to form their children out of sturdier, more practical material if they were to withstand the dents and scrapes that came with a life like hers. Her mother had formed her from mud and twigs and wrapped her limbs tightly with leaves, like moin-moin: pedestrian items that had produced a pedestrian girl. Ogechi was determined that her child would be a thing of whimsy, soft and pretty, tender and worthy of love. But first, she had to go to work.[49]

Here, the fantastical details of handmade babies and the materials women can choose to make them pivot to point toward realities of class we recognize in our own world too. By now, our hunch that we're in an alternate version of a real place, Nigeria ("Ogechi" is a Nigerian name), has been confirmed by Nigerian words we can either look up or infer from context: *danfo* a taxi, *moin-moin* a bean and pepper pudding wrapped in leaves. The third sentence ("Women like her …") could describe a working-class life in most times and places, where women "form their children" to be resilient, uncushioned by the privileges of "women of leisure." Ogechi herself has been formed—in imagery both literal and symbolic—from "mud and leaves … pedestrian items that had produced a pedestrian girl." Here the detail leads directly to the story's emotional significance: even as Ogechi loves and resents her mother, she dreams of using her own baby to make another kind of life for herself. (And because she's a hairdresser, who does skilled handwork every day, we suspect she'll have that dexterity; her job bears real weight in the story.) Her child won't be as ordinary and poor as she feels herself—because of her mother's "mud and leaves"—to be. And now we're back in a believable, significant emotional reality of mothers, daughters, expectations, hopes, and the choice of repeating the past or building a new life for ourselves. The yarn baby is not just a cool image—it does rich emotional work that couldn't have been done in this way without it.

Two recent novels—Colson Whitehead's *The Underground Railroad* (2016) and Mohsin Hamid's *Exit West* (2017)—speak of human oppression by building worlds in which everything is normal except for one thing: a magical means of travel that appears when a desperate person needs it. In *Exit West*—published soon after a photograph of three-year-old Syrian refugee Aylan Kurdi, drowned on a Turkish beach, shook the world—that device is a door that opens between the West and countries like the unnamed, war-torn home of the protagonists, Saeed and Nadia. Early in the novel, Hamid shows us how it works: from the darkness of an Australian woman's closet, which has suddenly become a travel portal, "a man was emerging:"

> He too was dark, with dark skin and dark, woolly hair. He wriggled with great effort, his hands gripping either side of the doorway as though pulling himself up against gravity, or against the rush of a monstrous tide. His neck followed his head, tendons straining, and then his chest, his half-unbuttoned, sweaty, gray-and-brown shirt. Suddenly he paused in his exertions. He looked around the room. He looked at the sleeping woman, the shut bedroom door, the open window. He rallied himself again, fighting mightily to come in, but in desperate silence, the silence of a man struggling in an alley, on the ground, late at night, to free himself of hands clenched around his throat. But there were no hands around this man's throat. He wished only not to be heard.[50]

Here, just as in real life, moving yourself from one world to another takes tremendous physical effort and risk, which also animate *The Underground Railroad*. Although Whitehead's novel takes place before the Civil War, it was written and published as the Black Lives Matter movement was leading a conversation about racism and violence in the criminal justice system and elsewhere, giving his enslaved protagonist Cora's struggles an uncomfortably current edge. As in *Exit West,* that readerly discomfort is the point, and it keeps the novel's magical conceit—the Underground Railroad is an actual train, with hidden stations, tracks, and conductors—from feeling merely whimsical. Here's Cora's first sight of the train as it pulls into the subterranean station, which escaping slaves Cora and Caesar have reached through a trapdoor in a safe-house floor:

> The locomotive was black, an ungainly contraption led by the triangular snout of the cowcatcher, though there would be few animals where this engine was headed. The bulb of the smokestack was next, a soot-covered stalk. The main body consisted of a large black box topped by the engineer's cabin. Below

that, pistons and large cylinders engaged in a relentless dance with the ten wheels, two sets of small ones in front and three behind. The locomotive pulled one single car, a dilapidated boxcar missing numerous planks in its walls.[51]

The hyper-realism of this locomotive—which looks exactly like a real train of Cora's time would have looked—heightens the oddity and the truth of its appearance here. Paradoxically, fiction helps us see reality more clearly by removing us from it a little. When police shootings, protests, and leaky rafts bearing desperate migrants across the Mediterranean flooded my screens in 2016 and 2017, I remembered Whitehead's chuffing subterranean train and Hamid's magical door, and I felt a heightened truth borne into my heart by story: suffering human beings long to escape from that suffering, by any means necessary. Slavery and the refugee crisis share a great human hope: to be taken from present danger and terror, to be somewhere else, to be free of being exploited and afraid. For a magical concept to really work, it has to speak to us of real—even painful and complicated—things.

Students are often surprised to discover that for this reason, writing fantastical worlds is not automatically easier than writing "realistic" fiction. In fact, it's often harder, since you have to invent and convey to us the details of your world according to a logic that makes sense on its own terms *and* on ours. You also must hearken to a recognizable human reality that fantasy can't dodge, using the distance *from* reality to say something *about* it. Margaret Atwood's *The Handmaid's Tale* (1986) channels 1980s conformity and religious repression into an enduring feminist dystopia, and Kim Stanley Robinson's *New York 2140* (2017) imagines how humans might live in a Manhattan flooded by rising seas—a real problem, as Hurricane Sandy showed in 2012. British journalist John Lanchester argues that George R. R. Martin's *Game of Thrones* series, with its dynastic battles and major characters' abrupt and violent deaths, reflect historical realities like the Wars of the Roses and the uncertainty of our own climate-change, politically doubtful moment, when things can change quickly and permanently.[52] Margaret Atwood writes that among the reasons for Ray Bradbury's enduring popularity is his sense for American psychological and historical reality:

> My own view is that in his best work, Bradbury sinks a taproot right down into the deep, dark, gothic core of America. It's no accident that he was descended from Mary Bradbury, convicted as a witch in 1692, during the notorious Salem witchcraft trials, for, among other things, assuming the form of a blue boar. (She was not hanged, as the execution was delayed until the

craze was over.) The Salem trials are a seminal trope in American history, one that has repeated itself over and over in various forms—both literary and political—throughout the years. At its heart is the notion of the doubleness of life: you are not who you are, but have a secret and probably evil twin; more importantly, the neighbors are not who you think they are.[53]

Without this rich sense of something at stake that we recognize from our real world—a fascinating darkness deep in our culture, like a troubled beast turning over in its sleep—Bradbury's concepts would still be cool but the stories wouldn't bite as deep. (I read *Fahrenheit 451,* "All Summer in a Day," and "The Veldt" in junior high—that time of peak social duality, conformity, and fear—and they've been seared into my brain ever since.) It's easy to get caught up in fanciful detail spinning (*Wouldn't it be cool if …*) or cliché (*the beautiful princess sighed as she thought …*) while evading the emotional heart of the story. But like any fiction, fantastical worlds must feel emotionally significant, driven by human desires even if those characters themselves aren't human. "Matters of the heart," writes Benjamin Percy, "make your world worth occupying. Especially when it comes to high-concept storytelling."[54]

Of course, Chekhov has some advice about this. In 1897, a seventeen-year-old girl who "described herself as an experienced writer who had been 'writing for many years'" sent him a story to which he returned the following critique:

> As far as your "Fairy Tale" is concerned, I wouldn't call it a fairy tale. It seems to me more like a conglomeration of words like gnome, fairy, dew, and knights—all of which are fake diamonds, at least on Russian soil, which has never known the tread of knights or gnomes and where you'll have trouble finding anyone who can picture a fairy dining on dew and moonbeams. Drop all that. You must be a sincere artist and depict only what exists or what in your opinion could be; you must paint coherent pictures.[55]

In other words, stringing together fairy-tale or young-adult-fantasy clichés won't automatically make a story; you need some connection with human reality and emotional significance. *Why* is the Wizard Clan fighting the Elfin Clan? *Why* does the young warrior/misfit/princess-in-disguise *want* to find and use the sword/magical gemstone/object du jour successfully? *Why* are we in a world of spells and pointy ears in the first place? The places your story touches our shared human reality through physical detail and complex emotion are the places it will touch your readers too. Go there emotionally—not just intellectually.

One of my students (let's call him Julian) discovered this for himself. In his story, the narrator visited his estranged brother's house to discover his brother was keeping a baby dragon in a box in the laundry room. While this charming, surreal image reminded me of Donald Barthelme or Aimee Bender, who heighten oddity with ordinariness, the story didn't really go anywhere, because the fantastical element wasn't adding any meaning; the dragon could just as easily have been a puppy. Julian and I talked about this, and his face brightened. "I see what you mean," he said. "It's not about writing what I know how to *imagine*. It's about writing what I know how to *feel*." Precisely. For the rest of the semester, he applied that new lens to his work. His final story was about a family conflict, sometimes funny, sometimes painful, with realistic details and dialogue and not a dragon in sight. His classmates and I felt more than just "entertained" when we read it—we felt as if we'd been taken on an emotional journey that mattered. The second story was harder for Julian to write, but it was much more rewarding for us to read—illustrating, just like Chekhov's orphans or Arimah's yarn baby, that when we trust details and tune in to the emotional truth behind them, our readers will trust us too.

# Exercises

1) Mine the images you have already brought to the page. Go back through your notebook material and circle the most interesting thing/s. Put that image, word, or phrase at the top of a new page and start writing.

2) Write at least one scene of a family legend or story you've heard a relative tell about his or her own early life, preferably before you were born. Make that relative the main character, and refer to the person by actual first name—not "Mom," "Grandpa," or "Aunt Dolores." It's a small change that makes a big difference in your writing.

3) Do the exercise I discuss regarding *Beloved* above; write a scene in which a character is doing one thing with her hands while thinking about and/or talking about something else. How are the two things, and the energies of writing them, related? What else do you learn about the character, her past, her world?

4) Make two short lists of pressures on your character: one immediate, one ongoing. (I say "short" because a character with too many problems will be as unbelievable to readers as a character with no problems at all.) How might they be connected to one another, and to what the character wants, what her secrets are, what she is afraid of? To raise the stakes in the story, raise the pressure in one or more of these areas.

5) Go outside, walk around for 15 minutes, and then put one observed detail from that walk into your work-in-progress—no matter what it is. This tends to enliven an imagined setting with the detail of an actual one, in a good way.

6) This is a classic exercise, but a good one: Write a scene in which an ostensibly neutral setting (the inside of a barn, a forest, a kitchen ....) is inflected by your character's state of mind, which will influence what details appear and how they're seen. See if you can "lean" the description in one emotional direction, then another, without ever naming the emotion (grief, anger, desire, nervousness) directly. Objects can also be used for this—I find that eggs work particularly well. (See Vladimir Nabokov's recipe for boiling eggs – reprinted as "Eggs a la Nabocoque" in *Harper's*, September 1999 – for an interesting example.)

7) Write a Renard-style encounter—200 words or less—with an animal that riffs on its observed appearance in the way he does.

8) Read the ending of James Baldwin's "Sonny's Blues" and watch what he does with the glass of Scotch and milk placed on Sonny's piano, right above his head. Using this as inspiration, kick-start a scene with an object in the following ways:

   a. Center it on an object that has some significance or becomes significant as the scene progresses. (One of the characters is picking it up, holding it, using it, looking for it, hiding it, throwing it at the other ...)

   b. Write a flashback scene that is connected to something your character is looking at or thinking about right now; show us a moment from his past that has gotten him where he is.

   c. Make a list of all the objects your character might be carrying in his or her purse or knapsack or toolbox, pick one, and write a scene in which s/he uses it, including, if possible, a detail you observed from having seen someone use that object in real life. What information do the other objects on the list give you about your character?

9) Try an exercise I give my beginning poetry students: Set in front of you an interesting object. Now generate three lists of detail, with three categories of information about it: (a) literal and sensory information (the quilt square is soft and colorful, with a faintly musty smell), (b) cultural and/or historical information (this is a quilt square like those made by the ladies of Gee's Bend, Alabama or Midwestern pioneer women, making art from the pieces of clothing that had seen hard use in other places, and (c) personal and/or familial information (my grandmother made a quilt like this and I slept underneath it as a child). Jot down as much information as you can in each category—you can take them in order or toggle among them—and then compose a poem or essay by writing down one item from one list, then another, then another. This will give you masses of specific and interesting material you can shape into a more finished piece of writing.

10) Walk yourself through this time-handling exercise I give my students to start building their stories; it's an adaptable scaffolding that will give you a solid set of images and scenes with more jumping-off points from within them, and it will teach you some of the basic ways to handle time in a story.

a. Write a paragraph that sets your point-of-view character in a place and time, with another character; something is happening in that immediate moment, preferably something that indicates an ongoing conflict or tension. Including at least some dialogue is good—especially since dialogue can reveal information you pick up on later in the story.

**Example:** *Mike followed his older brother Jerry out the door and into the backyard. It was Christmas time, and their mother's multicolored lights blinked from the windows. An inflatable Santa was collapsed near the rose bushes. Faint snow dusted the brown grass. "Come on," Jerry said over his shoulder. "Time to throw the ball around a little. Not every day I get to play catch with a college boy."*

b. Write a second paragraph of flashback beginning with a classic flashback-related verb tense: the past perfect (see Chapter 5), indicating an ongoing state of things that may still be going on. In cinematic terms, it's a *dissolve*, a signal that we're moving backward in time but still maintaining a connection with the present moment. Start with the phrase "It had always been this way," inside your character's thoughts. This will show us the source of ongoing tension within the story, which will interact with the immediate level of tension as both of them play themselves out.

> **Example:** *It had always been this way, Mike thought. From the time they were little, Jerry had been the athlete, Mike the scholar. Every day at recess he had stood on the sidelines of the ragged square of dirt that was McKinlock Middle School's baseball field, watching Jerry pitch. Out on the mound, his brother's glove rose just at the right moment to capture the ball; his long arm whipped it back into the catcher's mitt with a thwack. But Mike was really watching his brother's face, hoping for that moment when Jerry's habitual school frown, the lines in his forehead that appeared as he gripped his pencil and stared at the page, smoothed out and his eyes grew wide and clear and even from all the way across the field Mike could see that Jerry was happy.*

c. Try a flash-forward (yes, just like a flashback, it does exist: Stuart Dybek's short-short story "The Start of Something" is told entirely in flash-forward). Maybe this is only a line or two, but it lets you test where you think your characters might be headed. "Would" (a form of the future conditional verb tense, just in case you are wondering) can signal a flash-forward just as past perfect ("had") or the simple past ("threw") or a combination of both signals a flashback. You can move this paragraph around in your story or take it out completely (see Chapter 5), but it'll give you a nice confidence booster and open a door into the space of what's possible for your story and what's ahead for your characters.

**Example:** *For years afterward, Mike would wonder why it never happened for Jerry, why all the talent scouts only, in the end, said, "You got a lotta potential, kid," and walked away. He would wonder why Jerry could never find the same kind of happiness off the pitcher's mound as on it, why his marriage to Bonnie failed, why he spent more and more time between jobs, why Mike himself had been the only college boy in the family.*

d. Now, for super-transition-experimentation brownie points, insert a section break, which indicates a transition in place and time and a break between one part of the story and another. (In cinematic terms, it's like the cut between the end of one scene and the beginning of the next one, when we understand without being directly shown it that time has passed and the characters have moved to a new place.) The best way to indicate a section break on the page is to hit your return key after finishing your line of type, then insert some kind of symbol—I prefer the round black dot from the "symbols" menu in Microsoft Word—into the center of that empty line. This tells readers (and typesetters, if your manuscript is to be published) that your section break there is deliberate and should be preserved as white space on the page. I ask students to use the single black dot or, at most, three short lines like this—or asterisks like this *** to indicate section breaks. You want a visible but unobtrusive signal in the middle of the page with white space around it, not a solid barrier between sections (which lines or asterisks all the way across the page will create).

e. Now open a new scene with a paragraph setting characters and readers either back where we were at the beginning of the story OR another, related place and time. (For instance, Mike and Jerry could be either back in the yard or in their mother's kitchen. But since showing us that game will show us a lot we need to know about these brothers as the story develops, and since I want to avoid jumping around in time too much, I'm going to opt for the ballgame.)

**Example:** *The dry grass crunched under Mike's feet as he followed Jerry into the yard and stood in front of the steps. Snow clung to his sneakers. He shivered. But Jerry wasn't wearing a jacket; striding out across the yard, he looked strong, immune to the cold, despite the thickening around his waist and the bald spot on the back of his head. Mike swallowed and braced himself. When Jerry turned around, the ball would come at him without warning, and he wouldn't let Jerry see him flinch.*

And keep developing and adding scenes from there. Let yourself feel how information or images that emerge in one paragraph prompt questions or future scenes; this is how you build the story under you, step by step.

# 4

# Your Voice on the Page

In focusing on prose, word choice, and style, this chapter will also be grounded in my big theme from the rest of this book: always be mindful of your relationship with your reader, and of your language's relationship to cognitive and sensory reality. Are these words on this page in this order *actually* creating the effect on your reader that you want them to? It's a delicate dance. Some features of your prose feel essential to your voice, and to your delight in your own work. In revising to please everyone, you can also please no one, including yourself. But if you are writing for others, you do have to consider whether *these words on the page, in this order*, are having their richest, clearest possible effect in the reader's mind and, therefore, helping you achieve your goals for your work. Do these words in this order blur or sharpen a picture in your reader's mind? Do they sustain or break what John Gardner called "the vivid and continuous dream" fiction is meant to invoke in readers' heads? Do they carry this picture of *reality as your character understands it* into your reader's consciousness, with minimum friction and maximum accuracy? Are they wedging your own ego or assumptions between the reader and the thing described and damaging the reader's experience?

Writing and revising your best prose start with maintaining a relationship with the world beyond your own head. Fit your language to the images you mean to render with it, and if the language isn't clear enough, that may also mean the image isn't clear enough in your own mind yet or you don't know the precise words you need. Therefore, you may need to sharpen (and research, reobserve, or mentally enflesh, or read more good writing connected to) that internal image until you understand it better. To do this, you've fundamentally got to care about the world (and the people) beyond your head. This starts with being present in it, observing it, and then revising toward it and toward the other big thing you're responsible to: the reader. The fiction writer George Saunders says: "You revise your reader up, in your imagination, with every pass. You keep saying to yourself: 'No, she's smarter than that. Don't dishonor her with that lazy prose or that easy notion.' And in revising your reader up, you revise yourself up too."[1] Little by little, with each revision tweak, your writing gets better and so do you. Words are the place where this effort starts.

# Vocabulary: Precision and range

If I had a dollar for every apprentice writer I've heard bemoaning their lack of a "big vocabulary," I could donate my salary to my college—especially if I had another dollar for each writer I've heard bemoaning other people's lack of "big vocabulary." It's not always wrong to hold either of these beliefs. The problem is that they position "big vocabulary" as an end in itself, which leads kids to spelling-bee championships and leads everyone to pompous, vague writing. I suggest a shift in thinking: you don't want "big vocabulary," you want *word-range*, because range enables freedom and precision. Having a wide range of words (including speech registers) at your disposal increases your chances of being able to reach out and set your hand on the right one when you need to nail a precise shade of meaning to the page. (Sometimes you need to say, "I doubt the veracity of that statement," sometimes "For real?") Building a wide word-range comes from reading, and it also comes from observing and working to set language to what you see. Precision and a wide—not "big"—word-range go together because both enable and are products of a wide range of intellectual motion and freedom. Like a baseball pitcher's arm, your sense for words, when strengthened and stretched, can move better in all directions. Then, as you revise little by little toward your reader, you are more able to say exactly what you mean.

# Starting early: A sense for words

When I was a young reader, two writers honed my word-range by joining language to the world in my mind: Laura Ingalls Wilder (1867–1957) and Mary Ann Evans, who wrote as George Eliot (1819–1880). Madeleine L'Engle, author of *A Wrinkle in Time*, has said that writing for children is really not a different beast than writing for adults—the same principles of clarity, precision, and sensory detail apply.[2] Children can tell when an adult is lying to them, or when an adult has written a "children's book" driven more by ideas than by a real sense of how children feel (take something you think a child "should" be interested in, then revise your vocabulary down a notch, with predictably boring results), or when what's on the page doesn't quite match up with observed reality. While a good children's writer may seldom use words of more than two syllables, she never condescends; she enters fully into her imagined or remembered world so that young readers may do the same. Sensory detail is the bridge between her mind and theirs.

Like many other children, I was obsessed with Laura Ingalls Wilder, reading and rereading my precious paperbacks in their sturdy yellow box. Today, I notice just how good Wilder really is at narrative technique: layering the child's innocence with the adult's retrospective knowledge, she makes space for both. *Little House on the Prairie* (1935) describes the Ingalls family's settlement near what's now Independence, Kansas and their encounters with native people of the Osage Nation during 1869–1870. Each small moment glints with observed detail—frost on prairie grass, moonlight sparkling on wolves' fur, a lovely moment when Laura's father ("Pa") plays a fiddle duet with a nightingale. And, to Laura as they were to me, animals are carefully observed actors in the family's life. When the Ingalls's wagon, pulled by the mustangs Pet and Patty, pauses on the bank of a creek, the prose transmits to us exactly what Laura sees and hears: "The rushing sound of the water filled the still air. All along the creek banks the trees hung over it and made it dark with shadows. In the middle it ran swiftly, sparkling silver and blue."[3] As Pa and Ma debate whether the creek is safe to cross, we feel Laura's apprehension in her heightened attention to the horses who'll be pulling the wagon and the dog who's following: "Pet and Patty lifted their wet noses. They pricked their ears forward, looking at the creek; then they pricked them backward to hear what Pa would say. They sighed and laid their soft noses together to whisper to each other. A little way upstream, Jack was lapping the water with his red tongue."[4] (This is a great tension-raising technique: slow us down and make us linger in a moment by heightening detail.) The creek crossing turns out to be dangerous but luckily all is safe except for Jack, temporarily lost on the other bank, whose panic Laura imagines as many children (including me) have imagined their pets' feelings: "He had stood on the bank and seen the wagon going away from him, as if they didn't care for him at all. And he would never know how much they wanted him."[5] This effect exemplifies what Maryanne Wolf and others have written about children's literature; it teaches young readers to recognize others' emotions, and their own.

Heightened detail also indicates an emotional understory when Laura goes with Pa and her sister Mary to an abandoned Osage camp.

> There were ashes where Indian camp fires had been. There were holes in the ground where tent poles had been driven. Bones were scattered where Indian dogs had gnawed them. All along the sides of the hollow, Indian ponies had bitten the grasses short.
>
> Tracks of big moccasins and smaller moccasins were everywhere, and tracks of little bare toes. And over those tracks were tracks of rabbits and tracks of birds, and wolves' tracks.
>
> Pa read the tracks for Mary and Laura. He showed them tracks of two middle-sized moccasins by the edge of a camp fire's ashes. An Indian woman had squatted there. She wore a leather skirt with fringes; the tiny marks of the fringe were in the dust. The track of her toes inside the moccasins was deeper than the track of her heels, because she had leaned forward to stir something cooking in a pot on the fire.[6]

As in other encounters with native people in *Little House on the Prairie*, curiosity and melancholy blend in this moment. Just as Laura and Mary do, Pa (who shows a respect for native people that other white settlers don't) honors this woman's presence by noticing it with wonder rather than hostility, and by deploying the sharp-eyed observation anyone on the prairie needs to survive. But the detail also lets us ask a question Laura doesn't need to ask for us: Did the woman whose feet made those prints move on from that campfire willingly or unwillingly? And with that, a whole frontier history of exploitation and forced migration shimmers into view. By trusting her sensory detail, Laura Ingalls Wilder trusts the reader too. And there's not a "big word" in sight.

Another great treasure in my childhood word-hoard-building was a set of anthologies passed down through my mother's family: *My Book House* in six volumes, edited by Olive Beaupré Miller and published in the 1920s. They're beautiful, gilt-stamped black books, satisfyingly but not overwhelmingly large. Each volume features a glowingly colorful N. C. Wyeth painting on its cover but no paper jacket, which Miller believed would come between the book and the child. Miller, a 1904 Smith College graduate, founded the series in the belief that "To be well equipped for life, to have ideas and the ability to express them, the child needs a broad background of familiarity with the best in literature."[7] As a child, I slurped them down, flipping back and forth through the brittle pages with abandon. Now I see not only my own childhood rips and finger marks but Ojibway, Norse, Russian, Chinese, and African-American traditional stories, Dante, Shakespeare, Rabindranath Tagore, and all the Romantic poets (with a subtly tart biography of Shelley anticipating the same notes in Richard Holmes's *Shelley: The Pursuit* fifty years later). All the Victorians are here, too: both Brownings and Charlotte Yonge and Charles Kingsley and Lewis Carroll and George Eliot. *My Book House* introduced me to Shelley, Byron, and Keats—Miller's, and my, particular favorite—long before my graduate work in British Romanticism carried me back into their lives. The overall mood is one of mystery, magic, and a sensorily grounded narrative momentum I'd later recognize in J. R. R. Tolkein and C. S. Lewis. The real world is present—just as Laura Ingalls Wilder doesn't hide the dangers of rising creeks—but not in ways you can easily tie to the book's own moment. While there is loss, fear, hunger, and roiling emotion, there are no Model Ts, Spanish influenza, or jazz records. The books float free of a particular time and place while still developing the emotional muscles that will enable young readers to meet the world.

The moment when I made the connection between words on the page and the living world—indelibly as another childhood heroine, Helen Keller, with the pump-water pouring over her hands—came in *My Book House* Volume Four, "The Treasure Chest," which excerpted George Eliot's 1860 novel *The Mill on the Floss*. Tensions between rebellious heroine Maggie Tulliver and her prim cousin Lucy Deane enacted the same tomboyish-brunette-vs.-adored-blonde-good-girl dynamic I recognized from the *Little House* books and from real life: Mary-vs.-Laura, pretty-and-popular-girls-vs.-me, what you know you should be vs. what you are. But it's the real world, rendered with matter-of-fact vividness in Eliot's prose, that delivered the charge to me again and again. There's the moment where Maggie's brother Tom gives in to her pleading and cuts her long black hair: "One delicious grinding snip and then another and another, and the hinder-locks fell heavily on the floor, and Maggie stood cropped in a jagged uneven manner but with a sense of clearness and freedom as if she had emerged from a wood into the open plain."[8] (Like Tom Tulliver, I had also "tasted the forbidden pleasure of cutting the pony's mane" and recognized that finger-tingling shock in that "delicious grinding snip.") There's the adult consternation when newly shorn Maggie appears at the table, and her father's wonderful sympathy. And most of all there's the small moment when Tom and Lucy—pointedly excluding Maggie—sneak away to the forbidden pond, and Maggie boils over at last: "There were passions in Maggie at that moment to have made a tragedy, but the utmost she could do, with a fierce thrust of her small brown arm, was to push poor little pink-and-white Lucy into the cow-trodden mud."[9]

*Cow-trodden mud.* One phrase and the image of the walk-in path for our own cows at the creek bloomed before my eyes. This writer (back then I barely registered writers' names, happily lost in the verbal dream they delivered) had seen the same thing I saw every time we went out to drive the cattle across the creek and down the lane to the catch-pen for sorting and worming: thick mud pocked and jagged with cloven hooves, wobbly and sticky underfoot. Words showed me that the same reality existed for the writer and for me. Therefore, life was not only as it seemed to me in that moment. It could exist—and had existed—in the hazy country of the past as well as the moments my own thoughts were leading me into, one after another. Cradling Volume 4 now, I see that page is ever-so-slightly worn and loosened, missing its brittle bottom corner. The *cow-trodden mud* had set me on a path I still walk. How rich a memory it is, how precious an object: the childhood book into which you first dove, like Digory and Polly in the Wood Between the Worlds in C. S. Lewis's *The Magician's Nephew*, to come up again in a different world you still recognize as your own.

Many years later, I would recognize myself in Elizabeth Bowen's essay "Out of a Book" (1946):

The child lives in the book; but just as much the book lives in the child …
At any age, the reader must come across: the child reader is the most eager

and quick to do so; he not only lends to the story, he flings into the story the whole of his sensuous experience which from being limited is the more intense … For the child, any real-life scene that has once been sucked into the ambience of the story is affected, or infected, forever … . Such a thing, place or scene cannot again be walked past indifferently; it exerts a pull and sets up a tremor; and it is to indent the memory for life.[10]

# Saying what you mean: *Sprachgefühl* and the grown-up writer

Connecting the world and the word, as we've seen in our discussion of cliché in Chapter 2, matters as much for adults as for children. As a lexicographer for Merriam-Webster, Kory Stamper is responsible for reviewing, revising, and, when necessary, writing dictionary definitions of words, ensuring the language the dictionary describes keeps up with the language the culture is using. In her book *Word by Word: The Secret Life of Dictionaries*, Stamper describes the case of the word *nude.* One of its adjectival meanings was "flesh-toned," except the "flesh" in question was beige or pale tan—Caucasian flesh, since the dictionary defined "nude" as "having the color of a white person's skin." Obviously, nonwhite people also wear clothing designed to match their skin. Therefore, following a social media campaign in 2015, Stamper and the dictionary crew drafted a new definition that read "having a color (such as pale beige or tan) that matches a person's skin tones." Yet "nude" in that adjectival form describes things that are worn (hosiery, lipstick, shoes) because the person wearing them intends they will blend with her skin. Therefore, "the wearer" was more precise and accurate than "a person," and substituted accordingly. The definition now reads "having a color (such as pale beige or tan) that matches the wearer's skin tones," giving "nude pantyhose" and "nude lipstick" as examples.

Merriam-Webster's evolving definition of "nude" illustrates a good kind of thinking about language: a precise tailoring of words and phrases to the thing you're describing in its context. This is how prose-level revision proceeds—a continual checking of language against the world, as George Saunders and George Orwell describe, looking from your page to the thing described and back again, until you get it right. (And, of course, this doesn't happen in only one draft.) During this process, if you need to go to the thesaurus, do so to remind yourself *that* a word exists, not just to pull out any "big word." In *Word by Word*, Stamper invokes the German word *sprachgefühl* to describe the interior feeling for words, developed over a lifetime of reading, which sets off an interior alarm when a word is misused. "Sprachgefühl is a slippery eel," she writes, "the odd buzzing in your brain that tells you that 'planting the lettuce' and 'planting misinformation' are different uses of 'plant,' the eye twitch that tells you that 'plans to demo the store' refers not to a friendly instructional stroll on how to shop but to a little exuberance with a sledgehammer."[11] Kory Stamper's *sprachgefühl* makes available the word "wearer" out of her interior well of language, and she's able to recognize that "wearer" is more precise than "person" here. The instinct driving that back-and-forth glance can be developed, and it arises from your responsibility to your language and your world, which nudges you to clarify your words just a little bit more.

As an environmentalist and techno-skeptic, I think modern life is narrowing our word-range because it's narrowing our range of experiences of the world beyond our heads. As our language narrows, what we are able to describe, and to see, narrows too. Nature is a spring of metaphors and verbs and a whole sensory *sprachgefühl* we might not fully appreciate until it's gone.

# Unprettying: Writing, nature, and climate change

In 2007, a revised edition of the *Oxford Junior Dictionary* replaced words associated with nature—including *acorn, catkin, kingfisher, nectar,* and *pasture*—with words associated with white-collar, adult-driven technology, including *block-graph, bullet-point, committee, cut-and-paste,* and *voice-mail.*[12] When asked about the deletions, the then-head of children's dictionaries for Oxford University Press said, "When you look back at older versions of dictionaries, there were lots of examples of flowers, for instance; that was because many children lived in semi-rural environments and saw the seasons. Nowadays, the environment has changed." While acknowledging "a realism to her response," English nature writer Robert Macfarlane and others signed a public statement opposing the new dictionary changes, arguing that they show "an alarming acceptance of the idea that children might no longer see the seasons, or that the rural environment might be so unproblematically disposable."[13]

Online responses to that petition grouse about aging, idealistic writers, but I think those commenters miss a larger point about children, language, and writing that Olive Miller and Laura Ingalls Wilder understood: children need and want to engage reality in what they read, but they need some kind of distance from it. This can be time, like the gap between Laura's nineteenth-century world and an America gripped by the Depression. It can be narrative point of view, as I'll discuss in Chapter 5; Laura's first attempt at the material that would become the Little House books was the first-person ("I") narrative "Pioneer Girl," but the Little House books are written in third-person limited ("she"), which maintains a sense of both distance and closeness for young readers. It can be a distance of nonrealism, as seen in young-adult literature from *The Hobbit* to *The Giver* to *The Hunger Games*. Humanlike animal characters can help children learn to recognize and understand their own emotions better than they would if those characters were human. The child meets those fictional explorations on the common ground of her own body and her own senses, both thrilled and reassured by the fact they share a reality with her at a little distance.

By contrast, *block-graph*, *bullet-point*, and *committee* shove into the foreground our dismally corporate world, into which we're eager to initiate children despite our helicopterish worrying about their "innocence." In that world, docile corporate-technological subjecthood has become a new normal; an eleven-year-old texting, shopping, and leveling up in what she thinks is a game establishes an electronic identity trail that will track and shape her behavior for the rest of her life.[14] Meanwhile, even summer-camping activity time is shifting toward indoor crafts and away from hiking or swimming. Behind the dictionary change shimmers a blithe, dangerous cultural assumption: objecting to our screen-focused new normal is vaguely regressive, shameful, and backward-looking, so—even at eleven years old—we'd better get with the program. Yet cognitive and pedagogical research, not to mention our own experience and intuition, tell us differently.[15] Sure, it's a dictionary compiler's job to describe a culture's use of language as it is. But neither we nor our children have to accept a culture that pushes language—and, therefore, human minds—into technocorporate shapes.

Robert Macfarlane's worry about the junior dictionary is fueled by his work with vanishing rural dialects all over the British Isles—specifically their nature words, which are rooted in close observation and, often, earlier forms of a language. As described in his book *Landmarks* (2015), these words "act as compass; place-speech serves literally to en-chant the land—to sing it back into being, and to sing one's being back to it."[16] Hear just a few he shares with us: *quealed* (Exmoor; of vegetation, curled up or withered), *roddamy* (Fenland, to describe rolling land), *caochan* (Gaelic, from Old Irish "blind," for a small stream hidden in grass and therefore unable to "see out of its own bed"), or *wimpling* (from poet Gerard Manley Hopkins, the "rippling motion induced in a bird's wing feathers by the passage of wind"). The American version of Macfarlane's project is *Home Ground*, compiled by Barry Lopez and Debora Gwartney in 2006. Out of its wealth of language, my favorite term—which I heard in my own childhood—is "cowbelly," used to describe a fine, silty mud, found "along the banks of slow-moving creeks, where the current slackens completely" and where "the bottom is so plush that the sinking foot of the barefoot wader barely registers the new medium, only a second change of temperature."[17] With this word—remembered in my late father's voice—a wealth of memory and sensation wells up, like the eye of a spring: my own feet once sank in mud like that, soft as a new calf's fur before it had roughened in the grass and wind.[18]

As with our discussion of cliché in Chapter 2, this is one of those places where a door swings open between language and life: what humans can see is connected to what we can name and, in turn, to what we love and to who we are. "The nuances observed by specialized vocabularies," Macfarlane writes, "are evaporating from common usage, burnt off by capital, apathy, and urbanization"; such language isn't only to be mourned with platitudes about descriptivism and cultural change.[19] When your range of linguistic movement and your sense of what Macfarlane calls "the distinction between things" is reduced, so is your freedom of thought and self-understanding.[20] In *The Wayfinders: Why Ancient Wisdom Matters in the Modern World* (2009), anthropologist Wade Davis argues that when we lose a language, we lose a whole system of knowledge and ways of human being saturating its fibers. As the proverb says: when an old person dies, a library burns to the ground. And—as George Orwell described in his novel *Nineteen Eighty-four* through his imaginary Newspeak—when your language is narrowed, so is the personal interiority that you may use it to describe. Given how corporations loom expectantly in every corner of society, cracking their knuckles, we shouldn't fail to notice that here their language is encroaching on us too, supplanting the old distinguished ground of speech—the natural world and the body. If white-collar bureaucracy hogs ever-finer gradations of word-energy but landscape is named only in what Macfarlane calls "large generic units" like "woods," "hill," or "field," our attention will be redirected, and our feelings for nature dulled, accordingly. Some things are hard to love—even to see—if you can't quite put a name to them.[21]

Experience and emotion will sharpen your choice of words in a good way if you let them—even about something so grief-infused and hard to imagine as climate change. In July 2017, the radio program "On the Media," as part of a larger feature on environmental dystopias, invited readers to substitute their own words for what we are losing and how the world is changing.[22] A woman from Brooklyn submitted "wintersmell," which is exactly what it sounds like, the particular smell of snow and cold we are in danger of losing. Others submitted "hibernap" (as shorter winters will leave bears less time for the hibernation cycle they need) and "SPF'd," as in "we're SPF'd"—a pointed description of a not-so-future state when there won't be enough SPFs to put on to keep you from being burned. A man from Maryland, sadness obvious in his voice, contributed "verdone"—as in "it was once green and lush, but now it's verdone." (The sad echo of Verdun, the First World War battlefield, fits.) It's not just mashing syllables fancifully together but looking closely at a state of being, then trying to fit language to it.

While writers aren't always sure about how art can intervene in our climate crisis, my own hope is that sharpening our language and sharpening our sight can enable one another. As moral beings and as writers, it's our job to look at reality and describe what we see. When strained through the filter of careful observation, then sharpened with an astringent dash of complex emotion, language becomes a very bracing brew. Consider an interesting craft challenge: describing something unpleasant, alarming, frightening, or sad. Some of the most precise and effective descriptions of unpretty things I've seen lately have been written by women, who are so often trained to be "pretty" in life and on the page. Yet when we lift the glass cloche of expectation-to-please from over the little green shoot of our writing, it flowers and branches in unexpected directions, because its roots are going into the dark. The kind of restraint Chekhov describes—warmed throughout by emotion that may not be wholly pleasant or socially admissible—does good things for prose, sharpening it word by word.

Angela Carter's landmark story collection *The Bloody Chamber* (1979), feminist retellings of fairy tales, glows with her capacious, rebellious imagination and her ability to counterbalance excess with detail.[23] In "The Erl-King," haunted by the ghosts of John Keats, William Blake, and Christina Rossetti, a woman falls under the spell of a forest spirit who's both lover and jailer:

> Now the crows drop winter from their wings, invoke the harshest season with their cry.

It is growing colder. Scarcely a leaf left on the trees and the birds come to him in even greater numbers because, in this hard weather, it is lean pickings. The blackbirds and thrushes must hunt the snails from hedge bottoms and crack the shells on stones. But the Erl-King gives them corn and when he whistles to them, a moment later you cannot see him for the birds that have covered him like a soft fall of feathered snow. He spreads out a goblin feast of fruit for me, such appalling succulence; I lie above him and see the light from the fire sucked into the black vortex of his eye, the omission of light at the centre, there, that exerts on me such a tremendous pressure, it draws me inwards.

Eyes green as apples. Green as dead sea fruit.[24]

Claire Vaye Watkins's eco-dystopian novel *Gold Fame Citrus* (2015), set in a drought-stricken future California, contains similar passages of dark beauty:

Because sweet Jesus money was still *money*, and wasn't that something to celebrate? For now, enough money could get you fresh produce and meat and dairy, even if what they called cheese was Day-Glo and came in a jar, and the fish was mostly poisoned and reeking, the beef gray, the apples blighted even in what used to be apple season, pears grimy even when you paid extra for Bartletts from Amish orchards. Hard sour strawberries and blackberries filled with dust. Flaccid carrots, ashen spinach, cracked olives, bruised hundred-dollar mangos, all-pith oranges, shriveled lemons, boozy tangerines, raspberries with gassed aphids curled in their hearts, an avocado whose crumbling taupe innards once made you weep.[25]

Charlotte Wood's beautiful, brutal, and gripping dystopia *The Natural Way of Things* (2016)—set in a camp of imprisoned women on the Australian outback—forces us to confront a kangaroo in the trap the women have set in the hope of other food:

The roo is as tall as the girls. They can smell the animal breath coming at them, dank and afraid.

It stops struggling and stares straight at them. Ears vertical, twitching, quivering. The thick, muscular trunk of its tail presses into the dirt, supporting its great weight. The girls stand, unmoving, not speaking. Vainly, the kangaroo shifts and scuffles again. Then it lowers its head and lengthens its mighty neck, black eyes fixed on them, and lets out three long, hoarse snarls. Its snout fattens, nostrils flared. Panting with effort, it falls to rest back on the great stool of its tail. Little balls of shit lie everywhere about the clearing.

"Have to unclamp the trap," Yolanda whispers, and takes a tentative step toward the creature.[26]

In lesser hands, this kind of thing can easily become mere gross-out or prurience, more about an immature writer straining for effect than about a mature effort to look closely. But I think the fiction writer Megan Mayhew Bergman, who has written and has spoken about this issue in a workshop I took with her, is right: we can find a difficult and realistic kind of beauty in disorder and darkness, and that's where we need to look for a richer and wilder understanding of beauty and of life, particularly in our new reality of human-created climate change. This is the clear, all-encompassing gaze expressed by the Roman playwright Terence: *Homo sum, humani nihil a me alienum puto,* or *nothing human is alien to me.* It's also expressed, of course, by Chekhov. Here, in 1887, he's advising a novice writer against the temptation to prettify:

> Your statement that the world is "teeming with villains and villainesses" is true. Human nature is imperfect, so it would be odd to perceive none but the righteous. Requiring literature to dig up a "pearl" from the pack of villains is tantamount to negating literature altogether. Literature is accepted as an art because it depicts life as it actually is. Its aim is the truth, unconditional and honest. Limiting its functions to as narrow a field as extracting "pearls" would be as deadly for art as requiring Levitan to draw a tree without any dirty bark or yellowed leaves. A "pearl" is a fine thing, I agree. But the writer is not a pastry chef, he is not a cosmetician and not an entertainer. He is a man bound by contract to his sense of duty and to his conscience. Once he undertakes this task, it is too late for excuses, and no matter how horrified, he must do battle with his squeamishness and sully his imagination with the grime of life. He is just like any ordinary reporter. What would you say if a newspaper reporter as a result of his squeamishness or a desire to please his readers were to limit his descriptions to honest city fathers, high-minded ladies, and virtuous railroadmen?[27]

Expanding this lens of curiosity, generosity, and openness to a full range of emotion, including grief, equals confronting and continuing to live in reality. If each of us contains both a surgeon and a poet, words are the tools these aspects of our souls have in common. Words are the means with which we act upon the world, and the means by which we surrender to the world so it may act upon us. They are the knives with which we peel away the falsity and bloat of oblivion and lies and expose the slim nerves of reality, and they are indexes, like high water marks, of the means to which we have let ourselves be overtaken—the more precise the words, I hope, the greater the love and wonder they will register in their hearts, and ours.

# Verbs: Precise and lovely engines

If you have the right verb, you may not need an adjective or adverb at all, since a good verb can animate a character in a way that lets us think through our own bodies, build the picture in our minds, and read that for the detail you want. A verb is "kinetic," writes novelist Daphne Athas. "It is pure energy, and people respond to energy as moths to light … Movement satisfies as objects cannot."[28] When teaching sentence-level revision, I encourage my students to start with verbs, since they're a simple place to sharpen prose.

Good verbs start when you inhabit a moment with your senses, then try to render that feeling in a single word. An adult student in my community writing class, writing a scene in which her working-mom character is alone at home, crafted this lovely sentence: "Silence swelled through the house." That verb, *swelled*, conveys both the atmosphere *and* the sense of sudden spaciousness that opens up in unaccustomed quiet (which this writer, a working mom herself, was choosing a word very carefully to represent). Walking on a soft, post-thunderstorm evening, I saw a heron glide out of the sky and land in a dead tree-snag above the river. With one twist of its neck, it plunged its beak into its breast feathers—long, shaggy, floaty and gray as Spanish moss—and passed the tip of its beak through them, straightening them out. What could be a single verb to describe this motion? If you said *combing*, that's the verb I thought of, too. My grandmother once described our little tabby cat as "cantering out to meet me"; that verb's delightful, apt crossover quality (usually, only horses canter) has pinned it to my brain ever since. Of course, this works best if the motion's echo is precise, and/or if there is something creaturely or bodily about the "cantering" thing.

Applying an unconventional verb—or even using a noun as a verb—can jolt a sentence into fresh and startling life. Jonathan Lethem's novel *Motherless Brooklyn* (1999) is narrated by Lionel Essrog, an orphan with Tourette's syndrome who finds himself solving the murder of Frank Minna, his quasi-mobster boss. Exuberant and engaging, Lethem's language mirrors Lionel's—culturally omnivorous, hyper-articulate, erupting unpredictably in profanity, physical tics, and jazzlike riffs on the last few words he's heard. And in his voice, a noun as a verb is unconventionally apt:

"Boys," came the voice from the street side of the car, startling me and Coney both. "Frank," I said.

It was Minna. He had his trench-coat collar up against the breeze, not quite cloaking his unshaven Robert-Ryan-in-*Wild-Bunch* grimace. He ducked down to the level of my window, as if he didn't want to be seen from the Yorkville Zendo. Squeaky cabs rocking-horsed past over the pothole in the street behind him. I rolled down the window, then reached out compulsively and touched his left shoulder, a regular gesture he'd not bothered to acknowledge for—how long? Say, fifteen years now, since when I'd first begun manifesting the urge as a thirteen-year-old and reached out for his then twenty-five-year-old street punk's bomber-jacketed shoulder. Fifteen years of taps and touches—if Frank Minna were a statue instead of flesh and blood I'd have buffed that spot to a high shine, the way leagues of tourists burnish the noses and toes of bronze martyrs in Italian churches.[29]

Here, *rocking-horsed* unfurls a fresh visual image of the tilting, head-first hurtle of cabs through a potholed street, but (like the title) it also points us back into the heart of Lionel's character: his lonely childhood at St. Vincent's Home for Boys fuels his loyalty to Frank and will soon drive his search for Frank's killer. Significantly, Lethem doesn't overdo the special effects; "rocking-horsed" is the only quirky verb in sight. (Again, if everything is eye-catching or attention-demanding, then nothing is.)

Jon Day's *Cyclogeography: Journeys of a London Bicycle Courier* (2015) is animated by a sense of motion that drives sentence rhythms as well as particular verbs:

Riding a bike for a living means you learn to read the road too, calculating routes, anticipating snarl-ups, dancing around potholes almost unconsciously. It is an activity that forces you to think of the city in literary terms. With its signs and painted hieroglyphics the road is an encyclopaedia of movement: drive here, walk here, park here, no stopping here. Look down and the tarmac tells you what to do. Traffic lights regulate the entire mechanism like enormous clocks, telling you when to move and when to stop. Textures too are important: kerbstones separate walkers from the flow of traffic; knobbled paving alerts the blind to a coming crossing. Very soon the rhythms of the street become internalised. Traffic lights and vehicle indicators, the wails of sirens and car alarms, warn you to get out of the way or lure you on. Eventually you come to feel part of the city's secret networks, at one with its hidden rivers and its dead-letter drops, at one remove from its anonymous crowds of commuters.[30]

The simplest and best way to quicken your verbs—in several senses of that word—is to go through your manuscript and circle every verb and verb + adverb combination, then render that motion more precisely in a single verb. "Walked swiftly" can become "strode," "laughed loudly" can become "cackled" or "whooped" (depending on the quality of the laugh), "whispered softly" can simply lose the adverb (since a whisper is, by nature, soft). If you have one unconventional but apt verb—like Lethem's "rocking-horsed" above—let some time go by before you use another one; a little of that effect goes a long way.

# Similes and metaphors: Blurring or sharpening?

In a review of Wyoming writer Mark Spragg's first novel *The Fruit of Stone* (2002), journalist Jonathan Miles succinctly explains how a simile should work:

> Her face, Spragg writes, is "like the single track of an antelope," and when she stretches toward a hotel room ceiling, she "appears to be some misplaced and fatless sea mammal rising for a breath of air." Which prompts me to ask: What sort of tragic accident yields a face that resembles a hoofprint? And is there any sea mammal, no matter how misplaced, that's even mildly slender, much less fatless? Alas, "The Fruit of Stone" brims with such analogies: sunlit hair "flashes as a burl of volcanic glass would flash." A squirrel's tail is "fluffed and risen like a soft and oversized stinger." *In these efforts at lyricism, Spragg overturns the basic goal of an analogy; he blurs the world rather than sharpens it.*[31] [emphasis mine]

I brought this passage straight to my creative writing students, who'd been working with similes of their own. Near the back of the room sat a student named Dan, a gifted graphic novelist whose notebook pages teemed with words and pictures. As we laughed at the image of a squirrel with a stinger for a tail, Dan's eyes suddenly widened. After class, he presented me with a drawing of the creature who's been the unofficial mascot of my creative writing classes ever since: the Squirrelpion, a squirrel with back-swept, tufted ears, a wicked grin, and a segmented scorpion tail curling over its back. "Write proper similes," Dan's caption warns, "or the Squirrelpion will FIND you!"

Google "unintentionally hilarious similes" and you'll find lots of examples that would draw the Squirrelpion's wrath. Typically, *How Not to Write a Novel* offers some great ones: "Her nose perched on her face like a seagull, arching its wings to create two well-defined nostrils. The mouth below was thin as if actually consisting of only one dimension, like the loops which are the fundamental building blocks of all matter in string theory ... Her

**Figure 4.1** "Squirrelpion"—by Daniel Bruins.

stomach was as flat as the Earth was once believed to be."[32] Avoiding bad similes, though, isn't that hard. Critic James Wood writes that novelists like Faulkner, Dickens, and Henry Green "tend to produce the kind of similes and metaphors that, while successful enough in their own right, are also the kinds of similes and metaphors that their own characters might produce."[33] While a bad simile or metaphor rests on a superficial resemblance to something in the author's *own* world—the seagull has two wings, and, hey, the woman has two nostrils!—a good one arises from some concrete detail from within the *story's* world, observed and understood within its context by both the character *and* the writer.

Poet Dante Alighieri (*c.* 1265–1321)—better known simply as "Dante"— earned his titanic single-name status in several ways: cementing the language of his native town, Florence, as the version of Italian we still recognize; developing a multistory, circular scheme of hell; and writing similes that still help us picture those unimaginable torments down below in terms of the world up here. The souls of damned lovers in Canto V are compared to birds: "As cranes go over, sounding their harsh cry/leaving the long streak of their flight in air/so come these spirits, wailing as they fly."[34] When the Heavenly Messenger in Canto IX strides through hell, sinners scatter before him "as frogs before the snake that hunts them down/churn up their pond in flight, until the last/squats on the bottom as if turned to stone."[35] (When I stand on the Ponte Vecchio with my study-abroad students, I love to read these lines, then point down at the River Arno and ask, "Y'all reckon Dante saw any frogs down there?" World-recognition and delight bloom together in our laughter; a child of a river city most certainly saw birds, frogs, and nature going about its business every day.) Evoking a sturdy rural metaphor, a grieving Falsifier in Canto XXX describes "Inflexible Justice, that has forked and spread/my soul like hay, to search it the more closely."[36] As any farm kid knows, freshly cut hay has to be lifted and shaken to dry evenly, whether by machine or by hand. Just as in Dante's touchstone, the New Testament, parables, similes, and images of the known world—medieval Florence and its surrounding farms—help us understand the spiritual one.

Let's take a look at some more recent, and similarly successful, nonfiction similes, each of which arises out of an observed detail and the knowledge of the writer's subject in its historical context that pins that detail in place. I'll italicize the simile for emphasis each time. First, here's Rosemary Hill on Ida Nettleship (1877–1907), the beleaguered first wife of the English painter Augustus John:

> Ida sensibly argued with both parties that Edna was simply too young to know her own mind, which may well have been precisely the reason Clarke Hall and so many other 19th-century men wanted to marry teenage girls. Ellen Terry had been 16 when she married the 46-year-old artist G.F. Watts, Ruskin was the same age when he proposed to the 18-year-old Rose La Touche. More than the obvious attractions of youth or the anachronistic charges of paedophilia sometimes levelled against the Victorians, there was something like a desire to preserve that quality of indeterminacy, *to keep a woman like a bonsai specimen, clipped at the root to be perfect and miniature for ever.*[37]

Then, Robert Hughes on the brilliant, violent painter Caravaggio (1571–1610):

> Naturally this risky and exalted spontaneity seems to fit the picture of Caravaggio that his way of life offers, from what we know of it. He died of

a fever in 1610, at the age of thirty-nine, in Porto Ercole, then a malarial Spanish enclave on the coast of the Maremma, north of Rome. The last four years of his life were one long flight from police and assassins; on the run, working under extreme pressure, he left altarpieces—some very great, and none mediocre—in Mediterranean seaports from Naples to Valletta to Palermo. He killed one man with a dagger in the groin during a game of tennis in Rome in 1606, and wounded several others, including a guard at Castel Sant'Angelo, and a waiter, whose face he cut open in a squabble about artichokes. He was sued for libel in Rome and mutilated in a tavern brawl in Naples. *Saturnine, coarse, and queer, he thrashed about in the etiquette of early Seicento Rome like a shark in a net.*[38]

And here, the English nature writer Richard Jefferies (1848–1887), in "The Acorn-Gatherer," from 1884's *The Life of the Fields:*

Black rooks, yellow oak leaves, and a boy asleep at the foot of the tree. His head was lying on a bulging root close to the stem: his feet reached to a small sack or bag half full of acorns. In his slumber his forehead frowned—they were fixed lines, *like the grooves in the oak bark.* There was nothing else in his features attractive or repellent: they were such as might have belonged to a dozen hedge children. The set angry frown was the only distinguishing mark—*like the dents on a penny made by a hobnail boot, by which it can be known from twenty otherwise precisely similar.*[39]

As with Chekhov's children, notice how the detail of the fixed frown begins to tilt our view of the young acorn-gatherer toward pity and dread: that final simile, of the hobnail boot (traditional rural working man's footwear) stamping on something small and impressionable, confirms that view; by the end of the story, we've seen that abuse for ourselves. As with Hill and Hughes, the simile directs our gaze back into the world of the story, teaching us something about it and then asking us to apply that knowledge to the picture forming in our heads.

In her story "June Recital" (1949), about a mysterious German piano teacher, Miss Eckhart, in the imaginary town of Morgana, Mississippi, Eudora Welty's similes invoke the story's real subject—the relationship between art and provincialism. Her depiction of Miss Eckhart's piano studio suggests how an artist's freedom can disintegrate under the pressure of small-town obliviousness. "On the right-hand corner of the piano," she writes, "stood a small, mint-white bust of Beethoven, all softened around the edges with the nose smoothed down, as if a cow had licked it."[40] Evoking rural Southern textures I recognize—the chalky white mints set out in glass dishes for special occasions, then the rough, blurred edge of a salt block in a cow pasture—this simile works with a sharp-eyed subtlety typical of Welty: as critic Claudia Roth Pierpont writes, "It is part of Welty's engaging complexity that despite her obvious affection for Morgana, the town turns out to be stultifying for the more sentient whites who live there; many of her characters have the sense to dream, at least, of getting out."[41] A few paragraphs later, there's Miss Eckhart's music cabinet: "Whenever she opened the cabinet, the smell of new sheet music came out swift as an imprisoned spirit, something almost palpable, like a pet coon; Miss Eckhart kept the music locked up and the key down her dress, inside the collar."[42] This is the double bind of the small-town female artist: in safeguarding what's precious to her, the living, vaguely feral spirit of art, she "imprison[s]" it, and, by extension, herself.

Expressions are a form of similes, too—a neat way of explaining reality with an analogy that snaps an image and its associations into someone's head. Great examples can be found all over the world. The Sicilian mystery writer Andrea Camilleri offers: "When it rains it pours—*all'annigatu, petri di 'ncoddru*—or, 'rocks on a dead man's back,' as Sicilians call an unrelenting string of bad breaks that drag a poor stiff down."[43] Set in late nineteenth-century Nigeria, Chinua Achebe's *Things Fall Apart* (1959) includes this description of the hero Okonkwo leaving his clan: "As soon as he left, someone else rose and filled [his place]. The clan was like a lizard; if it lost its tail it soon grew another."[44] Rural Southerners—my people—are famous for this sort of thing. Zora Neale Hurston, who was born in Notasulga, Alabama, not far from my own hometown, recorded an expression I heard myself as a child: "Eatonville is what you might call hitting a straight lick with a crooked stick. The town was not in the original plan. It is a by-product of something else."[45] (Later, she wrote one of my favorite similes ever: "Love, I find, is like singing. Everybody can do enough to satisfy themselves, though it may not impress the neighbors as being very much."[46]) Historian Wayne Flynt relates a fellow Alabamian's description of a petite woman: "She's not as big as a bar of lye soap after a hard day's washing."[47] This is a kind of thinking with the body in its environment, and using what the body knows, that makes better writers and better readers.

# Editing: More ideas per square inch

When I edit my own prose and teach editing to students, my goal is *more ideas per square inch*—reducing filler or redundancy to deliver richer meaning in a smaller space, just as arrow-makers shave bumps from wooden shafts to make the arrows fly straight. The questioning process is the same as we'll see in the next chapter: Why have I written these words in this order, what do they actually mean, and can I sharpen rather than blur the picture they make? Am I piling on words to hide uncertainty? Consider the late Robert Silvers, editor of the *New York Review of Books*: "In one of my first articles," Robert Darnton writes, "I used the phrase 'in terms of.' He insisted on deleting it, because, he explained, writers used it as filler when they thought there was some relation between A and B but did not know what the relation was."[48]

Let me walk you through some prose revision in my *Eldorado, Iowa* novel draft to show you what I mean. In this scene, twin brothers Trygve and Oyvind, my Norwegian bachelor farmers (as Garrison Keillor would say), have come to Galen's office so that Galen, assisted by Sarah, his wife and my protagonist, can remove a benign tumor on Oyvind's shoulder. First, I revised at the level of the scene or paragraph. Can I make it more direct and visual? Are there side-glancing details I really don't need?

**Original:**
Trygve stands and swallows, hard, and rests his hand on his brother's back, avoiding the right shoulder, where a lump stands out under Oyvind's shirt. Twins feel each other's pain, Sarah has heard; each can tell what the other is thinking. In Miss Spofford's school, there were a pair of curly-haired twins, the Allston girls, who sat for each other's examinations sometimes, just for fun, and migrated, in their sleep, into the same small bed in the dormitory every night, to be found in the morning curled against each other, like puppies. When Galen cuts into Oyvind's shoulder, what will Trygve feel?

He doesn't want to go in the examining room, Sarah can see. Under his thick red hair, his forehead is white, and a film of sweat has started across his forehead and the tops of his cheeks. But he follows Galen and Oyvind across the front hall and into the doctor's parlor, and Sarah, carrying a kettle of hot water, comes behind them and shuts the door.

"Now," says Galen briskly, "we'll prepare. Sit on the table, here, Oyvind." He pats the top of the long oak bench that stretches down the center of the room, just wide enough for someone to lie down on, which Sarah keeps covered with a fresh white sheet. Oyvind sits, unbuttoning his shirt, and Trygve sits next to him, so close that Oyvind's arm bumps him in the ribs, but neither twin moves away. [**242 words**]

**Revision:**
Trygve heaved himself up reluctantly, gulped, and rested his hand on his brother's back. Supposedly, twins knew each other's thoughts, felt each other's pain. When Galen cut into Oyvind's body, what would Trygve feel?

Trygve's forehead was white under his thick red hair, and sweat filmed his cheekbones. But he followed his brother and Galen across the front hall and into the doctor's parlor. Sarah, carrying a kettle of hot water, shut the door behind them all.

"Now," said Galen briskly. "Sit on the table, here, Oyvind." He patted the sheet-draped bench in the center of the room. Oyvind sat, unbuttoning his shirt. Trygve sat next to him, so close that Oyvind's arm bumped him in the ribs, but neither twin moved away. [**157 words, reduction of 35 percent**.]

The flashback about the Allston twins drained some momentum from the scene, and I was able to avoid some of the description of the room here by seeding it into earlier scenes. (As I'll discuss in Chapter 5, notice how I also shifted the scene from present to past tense.) I pushed my verbs harder: "stands and swallows" becomes "heaved up and gulped." (I left that adverb on purpose, though.) Trimming this down has left me more room to linger on the operation itself, expanding that scene as I want it to expand in readers' minds (if all the scenes have roughly the same length and weight, they'll all feel equally important, and if everything is important, then nothing is). Notice, too, how I've removed the filter ("Sarah can see," "Sarah has heard") in favor of directly presenting what she sees or knows. I may flesh out this scene a little more, but paring it back helps me focus on what's happening and make decisions about it, rather than just rocking along at the same habitual level of detail from scene to scene.

Here are more examples of the same scrutiny working at the sentence level. Let's start here:

*Sarah looked out the window and saw there were three deer grazing on the lawn.*

As mentioned above, "looked out the window and saw" is a classic example of *filtering*, foregrounding a character's perception rather than the thing perceived. If you're close enough to your character's point of view, readers will understand she's seeing this thing. Let's adjust that.

*Sarah looked out the window. There were three deer grazing on the lawn.*

Better, but "there is/there are/there were" is a filler phrase which, like filtering, pads an image with a needless layer of presentation.

*Sarah looked out the window. Three deer grazed on the lawn.*

We're getting there, but now it's time—since our character is looking at something—to sharpen the picture of the thing she's looking at. Is "grazing" really what deer do, cropping grass evenly and methodically as cattle? And is that patch in front of Sarah's house (which we've seen in Chapter 3) a lawn, which brings to my mind an anachronistic carpet of machine-clipped green? Since we've bought ourselves more space by cutting the filler phrases, we have more room for weight-bearing, sensory language that contains "more ideas per square inch." Like Orwell and Saunders, we go back and forth between the words and the picture in our head. Let's lean on the verbs and, again, sharpen the picture:

> *Sarah glanced out the window. Three deer browsed in the tall, faded grass, flicking their tails.*

Now, the sentence feels driven by attention to the deer: in verbs ("browsing," nudging around in vegetation with their noses, is less clichéd and more accurate for deer than "grazing"), in gesture ("flicking their tails"), and in the sentence lengths (which prolong the reader's gaze, just like the character's).

Leaning on verbs can quickly tighten prose, especially if you remove empty presentational phrases like "there is" or "on [surface] there is":

He comes into the kitchen just behind Sarah, knotting his tie.

> → He *follows* Sarah into the kitchen, knotting his tie. ("Comes behind" literally means "follows.")

A trickle of strawberry jam runs slowly down his palm. (A trickle, by definition, runs slowly.)

> → Strawberry jam *trickles* down his palm.

On Trygve's face is a little boy's snicker, threatening to break through, but he stops himself.

> → On Trygve's face, a snicker threatens to break through, but he stops himself.
> → Trygve *snickers*, then stops himself. "It's a scary thing, true enough." (*Now I have room to show my character's voice in dialogue, too! More ideas per square inch!*)

Of course, too much minimalism may not even be possible, or desirable: you can wear away the life and energy from a sentence by paring it too far down, like the raccoon in Renata Adler's *Speedboat* (1976), "which in its odd fastidiousness would wash [a piece of] sugar in a brook till there was nothing left."[49] The novelist Rick Moody tells a story about his first boss, an editor, who led him through an editing exercise with an imaginary sign outside a shop: "Fresh Fish For Sale Today, Here." First of all, might not the presence of the sign in that location at that moment obviate the need for "For Sale Today, Here?" Fish for sale is supposed to be fresh, so why go to the trouble of saying "fresh?" Eventually you pare your sign down to a single word, "Fish," but even that could be replaced by the simple display of the object itself on its bed of ice in the window. Yet don't we still want the sign to help us direct our attention to reality, sitting there so patiently waiting to be beheld? And isn't it worthwhile to use our language to sing, to indicate some pleasure in reality, to have a little fun? Isn't that where a writer's *voice*, in all its unique *sprachtgefühl* and *sprezzatura* and word-delight, also lives? Consider another sentence from my manuscript, defiantly un-minimalist, that I've kept because I love its motion, its sound, and its window into my nineteenth-century world (look up "bustles" and see):

> *All around the house the chickens strutted and scuttled and quarreled, nestling their feathered bustles into their loose-dirt wallows in the yard, blissful as ladies settling into soft chairs.*

# Punctuation: The chocolate fountain

Think about the last wedding reception you attended: amid the pink monogrammed napkins and the bridesmaids dancing to "I Will Survive," there was probably a chocolate fountain. Resplendent in its silver tray, it gushed chocolate up through its center and then down the sides in three cascading tiers. When I'm talking to students about punctuation, I use the chocolate fountain as an image of how the energy of language cascades, with varying intensity and speed, up from within and then down over the surface of a poem or a piece of prose. Punctuation marks are among the tools you use to control its speed (and your reader's speed) along the way. Some will bring a reader to a full stop, while others will barely slow her down. Here's a visual guide: (see Figure 4.2.)

In the onward flow of a sentence, a comma will slow readers least, while a period will stop us most. Other marks fall somewhere in between, as you can see. The dash is a special case—as I've just demonstrated, it has a feeling like a kid playing freeze-tag, pausing dramatically and then sprinting off the mark again.

All of the punctuation marks in this chart can be used to combine clauses (smaller units of information) into complete sentences. The most common

## Using punctuation to control pace

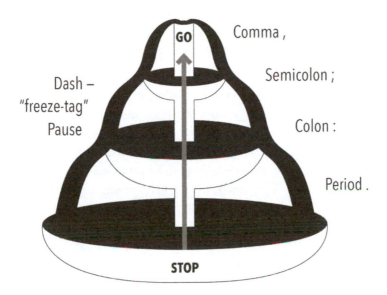

Figure 4.2 Punctuation: The chocolate fountain—illustration by Michael Bartels.

sentence-combination problem I see is the comma splice, which is attaching two complete sentences (or main clauses, subject + verb units) with a comma. If you want to hook two complete sentences together, you can use a semicolon, colon, or—for dramatic effect—a dash. If you have a comma in use, you need a dependent clause (which doesn't have a subject and a verb) on at least one side.

# Overwriting: More isn't better

Loving big rackety sentences can take you too far in the other direction— overwriting. "Some writers are convinced that since great modern authors like Joyce and Faulkner are difficult to understand, writing that is difficult to understand is therefore great writing," write Howard Mittelmark and Sandra Newman:

> This is a form of magical thinking, analogous to the belief that the warrior who dons the pelt of a lion thereby acquires its strength and cunning ... If the average reader cannot make sense of what you're saying, it is not a badge of honor; it is a badge of solipsism, and it's a safe bet your writing just doesn't make sense.[50]

Like our worst stereotype of a Victorian parlor, overwritten prose can pile up, all swags and decorations, until it smothers the shape of meaning underneath.

But pomposity and arrogance aren't the only reasons this happens. Overwriters sometimes have an endearingly sincere rationale: "I want to make writing that's pretty." They hearken to a Platonic ideal of writing—complex, wordy, "intelligent"-sounding—that exists in some parallel version of the nineteenth century. They love words and can put a lot of them together, fast. They've been praised by parents and teachers, since parents and teachers like to see kids writing rather than stealing gum from the convenience store. Therefore, overwriting students' habits have been reinforced by one of a bookish kid's drugs of choice: grown-ups' approval. The challenge comes when other readers—professors, classmates, editors—tell overwriters that there's not much content in all those pages and that their own words are blurring, not sharpening, what content there is.

Many of these writers developed their habits as bookish junior-high kids, when words were an escape hatch, intoxicant, and identity-formation tool. Words help them live more fully in the place they often find most rewarding: their own imaginations. And since words make them feel so good, more words make them feel even better. Writers write because it makes us feel real, alive, and important, with something to say. Therefore, the more we write, the more real we feel. However, a very significant gap can fall between what is fun for a writer to write and what is fun—or, even, literally possible—for a writer to read.

Imagine putting frosting on a cake. First, you start with your basic three-layer on its plate, solid buttercream coating all over it. Tasty, but a little plain. Pick up your frosting bag and pipe a thick streamer around the top edge. Then put crisscross latticework all around the sides. But that top still looks plain. How about a big frosting rose in the middle? Great. But it looks so lonely there! Let's put more roses all around it—one, two, three, four, five. A flower garden! Here's a big butterfly, made out of lollipops, that we can perch on top of the flowers. And some ladybugs made out of marzipan: one, two, three, four. But we're still not finished—here comes a big spun-sugar rainbow to arch over the whole thing. And—

Wait. Stand back and look at your cake. Some people will see it as a charming creation and be eager to take a bite. But most people, even frosting lovers like me, will be overwhelmed. Overwriting works the same way. Readers don't need *more* detail; they need the *right* detail. Plus, even a writer who knows how to put sentences together can get lost in her own clauses, tangling and burying information in a way that makes it hard to process. I see this often, but not exclusively, in fantasy writing.

Consider:

*The evil sorceress Alyris, her raven-black hair swirling wildly like a midnight storm cloud about her delicate frail shoulders, a cruel smile on her lovely face, lifted the Stone of Ithyrimore high into the air above her head and, beginning to recite the spell, brought it back down to the surface of the ancient granite table that had squatted grimly in the castle since the reign of Paramor with a loud crack.*

Notice some things here. Necessary information is buried. The moment when the sorceress begins to recite the spell is probably important for the plot and worth lingering on. For some reason, the writer also wants us to know how long the granite table has been in that room (although I don't really care about knowing that here—I care about the spell). Yet both of these things are shoehorned into the longer sentence in a way that minimizes their importance, since if it's in a dependent clause ("beginning to recite the spell"), it's syntactically subordinate.

Carried away by the cadences of that long sentence, the writer has let its literal meaning slip out of her control. Technically, "with a loud crack" is a misplaced modifier, a phrase meant to describe something but syntactically disconnected from it. Therefore, these words in this order literally mean that the table squatted with a loud crack. If you're giggling at this mental picture, you're not alone. (Unintentional humor is a sure sign of a misplaced modifier.)

The writer can't leave the language alone and let it work in peace: every noun has its adjective, every verb its adverb. But look how much of it you just don't need. By definition, "swirling" is already "wild," "raven" is "black," and "delicate" and "frail" just repeat one another, so each of those phrases is redundant. (Sorceresses are also evil, and long hair generally "swirls" around its owner's shoulders, so those could also be cut.) "Lifted" is, by definition, "high above her head," so maybe that phrase can come out. Given that the reader is already working hard to imagine dark swirling hair—a good and useful visual detail here—do you really need the "midnight storm cloud" simile (which is also redundant) for us to picture on top of that? Probably not. It may help you develop the picture of the character in your mind, and it may feel good to you to write it all in your first draft; that's your privilege. But when you revise it with a reader's needs in mind, take it out.

So, as we evaluate this sentence, let's ask: What blurs the picture in a reader's imagination, what sharpens it? And what do these words in this order actually mean?

Again, here is the original sentence:

*The evil sorceress Alyris, her raven-black hair swirling wildly like a midnight storm cloud about her delicate frail shoulders, a cruel smile on her lovely face, lifted the Stone of Ithyrimore high into the air above her head and, beginning to recite the spell, brought it back down to the surface of the ancient granite table that had squatted grimly in the castle since the reign of Paramor with a loud crack.*

And here is a possible revision:

*The sorceress Alyris, her black hair swirling, lifted the Stone of Ithyrimore. Between her fingers, its smooth surface glowed green. "Double, double, toil and trouble ..." she recited. "Fire burn and cauldron bubble." She slammed the stone against the granite table with a crack, and then she smiled. The castle had been Paramor's. Now it would be hers.*

Yes, the sentences are shorter. So is the overall word count—57 words compared to the original 72. But most importantly, once the redundancies have been trimmed and the clauses combed out, there's room for more detail and dialogue here (even if it is a borrowing from Shakespeare's *Macbeth*) that move the scene forward and help us, by the time we get to that smile, see it as sinister. This revision meets the "more ideas per square inch" goal and is cognitively easier to process than the first version is, with shorter sentences and more to see and hear. Version 1 is written to satisfy the writer. Version 2 is revised to meet the reader's needs too.

Remember what we said in Chapter 1 about making a mess? You'll probably make a similar mess on your printed page once you get into

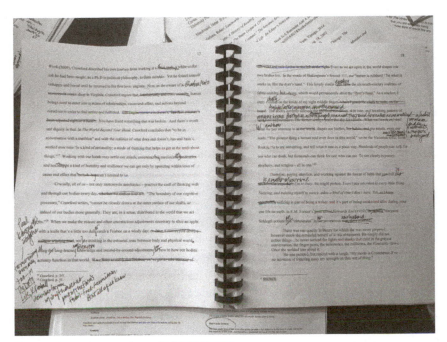

**Figure 4.3** Manuscript edit in progress.

editing—crossing out, writing in, circling and moving around—and that's a good thing. Here's a photo of some of my own edits to the second draft of Chapter 1 itself (see Figure 4.3):

In his essay "Going to the Tigers: Notes on Middle Style," novelist Robert Cohen muses on why we overwrite:

> Maybe it's a lack of faith, a frantic insecurity about language's ability to adhere to the real, that impels us to press more and more of it against the page, like a stoned teenager taping down the corners of an unruly poster. Either way the stuff won't stick. And the danger for the writer remains the same: that even as we sing our hymns and render praise unto our subjects, we only manage to obscure them, to fog the windows with the stains of our own breathing.[51]

But, as Cohen notes, what makes it hard is that the only thing we have to express our love for words is words themselves. Yet we have to keep trying, working toward more ideas per square inch. Revision that bends your prose in the direction of readers' needs is a reality for anyone who wants to have readers at all.

# Exercises

1) As with the description of the fox in Chapter 1 exercises, write a description of something you saw, felt, smelled, or tasted in language that conveys the feeling of it.

2) Go through your draft and ...

   • Circle every adverb (-ly word) you use. Is there a way to boil verb-plus-adverb combinations down to single verbs, and/or otherwise take your adverbs out?

   • Circle every verb. Does it describe a motion vividly and directly in a way appropriate to that motion, without personifying?

   • Thump every word and phrase for soundness to get toward "more ideas per square inch," as I showed in my passage from *Eldorado, Iowa*. Ask yourself: Why have I felt the need to say this? Am I burying important information? Personifying, falsely? Distracting the reader from the present moment with another image or bit of information that takes them away?

3) "Unbeautify" in words—describe something gross or sad that's nevertheless made worth looking at through language.

4) Invoke a smell in words.

5) Pick an abstract word, like "thing," and use it once in a description that's otherwise as precise as you can make it. What's the overall effect? This is inspired by Robert Cohen's discussion of the following passage in a Leonard Michaels story: "He yearned for his office and his desk and the window that looked out on the shining Pacific. He'd never gone swimming in the prodigious, restless, teeming, alluring thing, but he loved the changing light on its surface and the sounds it made in the darkness ..."

6) Reduce the word count of a particular passage by at least 30 percent.

7) Circle every flashback and ask yourself what it's doing there and whether you need it.

# 5

# Workshops and Revision

Now that you've built your draft, what do you do with it? How should you go about getting (and giving) feedback? What questions are the best ones to ask yourself, and to be asked by your readers? Since re-vision literally means re-seeing, how can we get under the skin of habit to see what our words are actually doing? In this chapter, I'll share some ideas that work for me and my students. Most of them are based on your relationship with your reader, and all of them are designed to help you gather information, since *gathering information in order to make decisions* is where revision starts.

# Workshops: (1) More like this, (2) This stops me, (3) Any questions?

I'll start by talking about how I run workshops in my classes for undergraduates and adults, because I think this will show the orientation toward revision that it's most productive for writers *and* readers to have. Workshops are not about leaning back in your chair, taking a thoughtful drag on your cigarette, and slaying the poor quivering wannabe in front of you. Neither are they about displaying your own critical acumen or telling the reader, "If this were *my* piece, I would …" Such actions feel like rigor but are usually just egotism. Rather, workshops are about readers helping the writer identify and work toward her goals, which means helping that piece, and that writer, succeed on the terms they have set out for themselves. If Jane is writing about a battle between robots on Mars, you help her write the best battling-robot story she can write, even if you yourself are writing about a father who's developed black lung from his life in West Virginia coal mines and his daughter, an anti-coal activist. You are there to give Jane the most valuable thing you can give—the testimony of your own experience as a reader, which will help her see the effect her words are actually having on readers and make decisions accordingly about what, and how, to revise.

Workshops function best when everyone approaches them with these realities in mind:

- Both writer and reader are taking a risk in the hope of a positive outcome. But showing another human being what we have created is risky because it involves self-exposure and vulnerability, just like making art in general does. Offering feedback is also risky, because you risk being misunderstood, which, when your intentions are good, is painful (as Nina Simone sang in the 1960s classic "Don't Let Me Be Misunderstood"). Therefore, both reader and writer want the workshop process to be productive.
- Most writers can't push our work to its full potential on our own, because we have no way of knowing how it looks to someone else unless we ask. When readers testify to their experiences with our words on the page, they help us see those words through someone else's eyes, giving us valuable information we can use to get closer to the effect we want. In turn, readers must remember they're here to help

a piece succeed on the terms it is setting out for itself, not to refashion someone else's draft in their own image.

- All of us, writers and readers, are responsible for bringing our best selves to the workshop. We're always looking through the lens of what's going on with us that day, but we've got to mind our tone and phrase our words in ways the writer can hear. Writers must remember that questions about their writing aren't necessarily questions about them as people, even if emotion can make it seem that way. Everyone shares the need to feel understood and respected as a fellow artist.
- Writers and readers have responsibilities and rights. The reader is offering the (responsibly phrased) testimony of her experience *as* a reader, which she has a right to do and which provides information for the writer that only she can offer. Similarly, the writer has the responsibility to listen to readers' testimonies but also the right to revise her work as she sees fit.
- Like writing itself, talking meaningfully about writing in workshops is a process that involves risk, failure, trying again, getting better, and doing the best you can.

I believe all these things, but as a teacher, I used to wonder how I could create a workshop framework that respected them and helped students move each other's writing forward. The answer emerged several years ago, when a colleague of mine from the Visual and Performing Arts Department gave me a short essay by the dancer and choreographer Liz Lerman. Entitled "Toward a Process for Critical Response" (1993) and developed in her book (with John Borstel) *Critical Response Process* (2003), the process is designed to bring the workshop process more into "the control of the artist."[1]

The first step in what Lerman calls "The Process" is "Statements of Meaning": "artists want to hear," she writes, "that what they have just created has significance to another human being."[2] Artist as Questioner comes next: "I'm working right now on the way I express a strong feeling, so what did you think of the closing section?"[3] Then, responders ask neutral questions: "What were you trying to accomplish in the final section?"[4] Step four is "Permissioned Opinions": a responder can indicate they have an opinion and ask whether the artist would like to hear it.[5] After this, if the piece raises other questions audience members and the artist want to talk about, a discussion can happen. Then, revision work on the piece can begin.[6]

Lerman's piece changed my thinking about workshops for good. As a teacher, I was particularly struck by the truth of step one: most of all, people want to hear that their work has communicated something to another human being. This squares with my experience of how vulnerable writers feel when they accept the risk of writing something and showing it to others. It's also a way to head off the dangers of workshopping—particularly other writers' obliviousness or arrogance—since it stresses "subordinating my response to the idea of another person's excellence" and shaping your response around the writer's needs, not yours.

Lerman's piece meshed with another great influence on my writing and workshopping life. As a participant in the Tin House Summer Writers Workshop in 2008, I heard the writers Steve Almond and Aimee Bender deliver a craft lecture they called "Writers on the Couch." It invited us to ask ourselves two questions about our work:

1) What are the moments or passages that make me want to write "more like this?" In other words, what are the places where my writing feels most precise, effective, significant, and alive—to myself and to my readers? Where do I think I was really "on," doing my best work? And what was my state of mind when I wrote those words?

2) What are the moments or passages that "stop me" as I read? In other words, where is the writing confused, sticky, lazy, kind of meaningless and blah, or just not right? And what was my state of mind when I wrote them?

3) In each case, how can I replicate or avoid the state of mind that produced that work to sharpen "more" of the piece to be "like this?

With Lerman, Almond, and Bender in mind, I fashioned a simple but durable and adaptable workshop process I've been using ever since. I want to help students approach the process with care and with rigor, neither as a simple feel-good session nor as an opportunity to sharpen one's claws on a classmate, and I hope they can learn to apply these lenses to their own work. This is the foundation for workshops in every course I teach, from first-year composition to introductory and advanced creative writing to adult classes, and it works well in all of them. As you read my summary of the process here, know that in all my workshops, I ask students to have copies of the work under discussion in front of them (preferably on paper) and a pen and notebook with which to jot notes as they listen, so both writer and reader are looking at the same manuscript during this process and the writer is taking notes. The reader has marked the writer's manuscript and written a summary note at the end, so the writer can take the manuscript away with her and read the comments when the workshop ends.

My workshops go like this. First, the writer enters what Megan Mayhew Bergman, a past workshop leader of mine, calls "the cone of silence," and the reader (or class) speaks. Although it's hard, the writer should listen and take notes, not talk, until later in the process. You can't helicopter-parent your writing through the world, and a nervous writer can easily take up the whole discussion time explaining her work rather than hearing what a reader has made of that work on her own.

The reader begins by pointing out the "more like this" moments: places she connected with/easily imagined/entered into/felt closer to what was happening on the page. If possible, the reader points out specific passages and word choices that are creating this response and analyzes their effect (like "Silence swelled through the house" in my community writing class, described back in Chapter 4). This satisfies the writer's need, in Lerman's words, to know that what she's created has meaning for another human being. Hearing "this paragraph was a 'more like this' moment for me" is more useful to many writers than hearing "I liked this paragraph," because it focuses the discussion on the writing rather than on individual taste and relaxes the writer at the beginning of the process. It also helps the writer ask, "What was my mode of thinking and working when I wrote this 'more like this' paragraph, and how can I 'make the whole piece *that*?'"

Next, the reader reports on "this stopped me" moments. These are places where something about the writing prevented her from engaging with it as fully as she wanted. Drawing on John Gardner's idea that fiction unfolds in the reader's mind as a "vivid and continuous dream," this helps writers see where their words on the page might be "breaking the dream" for readers, jolting them out of the experience the writer's trying to create. Again, the reader points to specific places in the text and analyzes their effect as much she can. As before, the reader resists the language of "like" or "don't like," "good" or "bad," testifying instead to her experience: "I didn't understand," "I couldn't picture," "I got confused," "This word doesn't mean what you think it means," "We do need this information, but not here."

After hearing the reader's testimony to "more like this" and "this stops me" moments, the writer can leave the cone of silence and ask the reader specific *questions* about the reader's experience of the piece, connected to problems s/he's working on: "I worked hard on these verbs because I wanted to create the motion and the sound of pheasants when they fly up from the ground; did that work for you?" "I wasn't sure about whether these characters would have this conversation here; what did you think?" Writer, you should be prepared to hear the truth of your reader's experience, and as hard as it is, you should also resist explaining your work too much. If readers aren't entering into your world in the way you're hoping they will, then you might not be giving them, on the page, the tools they need to do so. Interestingly, writers using this process in my classes seldom feel defensive by the time they get to this stage; progressing through steps one and two has made them feel taken seriously as artists and has, therefore, gentled them down out of their initial nervousness while focusing them on the work.

# The revision pyramid: Setting priorities

When you're facing revision, it's hard to know where to start, or what revision really means. Therefore, I offer my students in critical (first-year college writing and literature) and creative writing courses lists of priorities that focus them on the most important things about writing: thinking critically, taking a risk, knowing enough about your subject to write about it clearly, and developing something to say. (That's my working definition of education—becoming a self with something to say.) Without guidance, students may assume—as I used to—that "revision" is only a matter of correcting typos and comma placement. Yet if you have no thesis sentence and no argument, worrying about commas isn't the best use of your time. I've reproduced my ten-level "Grading and Revision Criteria" for academic writers in the appendix to this book. For now, I'll discuss my Revision Pyramid for creative writers, which focuses on the big, intangible things— significance, knowledge, "what is this really about?"—first as the foundation for the process and then works upward in the same way I teach critical writers to do. While you can toggle among the levels as needed, I do suggest approaching them at roughly this level of priority. Each has an exercise or two associated with it. And each involves bringing the habits of observation you're been honing as a writer to the observation of your own work.

**Level I (Foundation: First Priority):** Here, you confront the big questions and the deep engagement that will produce the most difficult but necessary revision: What is this really about? Is there enough at stake, lending my work a sense of emotional significance: will my reader care about what's

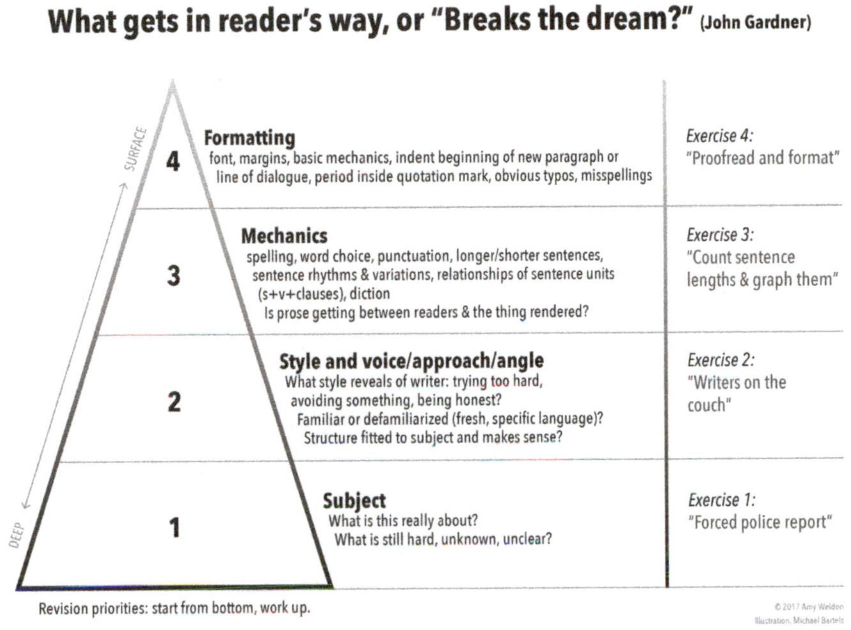

# What gets in reader's way, or "Breaks the dream?" (John Gardner)

**Figure 5.1** The revision pyramid—illustration by Michael Bartels.

happening in my story? What is still difficult for me to write about? Why? Are there aspects of this subject (types of scenes, etc.) I need to write about but haven't? Is my thinking about my subject as clear and un-clichéd as it might be? You can also approach this with the largest and most general question of all: Reading through my work, what do I notice?

> *Exercise: "The forced police report": Rewrite an important moment in your piece under the following constraints: a) sentences of no more than 15 words (including* a, and, *and* the) *each; b) words of no more than 2 syllables each; c) no adjectives except those of the five senses (rough, blue, bright, cold, sour, red). By forcing you to slow down and focus on the images in your mind, this exercise will show you pretty clearly what you might need to imagine or think through more fully. This knowledge can then influence the way you revise the rest of the work.*

**Level 2 (Second Priority):** Here, you look at the relationship between the words on the page and your understanding of your subject: what do the voice and style of your writing reveal here? Are you trying too hard, straining for a vocabulary that doesn't quite fit? Are you resisting cliché? Are the voice and structure of your piece fitted to the subject and the reader's needs as well as they might be? Structural questions can also be revealing: What types of scenes do you have or need more or less of? (For instance, if you have too many flashbacks, they'll drag the momentum of your story backwards, like a small boat trailing a big underwater net; if the real energy of your story is in that past time frame, it might make more sense to set the whole story there.) This may also be where you consider what to cut out. "Why have I felt the need to say this here?" is a great question to ask.

> *Exercise: Identify your own "more like this" moments and/or ask readers to do so. What was your state of mind when you wrote each of them, and how can you bring that state of mind to "making the whole piece that?"*

**Level 3 (Mechanics and Sentences):** Here, you look as closely and clearly as you can at what the words on the page are doing and whether they might do so more effectively: this is "editing" alongside the inner question, "why have I done this this way, and what is its effect on my readers?" This is where you consider the way your punctuation, sentence formations, and word choices are directing your reader's energy.

> *Exercises:*
>
> 1) *Read your whole piece aloud and/or have someone read it to you, making marks as you go (just to remind yourself where to look) but not stopping the reader. What have you noticed? What have you heard?*
>
> 2) *Select a passage and draw a graph of it: plot the position of each sentence (first, second, third, etc.) on the horizontal axis and the number of words in each sentence on the vertical axis. Then connect the dots. What do you notice about the shape your paragraph makes? Is it "flatlining," with all your sentences roughly the same length, and therefore monotonous? Is there a "barrier to entry," with the first sentence much longer than the rest? (As P.G. Wodehouse said, "Nothing puts the reader off more than a great slab of prose at the start.")[7] (See Figure 5.2).*
>
> 3) *Diagram your sentences (really!) and/or otherwise investigate your patterns of sentence construction; some variation is good. It's common, for instance, to fall into a "dependent clause, main clause" pattern: "Shouldering his backpack, he set off down the trail. Eyeing the hill in front of him, he prepared to climb." (Remember, if your dependent clause doesn't match the main clause, you may have a misplaced modifier—"Shouldering his backpack, the trail rose before him" is a misplaced modifier, since the trail can't pick up a bag.) You may be in a main-clause-only pattern: "He picked up his backpack. He put his backpack on his shoulders. He started walking." This may be a good time for you to review the rules of sentence construction, combination, and punctuation: what's a main clause, dependent/subordinate clause, or comma splice? What are conjunctions and conjunctive adverbs? What's the*

## Exercise 3: "Count sentence lengths & graph them"

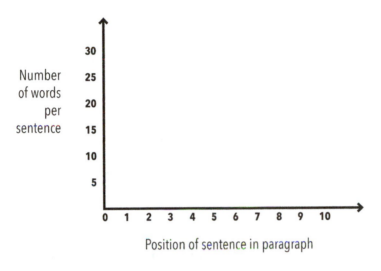

**Figure 5.2** Sentence graph—illustration by Michael Bartels.

*difference between how a semicolon is used and how a comma is used to combine sentences?*

**Level 4 (Manuscript Formatting):** This is where you apply the advice of my dissertation director: "You can't always control whether you've read everything or thought of everything, but you can control whether your commas are in the right places." *Control what you can* is great advice for the last level of revision, the most basic cleanup and format check before you show your work to someone else. If you don't care about your work, readers won't either. I've put formatting at the top of the pyramid because although it's the most visible level of problems in the manuscript and creates an immediate impression on readers, it's not the most important focus of revision energy; who wants a perfectly formatted manuscript that has nothing to say? Here's a sample checklist:

- Is your manuscript laid out readably and professionally: 12-point Times New Roman or similar font in sentence case, double-spaced, one-inch margins all around, page numbers in the top right corner, section breaks properly indicated, and, for poetry, single spacing between lines in a stanza unless you're using some other deliberate strategy? Have you included your title and name?

- Within your text, have you formatted content correctly: tabs at the beginning of each paragraph, punctuation marks inside quotation marks, "like this," smart quotes ("the curly ones") rather than straight quotes, each new speaker's dialogue beginning on a new line and avoiding the automatic capital letter Microsoft Word will add after a period ("Like this." She said. **should be** "Like this," she said.)

- Have you read your manuscript aloud to catch typos and wrong words? Spelling-and-grammar-check alone won't do it.

- Are you sure you're using punctuation—particularly semicolons and commas—correctly? See "Punctuation: The Chocolate Fountain" in Chapter 4.

# Windows into your world: Scenes, perspectives, points of view

As you work through levels 3 and 4 of the revision pyramid, you'll consider the windows you're giving your reader into your written world. This, for me, is what structural considerations like number and type of scenes, point of view, dialogue, and governing verb tense have in common—each positions your reader relative to your story in a certain way and gives her a particular angle of vision on it.

The kind of scenes you include and the information they show us—including your characters' actions or beliefs—will build our mental pictures of those characters in certain ways. Each scene is a portal through which we watch some unfolding action that will affect our sense of the whole work. Therefore, think about what you want readers to see in order to believe what you want us to believe. It may not be enough just to tell us, as your protagonist accompanies her eager children into the reptile house at the zoo, that she's afraid of snakes—you might also need to show us, in short flashback, the moment in fifth grade when her little brother put a garter snake down her neck. Along with this, consider whether you might have too many scenes that are too similar to one another in pacing, structure, or general function. In *How Not to Write a Novel*, Howard Mittelmark and Sandra Neuman point out that sex scenes follow this rule: they need to be different enough from one another or move character or plot along uniquely enough to justify the existence of more than one or two. (This can be true of characters, too, particularly minor ones; does your awkward adolescent character need to face six mean girls at the lunchroom table, or just three? And have you made their names or other identifying details different enough for readers to be able to tell them apart?)

**Point of view**—which character's eyes we're looking through, and which pronouns govern that angle of vision—is also important, because it can shape the level of distance between your reader and your character or narrator, and, consequently, the level of intimacy or access to that character's or narrator's thoughts. Basically, you have three options: **first person** ("I"), **second person** ("you"), and **third person** (character's or narrator's name, "she," or "he"). In nonfiction, "I" is understood to be the writer, more or less. But in fiction, a first-person narrator is not necessarily the actual writer and is not necessarily giving your reader the most intimate or honest window of access into the story. Consider the classic first-person stories "The Yellow Wall-paper" (1892) by Charlotte Perkins Gilman and "Why I Live at the P.O." (1941) by Eudora Welty. In each case, the first-person narrator, chatty and confiding, isn't giving us the whole story; we're figuring out what's actually going on in *spite* of what the narrator says, because we can't quite trust her. (This is why we call those narrators "unreliable," even though, as critic James Wood writes, "even the apparently unreliable narrator is more often than not reliably unreliable," since the novel or story "is teaching us how to read its narrator.")[8] By contrast, Katherine Anne Porter's "The Jilting of Granny Weatherall" (1930), written in third person, takes us into the mind and body of a dying woman, so that we experience her thoughts and memories almost as immediately as she does: "She was so amazed her thoughts ran round and round. So, my dear Lord, this is my death and I wasn't even thinking about it. My children have come to see me die. But I can't, it's not time. Oh, I always hated surprises."[9] (This kind of closeness is, appropriately, called close- or limited-third-person, which moves us into and out of the protagonist's thoughts; it is also called "free indirect style," which, as James Wood writes, allows readers "omniscience and partiality at once.")[10] Second person is a little more controversial; I find it useful for composite characters in nonfiction, writing about experiences several people share as if they're one person's experience (as in my essay "A Miniature Handbook for New Woman Activists"),[11] but in fiction, it can tend to come in and out of fashion and to strike some readers as annoying. Flip back to the excerpt from Larry Brown's *On Fire* in Chapter 1 to see second person at work.

Laura Ingalls Wilder's work shows how first or third person can tilt us toward memoir or fiction. As we've seen, the *Little House* books are told in third person, with "Laura"—a version of Wilder herself, experiencing Wilder's own memories—as the main character. Yet, as we saw at the end of the Introduction, Wilder's first attempt at the material that became the Little House books was a manuscript called *Pioneer Girl*, written in first person. Wilder's daughter Rose Wilder Lane, a professional writer, advised her mother, "You can not use the first person, because the 'I' books do not sell well" in the children's book market of the time.[12] Yet as Pamela Smith Hill, *Pioneer Girl*'s modern editor, writes, the shift from first to third "[gave] the series its unique, childlike voice," helping "[y]oung readers [see] the author's world from a single perspective, much like their own."[13] The shift from first to third also gave Wilder some freedom she needed to hover somewhere between fiction and nonfiction; while the Little House books are based on her own memories, she moves some timeframes and events around (she was around three years old during the time period of *Little House on the Prairie*, not six or seven, as "Laura" is in that book) and omits others entirely. In allowing her younger self to become a character, the third-person point of view also gives the adult author some freedom to put a distance, sometimes ironically, between her past and present selves; while young Laura doesn't wonder overtly what happened to the Osage woman hunkering next to her cooking fire, the adult Laura, whose subtle presence we feel, most certainly does—especially since, as with Pet and Patty on the riverbank, the heightened detail slows us down and focuses our attention on the footprints. "Thanks to free indirect style," James Wood writes, "we see things through the character's eyes and language but also through the author's eyes and language ... This is merely another definition of dramatic irony: to see through a character's eyes while being encouraged to see more than the character can see."[14] As I've mentioned, the third person also gives young readers that sense of slight distance they may need to process and enjoy Laura's experiences most. (Hill points out that J. K. Rowling's *Harry Potter* series also uses third person limited, as C. S. Lewis does in *The Chronicles of Narnia*.)[15]

Like point of view, the governing *verb tense* of a piece of writing can position readers and writers at particular angles as we experience its world. We rely on verb tenses to locate a sentence in time: when did this event happen? In relation to what other events around it? (When we learn our native language, we absorb these grammatical structures near-unconsciously and recognize them even if we can't name them.) For writers, tense shifts are markers of time, and of a consciousness as it moves through time. As readers, we need to have a character's consciousness and its location in time established for us before we can fully "join up with it" and use it to navigate the fictional world on the page. When we pick up a novel governed by past tense, we adjust ourselves to thinking in "past-tense-novel-dimension," calibrate our mental understanding of that world accordingly, and proceed to immerse ourselves in the story. A writer should pick a tense and stay with it, since a story that keeps shifting verb tenses is like a car that keeps popping out of gear—it stalls unexpectedly between "dimensions" while the reader repeatedly tries to readjust her mental framework. ("She walked down the porch steps and thinks that it's a beautiful day outside, but soon it would be getting cold, since fall is coming.") Therefore, tense shifts stop the reader and eject her from the story's world. Ouch.

Your choices for governing verb tense are essentially present tense ("She walks down the porch steps into the fall sunshine, kicking leaves aside as she goes") or past tense ("She walked down the porch steps into the fall sunshine, kicking leaves aside as she went"), perhaps also with excursions into past perfect to establish ongoing situations: "She had been inside all day, longing to come outside." (George Orwell's *Nineteen Eighty-four* is a one-novel masterclass in how to balance simple past and past perfect.) Past tense keeps the reader close but not too close to the character, giving us the psychic distance and range of motion necessary to walk beside and watch her while avoiding the claustrophobic closeness that governing-present can bring (see below). I think it also helps you achieve a certain vaguely "classic" maturity and polish in your style. For a novel, it tends to feel trustworthy, encouraging readers to settle in and go on the voyage. Some writers combine present and past tenses on purpose, depending on how they want to handle time: in *Frankenstein* (1818), Mary Shelley casts Robert Walton's letters (unfolding in the "now" of the novel) in present tense, while Victor's and the Creature's stories, recounting events gone by to Robert and to one another, are in past tense (but the overall logic of the novel, and consistency within sections, help readers accept this). Present tense can give a nice sense of immediacy and action unfolding in the present moment, enabling sharp, experimental effects in prose and very close psychic distance. It can also feel too-trendy or claustrophobic—readers might feel pressed against the surface of the action, unable to get a longer view of the character's past, or too close to a character with whom it's uncomfortable to share space for long. (That's why "The Yellow Wall-paper," told magnificently and uncomfortably in first-person present tense, works better as a story than it might as a novel; such intensity is hard to sustain.)

During your revision process, try a different character's point of view or a different governing verb tense; it might give you a whole new perspective on the window through which your readers will look into your world. For an exercise, select a scene you've already established in one character's point of view, then rewrite it in the voice and point of view of a different character who already appears in that same scene. Even if you don't end up changing the whole story, this can still give you interesting information that your main character might not have, but that another character does.

# The wrong detail: Blink and you're out

As we said in Chapter 3, readers react to a writer's staging of her imaginative world in surprisingly finicky ways; boldness and conviction, supported with precise detail, can lift us up and carry us into your story, but a wrong detail can shut the whole thing down. Lean us in the direction of a big unreal idea—women can make their own babies out of yarn, a closet contains a portal to another world, the Underground Railroad is actually a real system with trains, tracks, and stations—and, amazingly often, we'll go happily along. "The reader's conviction will follow the writer's," I tell my students. This is true of historical fiction too, by the way. Where we balk is if we don't get the right details to help us furnish and build this world, in sensory terms, in our own minds as we go. Strike the wrong note and we're out.

A member of one of my community writing classes found this problem in a draft of his dystopian novel, which is set in a decaying, not-so-distant-future version of Chicago. In one scene, a young female security agent is dressing up to go undercover as an upper-class, vice-prone party girl. This man is a great storyteller, with a strong sense of pacing and dialogue, yet when we got to the dressing-up scene, workshop members (all women) stopped short. His character was putting on a blue blouse with a knee-length floral skirt, pink lipstick, and a ribbon in her hair—more 1980s garden-party matron than futuristic sensualist. "I knew you all would be able to help me with this," he laughed. "I've been married for forty years, and my sense for twenty-something women's fashion is … lacking." With a few visual changes—black leather, spiked hair, blood-red lipstick, steel-toed stilettoes—the character sprang to life, and we followed the writer happily into the scene with nothing else to stop us.

The fifty-dollar word for this is *anachronism,* a detail out of place in time, which, again, comes from incompletely imagining your fictional world from inside that world itself. This is surprisingly easy to do. Writing a fictional scene set around 1814, I had a character describe meat as "rubbery." Whoops. Rubber wasn't made or used widely enough to become an adjective until later in the nineteenth and early twentieth centuries, so my character wouldn't have had that word available to her. What about *leathery?* But *leathery* would signal a dry, flexible, perhaps faintly crispy texture. I wanted to pin a particular gristly, moist, bouncy toughness to the page. So I went back to the image of that meat on the plate and showed a character acting upon it, with another textural word: "She took a knife to the gristly meat, pressing hard to force the blade through." Any day you can get a particular bodily, food-specific word like *gristle* into a sentence is a good day.

**Dialogue**—an art form discussed more fully in Janet Burroway's *Writing Fiction* and other craft books I list in my appendix—can be an inadvertent source of dream-breaking for readers too. A common error I see is *expository dialogue*—a character says something because the writer wants readers to know it, even if it's something no character would ever actually say. "Mary," John asks his wife, "didn't you say that your mother, Phyllis, who lives in Minneapolis, an hour's drive from us, is coming to dinner with us this Thanksgiving?" Like anachronism, it's a place where the writer's anxiety (*I want you to know this!*) is pressing into the story a little too much, striking that wrong note that wakes us from our fictional dream. You're better off separating this into dialogue and exposition:

> "Hey, Mary," John asked his wife, "your mom's coming, right?" Mary's mother, Phyllis, lived in Minneapolis, an hour's drive away, and she usually spent Thanksgiving with them.

Other common dialogue issues? The overly self-aware/psychobabbling speaker: "Reginald, I've made the decision to end my relationship with you because I feel the need for greater self-actualization than you can provide." The speaker who sounds like all the other speakers and/or the author: "Regina sighed as she thoughtfully pondered her unmet need for greater self-actualization. 'Reginald,' she stated, 'I have decided to end my relationship with you because I feel that your attention to my needs is inadequate.'" The phonetic speaker, usually an attempt at regionalism: "We wuz goin' down to the swimmin' hole when we seen Uncle Billy with his ol' hound dog walkin' t'other way." (Usually, regional speech is represented best with altered sentence rhythms and only the occasional "wrong" word—think

Ron Rash, Junot Diaz, Edward Jones, or Flannery O'Connor.) Explaining your own dialogue: "'Wait, I don't understand', she said, looking at him as if she didn't know what he meant." There's also such a thing as *too much dialogue*, particularly when it replaces action and gesture and other types of scene. Along with the rise of smartphones, texting, and Netflix, I've seen my students' fluency with dialogue and the amount of dialogue in their stories rising while their descriptive detail—and, therefore, the vividness of place and action—diminishes. If your dialogue muscles are strong, be sure you're cross-training to build up other skills too.

# Revising by reading: Pen in hand

So having just given you this massive list of things to look for as you revise, I'm going to suggest this: don't try to tackle them all at once. Pick one or two things you really want to focus on, then make a pass through your manuscript with pen in hand, focusing on one of those things at a time. With experience, picking up issues on more than one level as you read will get easier, but first, say to yourself, "I'm only going to look for lapses in verb tense this time through," or "I'm only going to look for expository dialogue now." One of my first-year composition students has a set of multicolored felt-tip pens she uses for this purpose, marking everything she looks for in a different color. And while we're on the subject, don't feel obligated to use red ink. In my first graduate-school writing pedagogy class, I was advised to use pencil, rather than red pen, to grade and comment on students' papers. (Yes, the research is in: red pen freaks people out.) Flush with the arrogance of youth, I regarded this as soft-headed pandering, *until* I met the girl I've told you about, paralyzed with fear of that giant red "Doo-Doo!" across the top of her paper. There's rigor, and then there's beating up on others to make yourself feel good. The red-ink phenomenon is real. So I use purple or green.

# Revising by hand: Paper, scissors, and tape

Yes, you read that correctly—cutting your manuscript apart and moving the pieces around can be fun, hands-on, and surprisingly informative, no matter what kind of writing you do. If you are writing a memoir like Abigail Thomas's or Nick Flynn's, which are composed of short scenes strung together like beads on a necklace, or a large research paper with several different sections, or a story in which you're juggling multiple layers of time, it's really useful to cut the manuscript apart along any lines that make sense to you (by paragraph, by scene, by section, or even by sentence) and experiment with rearranging them. You may decide your original order is best, and that's okay. But moving pieces by hand (which Susan Bell also discusses in *The Artful Edit*) lets you see and read different possible orders in a way you otherwise can't. As with your notebooks, the point is to get out of the vapor-lock of perfectionism, make a mess, and have fun. Here are some hands-on techniques to try:

- Cut your manuscript into pieces and sort it into piles based on categories that make sense to you (for example, "all my scenes about X, all my scenes about Y, all my scenes about Z"). Take a look at your piles and their relative size. Which is largest? Could that be the thing that your piece is really about? Which is smallest? Do you need to omit that category or write more about it or leave it the way it is?

- Make a "manuscript quilt" you can hang up on the wall or spread out on a table, look at all at once, and then write on. When I was revising *Eldorado, Iowa*, I printed out the whole manuscript in 8-point type and attached the pages together in order, left to right and top to bottom, to make one giant quilt I tacked to the wall. I was working with three different layers of time, so wrote shorthand names for them in pink, yellow, and orange highlighter over those passages. Looking at the patterns of color that emerged, I could see that I was either spending way too much time in one layer (long stretches of one color) or cutting among the three layers too quickly (a burst of colors together). As with the sentence-graphing exercise in the revision pyramid, ask yourself: is the pattern you're observing the pattern you really want to see?

- Cut your manuscript into shorter sections, rearrange them (on the floor or a table) and then tape them together in a new order that creates one long ragged piece of paper. This can be hung from a doorframe with tape (kind of like those 1970s bead curtains) or hung from a clothesline (a piece of string attached to your ceiling or wall) with clothespins. Then you can read the whole thing in a new order, top to bottom. If you have lots of small pieces of paper, you can use the clothespins to clip together scenes or scraps or even photographs that relate to categories of information or particular characters.

- If you need to expand a particular passage with more detail, cut it apart sentence by sentence, then lay the pieces out on a fresh piece of blank paper with gaps between them and write new sentences—preferably by hand—in the gaps. (This works *really* well for critical papers.) It helps you enact a useful revision tool: "write one more sentence about this."
- Cut the "most interesting thing" out of a typed page, tape it to the top of a blank page, and start writing by hand from there.
- Combine any or all of these techniques—or invent your own!

# Revising by voice: Reading aloud

Like cutting a manuscript apart, reading your work aloud is a great way to gather information. It may feel silly at first, but this sensation will pass. You can also have someone else read to you while you sit with pen in hand and make little tick marks on the page to remind yourself what you notice (don't stop your reader if you can help it.) When you finish listening, take a few moments to jot down your reactions and talk with your reader about what they noticed as they read (where did they run out of breath, where did they feel more or less engaged, where did they speed up or stumble?) and what you heard.

Reading aloud is useful in groups, too, since the ear is less forgiving than the eye. In all my classes, students and I read aloud from our course texts and one another's work. For a reading workshop, everyone brings one page of their own work, with a title but without the name. Then you "go to the floor" (as Missy Elliot advises, in another context)[16] in the center of the room and put your paper down. Pick up a page that isn't yours and return to your seat. Read the title and at least some of the prose aloud from the page in front of you, one by one, until everyone's work has been read. (If you're working on beginnings, focus on the first two paragraphs; if you are wanting to focus on other problem areas, people can submit other passages from their work—this exercise is very adaptable.) I usually ask everyone to jot notes as they listen (this helps conceal the writer, who'll want to take notes on her own piece) but not to pause too long between pieces. Then, after everyone has read aloud, we talk as a group about overall patterns we noticed. Where do readers stumble, where do they speed up, what images are memorable to us, and why? You may hear your work read by someone of a different gender, which can usefully defamiliarize it; I realized this when a male student picked up and read my own anonymous page.

# Revising by retyping: Once more from the top

Walking yourself through all these steps, you may find you've acquired a new direction or voice or angle of vision on what your piece should become. When this happens to me (in critical or creative writing), I've found it's usually better to close my old document in my computer, open a brand new one, and start retyping, from the beginning, *in* that new voice. It's the equivalent of an artist grabbing a fresh piece of paper. "Fixing up" an old document can hinder revision in surprising ways, because the old words and images and the self that conceived of them can linger and blur your new instincts, like the grubby traces of much-erased pencil on paper. You have the old sentences saved if you need them, but chances are, you won't.

Case in point: when I went to the Tin House Summer Writers Workshop in 2008, I was stalled out on a novel manuscript I'd been developing from a story I'd published in graduate school. At 150 pages, it just seemed to be losing more steam the more I wrote, even though I was doubling down on flashbacks to try to build the story and make it interesting. My workshop leader, Colson Whitehead, and workshop-mates identified three major problems immediately. One, my real main character was not this one but *this* one; two, the real first line of the novel was on page ten; and three, if the real energy of the novel was in the past (signaled by all those flashbacks), why not start the story *there*? A spasm of panic was followed by a surge of enthusiasm: once I saw what they meant, I saw that although the setting and characters would remain the same, the angle of vision through my new main character's eyes would be very different. Accordingly, I opened a new document and started (re)writing without looking at the old one, trusting that the images that belonged in the new version would migrate over on their own. Amazingly, they did. Fueled by a new energy and purpose, I rewrote all 150 pages in a month. That process was interrupted by the image that became *Eldorado, Iowa*, which that first education in novel-logic helped me complete. When you're a writer, nothing is ever wasted.

# Time: A writer's friend (Part 1)

At the risk of being patronizing, I will add one final point: none of these techniques will work if you don't give them enough *time*. Many student stories (and papers) fail to fulfill their real promise because the writers haven't pushed them through enough drafts over time. As I tell my first-year research-paper writers, writing is like athletic training: you go farther by working an hour or two per day for five days than you do in one ten-hour Saturday burst, even if you are technically spending the same amount of time each way. Of course, as I confessed in Chapter 1, I too have been that kid awake and writing at 4 a.m., sometimes literature-class papers, sometimes my "first novel." But even if you are a fluent night-before-it's-due writer, you'll probably find, as I did, that a habit of haste and/or halfassery *will* eventually let you down. (For me, this moment came in graduate school—the glib English major's Marine Corps—and I'm grateful each day for it.) I tell my students now that if you are turning in a first or second draft of anything, you are almost certainly turning in insufficiently revised work.

The difference between the "talented" writer and the person who has a writing career is that the person with the career is the person who has learned to apply pants to chair and words to page, routinely and without drama. That really is what it's about: walking the path, putting in the time, getting in the habit. Develop a work ethic and a standard and hold yourself to it as best you can. And the more time you give yourself to revise your work from that initial "shitty first draft," going back and back again to look for different things, the better it will be and the farther you will have progressed along your own particular writing path, for good. Get started writing and revising early. You'll be happier, and so will your readers.

## Exercises

Turn back through this chapter and select one exercise to try that will particularly help you with your manuscript right now. Not all of them will work for all manuscripts at all times, but try all of them at some point, and feel free to adapt them to your own project.

# 6

# Loving the Path

Let me tell you a story about what looks at first like failure.[1] Remember that novel manuscript of mine, *Eldorado, Iowa*, I talked about in the last few chapters? Here's what eventually happened to it.

In 2012—four years after that initial image-flash of a pregnant woman in a long dress, walking in the grass in my little Iowa frontier town—I finished my sixth draft of the novel and sent it to an editor I knew (let's call her Anne). I had published short stories and essays in journals but had never published a book. Counting the fragmentary beginnings and scenes I'd been toying with since my senior year of college, *Eldorado* was my fourth distinct novel manuscript and the first one I had finished. I felt more attached to it than anything else I'd written, having invested more in it in terms of emotion, craft, and time than I ever thought possible. I liked and trusted Anne, and although I felt nervous about sending *Eldorado* out, I knew I had reached a point where I couldn't do anything else with it. It was 286 pages long. And it was time to let it go.

Anne sent me back a thoughtful letter. She and her colleagues had read the manuscript and praised my prose style and sense of place, but they noted "insufficient narrative momentum," meaning "not enough happens." (This was my biggest challenge as a fiction writer: keeping a plot moving forward and the stakes high without getting lulled into flashbacks, descriptions, and other backwaters of distraction from the story, kind of like I've just done with this parenthesis.) I accepted this critique, with that same sense of relieved-yet-stomach-sinking feeling I always feel when someone has identified a flaw in my writing I'd hoped was invisible. I revised a couple more times. I added a villain—automatic stakes-raiser, right?—and rearranged and fleshed out some other scenes. I cut out a section of the novel set in modern times, as they'd suggested. I reread the whole thing aloud. And then I sent it off again.

On the morning of my thirty-eighth birthday, radiant with the light of early fall, a package thumped onto my porch: my manuscript was back, with a letter from Anne. Her verdict, gently phrased, was that she wouldn't be publishing it. I remember a cold crater opening in my chest, its edges crumbling in as it expanded out, and out. I cried. Eventually I chivvied myself back up to cruising speed: *be a professional, you've been rejected before.* Yes, but never for a project that meant so much, on which I had worked so hard, for which I had what I thought were such well-founded hopes. *You'll write other novels.* Yes, but I had given this one my heart, and what I still think is some of my best writing. (James Salter felt the same way about his classic novel *Light Years:* "Some things I love in [this book]," he wrote, "I love as one loves a woman."[2]) Now I had a broken heart, a too-familiar way of talking about the pain of the fact that reality has denied you your vision of a state of being that, if achieved, could change your life for good.

Of course I kept on teaching, writing (mostly nonfiction that would become my book *The Hands-On Life*), and trying not to let the downward suck of that grief—and it *was* grief—draw me in. I couldn't look directly at that cold crater inside, or at the mute, innocent manuscript in its yellow padded envelope with the publisher's logo. I knew, and I still know, that the book has other flaws, that Anne's verdict was not unfair, that Anne is a good person and a fair reader. (Which she is.) Each time I think I'll go back to it and take another look, another book comes along: first *The Hands-On Life*, then this one you're reading, and now also a new novel manuscript with which I am in love, and on which I am working with the techniques and overall vision of time and structure *Eldorado, Iowa* taught me. In my head I still feel Sarah and the other characters walking around their little town, tugging like children at the edges of my attention: *What about us? You haven't forgotten us?* No. No, I haven't. And I won't.

My students' eyes widen when I tell them this story: *you, our teacher, also get rejected?* Yep. *You did all that work for nothing?* Not for nothing, since nothing is ever wasted when you're a writer. Experiences and emotions silt down through the soil of your self into the vast, never-fully plumbed aquifer of words and images and impulses inside you. Each draft gets you closer to the next one, even if you are starting from scratch each time. Even if you (meaning me) write 150 pages of a novel and then your workshop leader and workshop-mates suggest to you (accurately) that your main character is too passive to carry the novel and that another character might actually be the *real* protagonist and then you rewrite all 150 pages with a new character at great and excited speed only to be interrupted by the image of a woman walking through the grass that becomes a whole *new* novel that takes over your imagination and your life, nothing has been wasted there. Rejection and revision are facts of life that experience and time can never remove but definitely do soften and teach you about. Being told *no, thanks anyway* by an editor is not and will never be easy, but it doesn't flatten me anymore. Despite what our youth-obsessed culture would like us to believe, being more than forty years old, with a fully functioning frontal lobe, is a good thing.[3]

But, as you can see, this long ramshackle process of writerly growth takes *time*. It takes many thousands of pages—drafts, notebooks, journals—written over many days, and it takes multiple drafts of revisions of most of those pages. It takes the ability to feel and accept emotions without being derailed by them. And, as Sonya Chung says, it takes a very high tolerance for uncertainty. If you do not have this tolerance for uncertainty, and you do not hang in there with this process, for however long it takes, usually without much (or any) signs of external reward, you will probably not be able to live as a writer. Because, if you are a writer, this is just how things are. Underneath it all, though, is another truth: *not* writing is worse. The uncertainty, the work, the fretting, the neurosis—these are, to borrow a phrase from James Baldwin, the price of the ticket to doing this thing we love to do. Victorian art critic John Ruskin observed, "The highest reward for a man's toil is not what he gets for it, but what he becomes by it." I think he's right about that.

Just about every novelist I know has a story like mine. It's very common to write much more than you publish, and to write multiple novel manuscripts (whole ones or pieces) before you write one that sells. Patrick Hicks, author of the novel *The Commandant of Lubizec* (2014), the story collection *The Collector of Names* (2015), and three poetry collections, *Adoptable* (2014), *This London* (2010), and *Finding the Gossamer* (2009), puts it this way: "When people congratulate me on publishing my first novel, I smile, say thank you, and think about the five novels I wrote *before* this one. This is novel number six. It's just the first one that got *published*."

The reality is this: love of writing, not the desire to be published, has got to be your reason for writing. Doing this work will challenge and excite you and reinvent your inner life and break your heart. You have to love walking the path—you can't set out with your eyes fixed only on the goal up ahead, not on the ground under your feet, the daily work, since that goal might never happen. You will see writing published that breaks every Law of Good Writing I've described, and then some. You will see your work rejected for reasons and in ways that seem to you misguided at best or unprofessional at worst. But you have to keep at it. My former teacher, the late, great Barry Hannah, said, "But I'll say now, having been close or on the deathbed briefly, THAT WE'RE ALL BUSY DYING. Cut the crap, get to work. But not unless you love writing deeply, feel the angst of vacuum without it." Ultimately, if you are making art, you have to be content with a certain degree of mystery.

The literary industry moves so fast and there is so much advice out there that I'm not going to try to offer more than a few guidelines and realities as I understand them and as I discuss them with my students. Betsy Lerner's *The Forest for the Trees: An Editor's Advice to Writers* and the editor and agent interviews in *Poets and Writers* Magazine (archived online) are also wonderful resources.

# Literary journals

Most of us still get started as writers by submitting our work to literary journals and accumulating a list of publications. I published my first short story in 2001, back when "submitting" still meant sending the journal a copy of your manuscript with a self-addressed stamped envelope for their reply. A few years later, I became editor of the *Carolina Quarterly*, based at the University of North Carolina (where I was a graduate student) and saw for myself that most literary journals get stacks and stacks of submissions per month. For us, that number was around a hundred submissions (fiction, poetry, and nonfiction) per month. Now most journals accept submissions through online portals like Submittable, which means that at times they may be dealing with a hundred submissions per *week*. Even when the journal charges reading fees, attaching a file and hitting *submit* is easier (at least for writers) than printing pages, stuffing an envelope, and paying postage.

The odds are long, particularly as online submissions swell the numbers of manuscripts editors are considering and many journals still remain staffed by un- or underpaid volunteers, but you can help yourself in basic ways. Most importantly, be sure your work is as good as you can make it before you send it out. Then research the journals to which you're sending work to be sure your writing and their mission are aligned; carpet-bombing everything with *journal* in the title, even if you've never read a single issue, is a classic rookie mistake. So is failing to read and abide by the journal's guidelines, which will tell you what kinds of work they do and don't publish, when they are accepting submissions, and whether they have policies against simultaneous submissions (a story sent to more than one journal at a time.) You can find lists of journals or places to send work through online sources like *Poets & Writers* Magazine, Submittable (an online submission portal), and the Community of Literary Magazines and Presses (clmp.org). A good library, particularly at a college or university, will also have literary journals to browse in its Current Periodicals section.

Here's a basic template for a submission letter to accompany your manuscript to a literary journal:

**Your Address**
**Your City, State ZIP**
**Your Phone Number**
**Your Email Address**

DATE

Editor's Name
*Journal Title*
Address Line 1
City, State ZIP

Dear Mr./ Ms. Editor's Last Name,

Enclosed/attached, please find my story/essay "Title" (1234 words), which I am submitting to *Journal Title*. It is not a simultaneous submission.

Thank you for your consideration.

Sincerely,
Your Name

And you're out. You've performed a basic, courteous professional handshake, and now your manuscript will speak for itself. As with Chekhov's police report, clarity and brevity signal professionalism (and respect for an editor's very scarce time), especially if you have also spelled the editor's name correctly. (Hey, some people don't). If you aren't sure of the editor's gender identity, "Dear A.B. Carter" is fine.

Wait, you may protest. Shouldn't I be giving them a summary of my story? No, unless you're writing a query or submission letter for a book manuscript (discussed later); in that case, the purpose of that summary is to help the editor or agent see how your book compares to similar ones and, therefore, how she might pitch it to colleagues. But a story needs to be let alone to do its work on its own terms. Furthermore, the temptation to summarize your story bleeds too easily into the temptation, which *must* be resisted, to "sell" it to the editor or tell her how to read it ("This is a moving tale of two robots in love, which will warm your readers' hearts … "). But what about a biographical note, you might ask—do I need a bio? Here, too, limit yourself to what is professionally relevant. If you don't have publications or experience connected to the work you're submitting ("This story is informed by my experiences as a community organizer on the South Side of Chicago"), then you don't really need a biography. If you do, it should be short and focus on your publications: "Currently, I'm associate professor of English at Southwest Northeast State University. My essays and short fiction have appeared or are forthcoming in *Journal A*, *Literary Magazine B*, and *Additional Publication C*." (Do yourself a favor and avoid the misplaced modifier: "Currently associate professor of English at Southwest Northeast State University, my essays and short fiction have appeared in … .," since no publication, as far as I know, has ever earned a job on its own, much less tenure.) Don't apologize for flaws that are probably larger in your own head than the editor's: "I know that at my age I should have written more, but … ." (Every writing path is different, so, as Billie Holiday advised, don't explain.) Don't talk about your weekend hobbies or your family. Don't puff yourself up, ("I am complex and intuitive, just like my stories," "My work is not for the average, mindless reader." This signals the *opposite* of the specialness you feel yourself to possess.) And did I mention the biography should be short?

Let's see: what else should you avoid? I don't like "I look forward to hearing from you" in any context, since it can come off as peremptory: "hey, you lazy so-and-so, get cracking!" Don't ask the editor for feedback: "if you have any thoughts on how my manuscript might be improved, I'd appreciate … ." I understand the temptation when you're facing what can feel like the blank wall of the literary world. But please, please, please resist; as editor Betsy Lerner writes, "you are seeking professional, not educational, services."[4] If for some reason you're lucky enough to get a "positive rejection" ("we liked this but aren't taking it, and here's why") or any other form of personal communication from an editor, please thank her for her time if you can, because that's a pretty big deal.

# Book publishing

Again, this is a very basic introduction to the process, as more exhaustive and up-to-date resources are appearing (particularly online) all the time, and I've seen this process shift even in the last decade. These days, the typical path is for a writer to polish her work as much as she can, then (perhaps using her existing publications and other credentials in addition to the quality of the work) acquire a literary agent. Often, that agent will work with the writer to polish the work further. Then, using their professional networks and their knowledge of who likes projects similar to yours, who is looking for new projects, and other factors, agents will approach editors at different publishing houses on your behalf. If an editor decides to acquire your book, she and the agent (and you) will work out a contract, including an *advance*, or the amount of money paid out directly to you from the publisher when you sign the contract for the sale of your book. As its name indicates, this is literally an "advance" on the amount of money the publisher expects your book to earn, and it's yours to keep. If your book sells well, it will "make back its advance," and then royalties will begin to accumulate on top of that, with some to the publisher and some to you depending on your contract. But if book never earns back its advance, that advance (minus the agent's fee of around 15 percent) may be all you ever earn from it.

A note about the business model of publishing and editorial work—detailed more fully in Jason Epstein's *Book Business*, Robert Gottlieb's *Avid Reader*, Al Silverman's *The Time of Their Lives*, and A. Scott Berg's *Max Perkins: Editor of Genius*—may be helpful here. Publishing isn't and never has been very profitable as most corporations define that term. In fact, it used to be known as a "gentleman's game," since editors and publishers (often well-educated, well-heeled men and women) could afford to keep going for art's sake, because they had other sources of income. The business model of a publishing house rests on a relatively small number of bestselling authors (the John Grishams, Stephen Kings, and Jodi Picoults of the world, and more power to 'em) who bring enough cash into the house to enable its editors to acquire and issue advances to other books that won't sell on that scale. Therefore, like a marine ecosystem, publishing is a vast, intricate food chain resting on the backs of some very big fish. And like most other industries these days, it's subject to pressure from ever-larger conglomerates, the "disruption" (talk about a cliché!) of electronic media, and the thousand natural shocks that twenty-first-century capitalism is heir to. Yet I often hear it said that there are more good books to read, in more channels (in print and online) than there have ever been, and there's some truth to that. Writers get understandably frustrated with the industry, but it's also useful for us to remember that like college professors (ahem), most editors and agents aren't getting rich; they're doing this work because they love books and there's nowhere else they'd rather be.

With that encouraging fact in mind, let's talk about how the book submission process works. Frequently, unless you're publishing short stories in big-name journals like *The New Yorker*, editors or agents will be willing to take on a story collection only with the promise of a novel to follow. If you're submitting a novel, be aware that many agents and editors will prefer to see only part of the manuscript to begin with, and your manuscript should be complete as you begin the submission process. Book-length nonfiction, by contrast, can sometimes be sold on the basis of a proposal (a detailed summary and outline of the book), without a complete manuscript. Different fields like children's books and young-adult will have their own rules, too. The agent's or editor's/publisher's guidelines will specify what to send and when. Please don't ignore them.

Like a literary journal submission, a submission to an agent or editor needs a query letter, or cover letter, introducing yourself and your book to the editor or agent and asking if she would like to read it. Again, your goal is not to write jacket copy ("moving," "thrilling") but to introduce yourself professionally and give the recipient a sense of the following things: why you're approaching him or her (indicating familiarity with that press or agency's clients, and thus an ability to compare yourself accurately with others), what happens in the book; whether the book is finished and polished or is likely to be so in the near future; what other books it's like (this will help her envision where your book might fit in the market and how she might pitch your book to other colleagues and to booksellers); and—this emerges between the lines, and in your biography—whether you will be honest, pleasant, professional, and promising to work with as a writer. This letter will shape this editor's or agent's first impressions of you, and therefore you want it to have a sense of your voice, but you don't want it to feel gushy, rambly, or puffy and, above all, not cutesy, spacey, crazy, or self-involved. Strive for professionalism, clarity, and brevity, or, as Chekhov put it, a tone that's "sober, rapid, unaffected." Here is a model I suggest (all details, of course, are placeholders):

Your Address<br>
Your City, State ZIP<br>
Your Phone Number<br>
Your Email Address

DATE

Editor's/Agent's Name
Editor's Press/Agent's Agency Name
Address Line 1
City, State ZIP

Dear Mr./ Ms. Editor's/Agent's Last Name,

As a longtime reader of Your Author/Client, I am writing at the recommendation of Your Other Author/Client to ask if you might be interested in reading my novel *Title* (complete at # of pages and # of words.) Reminiscent of Other Author's Novel 1, Another Author's Novel 2, and A Third Author's Novel 3, *Title* is a brief descriptor that shows your grounds for comparison with those three. It is not a simultaneous submission.

Title tells the story of Character, a character who finds herself abruptly doing interesting things on the eve of a Major World Event Readers Will Recognize. In the company of Sidekick, described in this dependent clause, and Third Character, described in this additional clause, Character does something actual while doing, on the inside, something psychological indicating an arc of development. Avoiding fake-suspenseful questions, I will write a sentence here that indicates, generally, how things turn out. If your guidelines permit it, I will add another sentence here indicating that I have attached/included an excerpt of *Title*, which, by giving you only this relatively brief summary here, I will signal my professionalism by allowing to speak for itself.

I'm currently associate professor of English at Southwest Northeast State University in Town, State. My short fiction and creative nonfiction have appeared in *Journal, Another Journal, Still Another Journal*, and *Journal Number Four*. In Year, I won this award, and I have been a fellow at this writing program, arts center, or writers' conference.

Thank you for your consideration.

Sincerely,
Your Name

There are a million models of how to write cover letters out there, and requirements may vary by genre, but for a literary fiction or nonfiction manuscript, something like this—short, polite, professional—is the way to go. Don't lie or exaggerate connections, which can be easily checked. As with Chekhov's police report, you're letting the details (and your manuscript) speak for you. Given the very wide range of self-promotional strategies that cross editors' and agents' desks every day, rife with anxiety, arrogance, naiveté, and straight-up unprofessionalism, a little understatement will stand out in a good way.

Format your query letter according to the standards of manuscript professionalism described in Chapter 5 (although single-spacing is OK) and be sure your email address is a professional one, not "ChildhoodNickname123@ yahoo.com." Once you've sent your query, resist, at all costs, the temptation to write and ask, "Did you get my letter?" unless you haven't heard anything for at least six months. Do whatever it takes—like the four-year-olds with the marshmallows in that delayed-gratification study I'll talk about in a little while—to avoid hounding the person. But resist. And wait.

# Self-publishing

If you are paying someone to print in book form a manuscript you submit to them, you are being *self-published*. You are not being "published" in the sense that the mainstream literary industry and creative-writing professors like me use that word: an editor and the press or journal with which she's associated have used their professional judgment to decide to enter into a contract with you to bring your work into print, without payment to them from you. Neither are you being "published by an independent press" or "indie-published," since an independent press, technically, is one like Graywolf, Sarabande, or W. W. Norton (to name only three) that are nonprofits and/ or not owned by a larger corporation. While self-publishing may make you money more immediately than the long process of writing and submitting your work through conventional channels (and, unlike that process, it *will* ensure a printed book in your hands), self-publishing can artistically stigmatize a writer, since self-publishing platforms usually just print what you send them, with little or no editorial supervision. Yes, there are stories of self-publishing success, and yes, this is a complex topic, but in the world of literary fiction, poetry, and nonfiction in which I operate, self-publishing will usually shut the door between you and any reputable publishing house. Self-published books don't get distributed through the channels that build reputations in the sense that most writers think of doing so; for instance, your self-published book won't be reviewed in the *New York Times*. If you're considering self-publishing, be clear what your goals and motivations are and what taking this course of action will mean for you professionally. If you just love writing, want your family and friends to have access to your work, and don't need to build an academic or literary reputation, self-publishing can be a good choice. But in the eyes of agents, editors, and (in my world) tenure review committees, self-publishing is not the same as *being published* and does not carry the same professional value.

# Writing community and literary citizenship

As you can probably gather from my discussion of advances and big fish above, the book world, like the rest of society, is a place where voting with one's dollars can make an impact—and casting such votes responsibly is an act of good *literary citizenship*. Buying from a local independent bookstore is obviously good for local economies, but it's good for authors in ways you might not see; as Betsy Lerner describes in *The Forest for the Trees*, independent booksellers play vital roles in the publishing ecosystem, since they can support the success of authors and books that get lost in (ahem) the Amazon jungle, and an author's sales figures (including her record at independent bookstores) can determine where, and for how much, her next contract is coming from. Purchasing books through a small press's online portal is a good way to support them directly (they get more of the money that way). But book buying, while important, isn't the only way to be a good literary citizen. Attending readings and book signings, subscribing to literary journals and magazines, being a good workshop participant, observing good professional manners—all these are forms of literary citizenship too.

With citizenship comes *community*, which all writers need in some form but which can be hard to find if you aren't enrolled in a writing class. First, it helps to see yourself as part of a professional community, and, therefore, to read professional periodicals to keep up with its conversations. I regularly read *The New Yorker*, *London Review of Books*, *New York Review of Books*, *Orion*, *Harper's*, *Poets & Writers*, *The Writer's Chronicle* (the official publication of AWP, of which more below), *The American Scholar*, Lithub.com, *Tin House*, *Granta*, *The Common*, *The Sewanee Review*, and *The Paris Review*, and I subscribe to almost all of these. *Poets & Writers* is an excellent source for news and perspectives on the writing life, including interviews with authors, editors, and agents and an updated calendar of submission opportunities (which you can also find through Submishmash, the online newsletter of Submittable.com). Other journals on my radar are *Ploughshares*, *Georgia Review*, *Southern Review*, *A Public Space*, *Creative Nonfiction*, *Guernica*, *New England Review*, *Kenyon Review*, *Ecotone*, *One Story*, *Image*, *Lapham's Quarterly*, *Five Points* ... And on and on. I like to read email newsletters from a variety of sources, including Atlas Obscura (weird, cool stories that may spark some writing), Publishers Lunch (news from within the industry), and presses like Persephone, New York Review Books, and Farrar Straus Giroux. You may also consider joining the Association of Writers and Writing Programs (AWP), which sponsors a massive annual conference with craft discussions, professional advice, and a book fair where you can browse and learn about literally hundreds of journals and presses. In recent years, AWP has also developed a Writer to Writer Mentorship Program, for which application and participation are free, and through which one of my adult writing-class participants has acquired a mentor.

Writers' conferences—basically summer camps for writers, to which you submit a manuscript-in-progress to apply—are great portals into the wider literary world. Amid craft lectures, and opportunities to connect with editors, agents, and other writers, the heart of the conference experience is a workshop including about a dozen other writers and led by a faculty member who discusses each workshop member's manuscript in turn. I have been and continue to go to conferences like the Bread Loaf/Orion Environmental Writers Conference, the Bread Loaf Writers' Conference, Sewanee Writers Conference, and Tin House Summer Writers Workshop. (Information about these and other conferences is available online and in *Poets & Writers* and *The Writer's Chronicle*; many offer scholarships.) For me, a writers' conference is like a shot of oxygen after one school year and before the start of the next. I come away with fresh perspectives on craft, good feedback from my workshop, and new professional and personal connections, particularly with my fellow workshop members.

Community writing classes—like the ones I teach in our town, or those offered through literary centers like The Loft in Minneapolis—can also be a good way to build your skills and connect with other writers. Many colleges allow non-degree-seeking students to take classes, paying a certain fee per credit hour. Author readings and events at literary centers, libraries, or bookstores can help you connect with like-minded people; so can online writing groups or methods like Google hangouts to workshop with faraway friends. Getting together with a local group to workshop your pieces and/ or work your way through the exercises in a textbook like *Tell It Slant*, one of the other writing guides listed in my appendix, or (I humbly suggest) this one can also be useful.

# MFA: Yes or no?

If you're searching for a more formal writing community, you may be pondering whether to get your MFA, or Master of Fine Arts degree, in writing. Focused on intensive workshops, MFA programs typically last about two years. Traditional programs require you to attend and take classes at a campus location; low-residency programs pair students with mentors with whom they confer online or by telephone, then meet in person during a few intensive short-term sessions (like a week or ten days on site) each year. Some MFA programs also offer teaching assistantships, which means their graduates emerge with degrees in hand, teaching experience, and (ideally) manuscripts ready to send out into the world. A great benefit of MFA programs is the network of professional connections they offer, as classmates move out into the world and stay in touch with one another and "I have an MFA from X University" may open some doors a little wider.

But at the risk of seeming overly blunt, I must dispel a myth still lurking in some corners of the MFA world: that an MFA will automatically qualify you for a college teaching job. Full disclosure: I have a PhD in nineteenth-century British literature but no MFA, and I applied for my tenure-track job in 2004 (which was advertised as combining literature and creative writing) with that degree, with critical and creative publications, and with teaching experience. As higher education contracts and the number of positions (tenure-track and fixed-term or adjunct) shrinks along with it, most departments will hire the highest level of qualification and teaching experience and the most versatility they can get, and since there will usually be PhDs in any applicant pool, they'll often make that choice. Even though an MFA (with publications) may be sufficient for a creative-writing-only teaching position at a large school, many schools (including mine) need a new hire to teach several kinds of courses in literature, composition, *and* creative writing, and, thus, they need a candidate to show a wider intellectual and pedagogical range than the average MFA program prepares many graduates to offer. A PhD in creative writing, unfortunately, may be subject to the same realities.

Again, this is a complex topic, and, in the words of Jane Austen, I'm a "partial, prejudiced, and ignorant historian," but I'm convinced you should only get an MFA these days if (a) you're obsessed with writing and want to read a lot, write a lot, talk a lot about writing, and try to get better at all of these, (b) you are already at least trying to write on your own, without a formal academic structure (this is *crucial*); (c) you're prepared to pay the tuition, take on debt, or find a program that will support you without debt; (d) you understand that an MFA will not automatically result in a teaching job, or in publication, or in finding an agent, (e) you're determined to avail yourself fully of your program's teaching and professional opportunities, polishing your professional identity in a responsible way, (f) you've chosen the right program for yourself out of the many available, and (g) you understand what your goals for the experience are. I know a retired teacher in her sixties who got an MFA just for the love of writing, because it was something she'd always wanted to do. I know a man in his thirties, a husband and father of three, who completed a low-residency MFA and published his first book after a decade of taking local writing classes, working full-time, and writing steadily on his own. Both these people are awesome. What's even more awesome is that they knew themselves and their goals and chose the MFA path on purpose, out of a devotion to writing that would be there whether they were in an MFA program or not.

# How to be a good literary citizen: Some codes of conduct

Buy books, subscribe to magazines, attend readings, sign up for classes. Vote for your values and for a continued space for literary work with your money, your time, and your attention—or, as we say at my church, "your prayers, your presence, your gifts, and your service." What you can't buy, get from your local library or interlibrary loan, and say thanks to the librarians.

Be polite and professional, and get your ego in check. For real. The literary world is amazingly small, and reputations—good and bad—spread in surprising ways. When the noise of your own emotions is loud in your head, it's hard to remember that everyone else doesn't feel the same way. But they don't. Nor does anyone owe you a reading of the work you've just finished and which, therefore, is currently dazzling you with its brilliance. (Give it a week and see how you feel about it then.) For this reason, **never** write to professors or authors out of the blue and ask them to read your work, just as you wouldn't ask an accountant to do your taxes or a carpenter to build your deck unless you had contracted with and agreed to pay them. Yes, we do the work of writing and teaching because we love it. (So, ideally, do accountants and carpenters, yet people often assume that anyone in an artistic field must be "doing it for love" and therefore—an interesting *therefore*—money is out of the equation.) But as writers and teachers, we're busy all year round with our own teaching, mentoring, and advising, other professional duties (like manuscript review for presses and journals), committee and administrative work, family and personal lives, and, oh yeah, our own writing. Every bit of this continues in some form through the summer, which is when teaching writers double down on our own writing, trying to get words on the page in advance of the coming academic year. We simply don't have time for other requests.

Along those lines, don't impose yourself on journals, editors, or literary agencies whose mission obviously doesn't align with your work. Read the guidelines, and read the journal or the press's other books. The Internet makes it easy to carpet-bomb unsuspecting editors with your only-tangentially related or outright inappropriate-for-them submissions. Don't send your young adult novel about space cowboys to a small press that's known for its translations of literary fiction by international women authors. That wastes everybody's time.

Don't focus on developing a professional "brand" at the expense of your writing itself. This is more important the earlier on your writing path you are. More than once I've talked with would-be writers for whom the mental noise of *get an agent! Get a website! Pitch my book!* was so loud that they had trouble hearing their own prose still needed work. Overinvestment in the professional side of things is easy, because it feels like something you are "really doing to help yourself" and, unlike writing, feels like a definable task you can control. But put your energy in the wrong place and you'll end up with zealously maintained social media accounts you use primarily to complain about why your novel isn't getting picked up—perhaps because you are spending more time on the Internet than writing.

While we're on that subject, let's talk a little about writers and the Internet, about which my basic (and typically Luddite)[5] belief is this: too many folks, particularly those looking to break in, use "building an online presence" as a substitute for writing, with the result that they have no meaningful writing to use the Internet to promote. But it's not their fault entirely: as publishing, like many other industries, contracts, writers are being asked to do much of the publicity work that used to be handled by employees of the publishing house itself. Most everyone agrees that once you have a book coming out, or if you have online articles to link to, a website is good for you. Regarding social media, opinions vary—there are editors and agents who break out in hives when a writer says, "I don't really do that stuff," and others who accept it. But the general consensus is that for a writer's social media and/or Internet presence to be successful, it must be authentic. If you don't like that stuff, don't do it.

# Time: A writer's friend (Part 2)

In the 1960s, a Stanford psychologist named Walter Mischel conducted a famous experiment known as the "marshmallow test," in which small children were told they could either have one treat (like a marshmallow) immediately or two treats if they waited just a few minutes more. Children who could hold out for both marshmallows rather than grabbing at one showed a higher development of "executive function," predictive of future academic, physical, and professional health, than those who could not.[6] They could manipulate their own perceptions to calm themselves down and stay the course. Successful children put their hands over their eyes (so they wouldn't see the tempting marshmallow in front of them), turned their backs on the marshmallow (for the same reason), hummed or sang a song to themselves, or even said aloud, "I do not want the marshmallow!" "The key, it turns out," writes journalist Maria Konnikova,

> is learning to mentally 'cool' what Mischel calls the 'hot' aspects of your environment: the things that pull you away from your goal ... by putting the object at an imaginary distance (a photograph isn't a treat), or by re-framing it (picturing marshmallows as clouds not candy). Focussing on a completely unrelated experience can also work, as can any technique that successfully switches your attention.[7]

If we can learn to calm ourselves down and look beyond the noise of the present moment to fix our eyes on the long-term goal or larger reality, or jump the tracks of the habitual thought that always takes us to the same dismal place, we can decide how to *respond*—not just *react*—to that moment in ways that move us toward our goals in ways that respect reality and other people.

In my own ongoing effort to "cool" the distractions, realities, emotions, moods, impulses, and imperatives (genuine and false) of the writing life from inside my own mind, I've learned that *time* is a great friend—perhaps the greatest friend, aside from sympathetic readers, that writers can have. With age (and a maturing frontal lobe) come emotional and psychological maturity, along with more life experiences and more nuanced understanding of ourselves, the world, and other people. Often age reduces our fears of others' opinions while increasing our empathy and concern for others. Age can also increase our desires to be honest with ourselves and others, on and off the page (as Robert Cohen discusses in his essay "Going to the Tigers"). Unlike racehorses, fashion models, or gymnasts, writers get better with time, developing, in the words of my Introduction, something to say and a voice to say it in. I've also made peace with the realities of a writing life that I used to struggle with much more: solitude, focus, anxiety-and-mood management, health management, inevitable setbacks. Many of us find as we get older that maturity brings resilience, helping us, however painfully, rebound from events that would have flattened our twentysomething selves—the death of a parent, illness, financial trouble or job loss, struggles with faith, the end of a marriage, and, yes, rejection of our work. We get older and our shoulders get wider, carrying loads that can sometimes be heavier than we dreamed. We learn to hearken to that small voice inside: *keep going. You've been in hard times before. And look—you're still here.*

As a thousand writing-residency advertisements (and the realities of our lives) testify, writers also need time in a very literal way: uninterrupted hours in which to ponder, dream, reflect, and put words on the page. As I discussed earlier in this book, this requires a balance of difficult things: taking ourselves seriously enough to ask ourselves and others for this space, holding ourselves to the high standards in which we believe, and rearranging the realities of our lives and our available energies to create the circumstances under which we can write.

Yet literary-industrial imperatives as preached or perceived these days—not to mention the publish-or-perish dynamics of my own academic world—can push writers toward a speeded-up mode of thinking, working, and self-development that isn't necessarily best for our writing itself. Typically, the Internet has made all of this worse. I don't blame writers for this state of things, and I don't blame editors or agents, not really. I know how it is to want it, and to be one of the people crowding into the big rooms at AWP's annual conference, where editors and agents offer advice. Hard work and at least a little self-promotion are basic to a writing life. But the time has come for all of us to say to ourselves, and each other, *Enough. Is all this professional chatter and online-focused anxiety really helping me grow into a better writer, and do the work I am capable of doing? Am I really ready for this "career" step I am pushing myself, or being pushed, to take? Is all this stuff—really—good for books, and good for people?*

If you're an historically minded corporate- and Internet-skeptic like me, you might find grim comfort in the fact that the literary industry's always been like this in one form or another. And so, perhaps, has the world. William Wordsworth complained in his *Preface* to the second edition of *Lyrical Ballads* that people needed the honesty of good writing more than ever, because

> a multitude of causes unknown to former times are now acting with a combined force to blunt the discriminating powers of the mind, and unfitting it for all voluntary exertion to reduce it to a state of almost savage torpor. The most effective of these causes are the great national events which are daily taking place, and the increasing accumulation of men in cities, where the uniformity of their occupations produces a craving for extraordinary incident which the rapid communication of intelligence hourly gratifies.[8]

As descriptive of our own time as this sounds, it was published in 1800. The struggles of professional writers also echo from that time to ours. William Godwin—husband of the feminist writer Mary Wollstonecraft, who died soon after the birth of their daughter, Mary Shelley—wrote in his *Memoir* of Wollstonecraft (1798) that, kind of like Facebook, writing lots of small assignments for money can dissipate one's energy for larger creations: "The writer is accustomed to see his performances answer the mere mercantile purpose of the day, and confounded with those of persons to whom he is secretly conscious of a superiority ... He is touched with the torpedo of mediocrity."[9] George Gissing's 1891 novel *New Grub Street* tracks a mix of idealists and cutthroats through the literary world of late-Victorian London as they battle the same issues of time, money, jealousy, publicity, and motivation writers recognize today. In 1936, the legendary editor Maxwell Perkins rejected a manuscript by indicating, among other things, that the writer had tried to rush his project too much: "We ought to tell you at the outset that we think you are both creating and writing too hurriedly, which is not fair to your unquestionable talent," Perkins writes. "Your novel seems to us to show the consequences of this in both conception and execution .... We think that your rapid writing for income has got you into an attitude toward your material that you will have to lose."[10] Perkins closes by recommending the writer apply for a Guggenheim Fellowship to give him the necessity of time and remove the pressure of money. Crucially, though, he also counsels patience: "If you write another novel, we believe that you ought to put it away, once you have finished it, until the impulse that led you through it has gone quite cold; then take it up again and see if you are ready yourself to accept it."[11]

Like the commercial-fiction markets of the 1930s, the Internet's creating habits of haste and early exposure in writers that come from what feels like necessity but aren't ultimately good for us or our art. Essayist Meghan Daum described this in a 2014 interview: "There is a sense of looking over your shoulder as you're writing and expressing an opinion, because you have this anticipatory anxiety about what the comments are going to say or who's going to tweet something or call you out on Twitter." Writing has begun to feel "sort of at once disposable and nonbiodegradable," like Styrofoam. "[Y]ou don't need it after five minutes," she says, "and yet it's never going to go away. It will never break down and be reabsorbed. And that's a very different kind of experience as a writer" than in pre-Internet days.[12] Editor and agent Betsy Lerner, in *The Forest For the Trees: An Editor's Advice to Writers*, believes professional pressures are similarly stunting writers' voices and self-perceptions:

> I believe that a certain amount of innocence is as critical to the creative development of an artist as amniotic fluid is to a fetus. There is a necessary gestation period during which a writer should protect his work, because the minute he sends it out, or joins a writing group, or enrolls in an MFA program, he engages the part of himself that is focused on the result more than the work. For some people it's a quickening experience that can heighten their ambition and potentially improve their work. For others it's disastrous.[13]

I've been that writer, too, like Lin-Manuel Miranda's version of Alexander Hamilton, "writing like I'm running out of time"[14] and hustling for another publication credit, the next rung on the academic ladder, the next brick in the wall of the writerly identity I think I need to build. But now, on the threshold of early-mid-forties and full professorship, I'm beginning to think it's time to let myself ease up a little. Stop looking over my shoulder. Bring what I know from my kitchen into writing: let it cook, and enjoy it mindfully. Stop opening the oven door before the timer goes off to see whether the bread is finished. Once it does come out, let it cool before you cut it or you'll squish the crumb. Stop hustling through drafts and shortchanging your own projects. Give them the time they need. Give yourself time to geek out, read, and just enjoy words—the reason why you're doing this work in the first place. And remember: there's a reality beyond your own head, and, in some bracing ways, you are not unique. "I can't accept the idea of 'our nervous age,'" wrote Chekhov in 1895, "because people have been nervous in all ages. Anyone who is afraid of being nervous should turn himself into a sturgeon or a smelt. A sturgeon can make a fool or a blackguard of himself once and only once, by getting caught on a hook. After that he goes into soups and pies."[15]

Of course, all this takes me back into the self-analytical processes that are basic to writing and to life. Be willing to be alone with your work for a while, and to work by yourself. Otherwise you're like a child making crafts, desperate for approval, toting each new macaroni collage to your mom before the glue is dry: *Look what I did!* We are indeed driven by our need to know what we've made has meaning—to send that draft immediately to a friend or post it online somewhere. But this is still a need for approval and external validation that keeps you from learning to develop these qualities in yourself. Be patient; don't leap too soon. Sit on your hands and don't look at the marshmallow. This obviously goes for showing work to peers and editors and agents. Give it some time. Be fair to it, and to yourself.

You have to find ways to calm yourself down, manage your own relationship to time and others' expectations—family, friends, the imaginary voice that insists *They* are all getting Twitter accounts/agents/publishing deals and you're not. Hang in there and strike the balance between responsibility to Them and to yourself. Walk your path, which only you can walk in the way that is right for you. "Do the work. Keep the faith. Be true blue," advised Cheryl Strayed in her famous "Dear Sugar" advice column. "Your book has a birthday. You don't know what it is yet."[16] Ultimately writing your book your way and giving it the time it needs is your decision, your prerogative, your necessity, and—however real and difficult the ups and downs—your joy.

# Grading and Revision Criteria and Grading Philosophy (For Academic Writers)

*These are included on my syllabi, as discussed in Chapter 4, to help students in critical/literary writing courses set revision priorities. I reproduce them here in hopes they'll help students bridge the gap between critical and creative writing. Please don't reproduce them (or any of the other diagrams in this text) without permission and without crediting this book. Thanks.*

During revision, focus on the following criteria, one at a time (listed in order of importance, from most (1) to least (10)), and be sure you are fulfilling one before you move down to the next. Always try to "cover" as many levels in each paper as you can, but prioritize the most important levels of the list. With each paper assignment, you will be expected to work at more of these levels simultaneously; this will get easier, especially since we will address each of them in class. Save this list beyond this course, too; these are the general expectations for college writing. (I wrote the first version of this in graduate school and have revised it over the years as work with students, colleagues, and my own teachers have taught me even more.)

1 Doing what **the assignment** really asks for. Refer back to the original assignment throughout your writing process (and ask your professor if needed) so you understand what you're really supposed to be doing.

2 **Thinking critically and analytically** and **demonstrating some intellectual ambition**, not just summarizing or regurgitating the text or lecture. Your reader should be able to feel a real mind—and

hear a real voice—at work when she reads your paper, which should represent you as a lively thinker considering an issue in depth. Good papers make readers feel "taught" as they read, and even make them feel eager to read the paper again. And they actually have something substantial to say. No amount of "elegant"/pseudointellectual language can conceal a deficit of content.

3 **Organizing** the paper logically. Your reader should be able to follow your chain of reasoning, just like we'd be able to follow you if you were telling us a story, and not feel jerked around between out-of-order ideas. You may need to rearrange paragraphs or fill in gaps with new paragraphs to address this issue.

4 Setting forth a **thesis sentence** that makes a distinct claim, conveys the focus and content of the paper, and includes a "so what?" element. I define the "so what" element as an answer to the question "why is this important?" or "how does it connect to a larger context or purpose?" A thesis sentence needs to say not only THAT something exists but WHY it exists, telling us something we might not necessarily "get" on our own. One of my former students refers to the thesis as a "spoiler alert for your paper—it gives you the 'answer' to what you're supposed to believe right up front."

> For instance, an unsatisfactory thesis sentence for a paper analyzing the movie "The Godfather" is "*'The Godfather' uses images of confined spaces and dim lighting*." (Well, we can see that already just by looking at the film.) A satisfactory thesis sentence says, "*'The Godfather' uses images of confined, dimly lit spaces to emphasize the social exclusiveness and moral darkness of the Corleone family, which eventually bring about its decline*." The first thesis sentence lists qualities of the film but doesn't say what their larger purpose is. The second thesis sentence takes the extra step to do so, giving us an analysis of the film (and going on to prove it) we might not have thought of on our own.

A thesis sentence is your whole paper in capsule form. Test yourself during the revision process by putting your thesis sentence on a blank sheet of paper and giving it to someone else to read. Ask her, "based on this sentence, what do you expect to read about in my paper?" If she doesn't mention a major aspect of the paper you've already written, revise the thesis to mention that aspect in addition to the others. Remember that a sentence can be long yet still effective if it's mechanically correct.

5  Framing each **paragraph** with clear **topic and concluding sentences**, each of which relates back to the thesis, and making the information in each paragraph feel like it goes together. Each paragraph needs a topic sentence that signals what role that paragraph will have in the overall argument (what information readers can expect to get from it) and a concluding sentence that restates or "wraps up" that paragraph's main ideas (what they are supposed to have gotten from the paragraph they've just read). A paragraph's topic sentence does the same thing for a paragraph that a thesis sentence does for a whole paper.

6  Using accurate, specific, and correctly cited **evidence** to support the paper's claims, including quotations and analysis from the text and outside (secondary) sources when appropriate.

7  Making good **transitions** between sentences and paragraphs, which good topic and concluding sentences can really help to create.

8  Writing clear, effective and pleasantly varied **sentences**.

9  Using correct **grammar** and choosing the right words—not the almost-right ones or the $50 ones.

10  **Spelling and punctuating** correctly as part of a paper's overall professional finish (including correct and readable formatting).

## Grades and Comments

The grading and revision list above will guide you and me in commenting on work in progress, and it will guide me in grading. Think of a grade as a measure of how many levels of the list your papers successfully handle at once. The lower the grade, the more fundamental—the lower on the list—problems with the writing start to show up. An A-range paper shows skill in all the levels of writing that the list represents, managing them smoothly and simultaneously. (In athletic terms, this is a paper with agility, strength, *and* speed.) A B-range paper may manage only up to, say, level 5 or 6 before problems start to appear. (Pretty strong, but needs to work on speed.) A C-range paper may run into problems at level 4 or below. (Needs some basic training in all three areas.) While this isn't an exact formula, it's a good representation of the way teachers think about grading. The good news is this: writers, like athletes, can—and do—get stronger with practice. On each draft—graded and ungraded—you get back from me, you'll see comments in the margins (responding to specific issues in the paper's text) and a longer comment at the end that summarizes the paper's major strengths and weaknesses and gives you suggestions of what to work on next. Read them carefully! And by the way, I don't believe in red ink. Ask me why in class. ☺

# Notes

## Introduction

1. Miriam Balmuth, "Female Education in 16th and 17th Century England: Influences, Attitudes, and Trends." *Canadian Woman Studies* 9:3 and 4 (1988): 17–20. cws.journals.yorku.ca/index.php/cws/article/viewFile/11719/10802.

2. July 31, 1763; from James Boswell, *Boswell's Life of Johnson: Vol. I: The Life (1709–1765)*. Ed. George Birkbeck Hill (Oxford: Clarendon Press, 1934), 463.

3. Virginia Woolf, *A Room of One's Own* (1929; New York: Harcourt Brace Jovanovich, n.d.), 50–51.

4. Ibid., 38.

5. Zora Neale Hurston, *Folklore, Memoirs, and Other Writings* (New York: Library of America, 1995), 717.

6. Ibid., 4.

7. Anne Lamott, *Bird by Bird: Some Instructions on Writing and Life* (New York: Pantheon, 1994), 27.

8. Hurston, *Folklore, Memoirs, and Other Writings*, 829.

9. Zora Neale Hurston, *Their Eyes Were Watching God* (1937; New York: HarperPerennial, 2013), 14.

10. Adrienne Rich, "Claiming an Education." In *On Lies, Secrets, and Silence: Selected Prose 1966–1978* (New York: W. W. Norton and Co., 1979), 233–234.

11. Ibid., 234.

12. Tammy Lytal and Richard R. Russell, "Some of Us Do It Anyway: An Interview with Harry Crews." In *Getting Naked with Harry Crews: Interviews*, ed. Erik Bledsoe (Gainesville: University Press of Florida, 1999), 286.

13. Maryanne Wolf, *Proust and the Squid: The Story and Science of the Reading Brain* (New York: HarperPerennial, 2007), 22.

14. Sonya Chung, "What We Teach When We Teach Writers: On the Quantifiable and the Uncertain." *The Millions*, October 29, 2010 (http://www.themillions.com/2010/10/what-we-teach-when-we-teach-writers-on-the-quantifiable-and-the-uncertain.html).

15. Laura Ingalls Wilder, *Pioneer Girl: The Annotated Autobiography*. Ed. Pamela Smith Hill (Pierre: South Dakota Historical Society Press, 2014).

# Chapter 1

1. Wordsworth, *The Prelude: 1799, 1805, 1850*. Ed. Jonathan Wordsworth, M. H. Abrams, and Stephen Gill (New York: W. W. Norton and Co., 1979), 432. (Book Eleventh, lines 269–271.)
2. See also Wendell Berry, "Faustian Economics." *Harper's* (May 2008): 35–42.
3. Matthew Crawford, *The World Beyond Your Head: On Becoming an Individual in an Age of Distraction* (New York: Farrar Straus Giroux, 2015), ix.
4. Ibid., 175.
5. Ibid., 241.
6. Paul Kingsnorth, *Confessions of a Recovering Environmentalist and Other Essays* (Minneapolis: Graywolf Press, 2017), 127–128.
7. Kristin Kimball, *The Dirty Life: A Memoir of Farming, Food, and Love* (New York: Scribner, 2010), 158.
8. Ibid., 5.
9. Henry David Thoreau, *The Journal 1837–1861*. Ed. Damion Searls (New York: New York Review Books, 2009), 21.
10. Larry Brown, *On Fire: A Personal Account of Life and Death and Choices* (Chapel Hill, NC: Algonquin Books, 1994), 167.
11. Crawford, *The World Beyond Your Head*, 51.
12. Alice McDermott, "Only Connect." *The Sewanee Review* 125:2 (Spring 2017): 442.
13. Wordsworth, "Lines Written Above Tintern Abbey," lines 65–66. In William Wordsworth and Samuel Taylor Coleridge, *Lyrical Ballads* (1798), ed. W. J. B. Owen (Oxford: Oxford University Press, 1969).
14. Wordsworth, *The Prelude* (1805), 430–432, lines 208–216.
15. Ibid., 430, lines 223–226.
16. Wordsworth, *The Prelude* (1850), Book First, lines 398–400, 51.
17. Ibid., Book Twelfth, lines 317–335, 437.
18. Wordsworth, "Ode: Intimations of Immortality from Recollections of Early Childhood," lines 4–5. In *William Wordsworth: A Critical Edition of the Major Works*, ed. Stephen Gill (Oxford: Oxford University Press, 1984), 297.
19. Flannery O'Connor, *Mystery and Manners: Occasional Prose*. Sel. and ed. by Sally and Robert Fitzgerald (New York: Farrar Straus Giroux, 1969), 84.

20. Mary McCarthy, "A Guide to Exiles, Expatriates, and Internal Emigres," *New York Review of Books,* March 9, 1972 (http://www.nybooks.com/articles/1972/03/09/a-guide-to-exiles-expatriates-and-internal-emigres/).
21. Wordsworth, "The Tables Turned," lines 15–16, *Lyrical Ballads,* 105.
22. Henry David Thoreau, *A Week on the Concord and Merrimack Rivers; Walden; or Life in the Woods; The Maine Woods, Cape Cod* (New York: Library of America, 1985), 646.
23. Neil deGrasse Tyson, *Astrophysics for People in a Hurry* (New York: W. W. Norton and Co., 2017), 13.
24. Lamott, *Bird by Bird,* 22.
25. Ibid., 28.
26. This hearkens to a haunting image in Terry Tempest Williams' memoir *When Women Were Birds* (New York: Sarah Crichton Books, 2012)— shelves of her late mother's journals in a closet, all blank. Jean's story has a happy ending; see the Exercises at the end of this chapter.
27. Jay Griffiths, "Artifice vs. Pastoral." *Orion* March/April 2009: 20–27, 26.
28. Ibid., 26.
29. Dean Young, *The Art of Recklessness: Poetry as Assertive Force and Contradiction* (Minneapolis: Graywolf Press, 2010), 11–12.
30. Ibid.
31. Wolf, *Proust and the Squid,* 87.
32. J. R. R. Tolkien, *The Hobbit* (1937; New York: Houghton Mifflin Harcourt, 2012), 199.
33. Ibid., 171.
34. Ibid., 198.
35. Helen Macdonald, *H Is for Hawk* (New York: Grove Atlantic, 2014), 4.
36. Ibid., 5.
37. Wordsworth, *Lyrical Ballads,* 157.
38. Thoreau, *The Journal 1837–1861,* 259.
39. George Orwell, *Essays.* Sel. and intro. by John Carey (New York: Knopf/Everyman's Library, 2002), 1085.
40. Terry McDonell, *The Accidental Life: An Editor's Notes on Writing and Writers* (New York: Vintage, 2017), 16.
41. Anton Chekhov, *Letters of Anton Chekhov.* Trans. Michael Henry Heim and Simon Karlinsky (New York: Harper & Row, 1973), 332.
42. Marie Howe, *The Kingdom of Ordinary Time* (New York: W. W. Norton & Co., 2008), 62.
43. Mollie Panter-Downes, *London War Notes* (London: Persephone Books, 2014), 113–114.
44. Orwell, *Essays,* 967.
45. Susan Bell, *The Artful Edit* (New York: W. W. Norton and Co., 2007), 52.
46. Ibid.

47. Ibid.

48. Ibid., 54.

49. Ibid., 55.

50. Ibid., 54–55.

51. See my discussion of this in my book. *The Hands-On Life* (Wipf and Stock/ Cascade, 2018).

52. Ralph Waldo Emerson, *Selected Journals 1841–1877* (New York: Library of America, 2010), 896–897.

53. Thoreau, *The Journal 1837–1861*, 15.

54. McDonell, *The Accidental Life*, 32.

55. Joan Didion, *We Tell Ourselves Stories in Order to Live: Collected Nonfiction* (New York: A.A. Knopf/Everyman's Library, 2006), 104.

56. Orwell, *Essays*, 1084.

57. I learned about Perec and "exhausting the place" from Stephen Tuttle's paper "Beyond the Postcard: Teaching Students to Exhaust a Place" on the "Innocents Abroad: Essaying with Study Abroad Students" panel at the Association of Writers and Writing Programs (AWP) annual conference in Washington, D.C., on February 9, 2017.

58. Georges Perec, *An Attempt at Exhausting a Place in Paris*. Trans. Marc Lowenthal (Cambridge, MA: Wakefield Press, 2010), 13.

59. Ibid., 5–6.

60. Ibid., 20.

61. Ibid., 22–23.

62. Ibid., 34.

63. Henry David Thoreau, *Selections from the Journals*. Ed. Walter Harding (New York: Dover Publications, 1995), 2.

# Chapter 2

1. Susan Orlean, "The Walking Alive." *The New Yorker*, May 20, 2013 (http:// www.newyorker.com/magazine/2013/05/20/the-walking-alive).

2. Wolf, *Proust and the Squid*, 121.

3. Alberto Manguel, *A History of Reading* (New York: Viking Penguin, 1996), 37.

4. Wolf, *Proust and the Squid*, 14.

5. I'd like to acknowledge a debt to novelist Anthony Doerr, whose craft lecture on defamiliarization at the Tin House Summer Writers Workshop 2008 introduced me to Victor Shklovsky and Graham Rawlinson's scrambled letter and started me thinking about neuroscience for writers. I first saw a version of this illustration on a handout created and distributed by Anthony Doerr during his lecture at the Tin House

Summer Writers Workshop 2008. This illustration was recreated for me by Michael Bartels from that model. The proverb about habits appears in Doerr's lecture too.

6. Graham Rawlinson, "Rebadailty." *New Scientist*, May 29, 1999 (https://www.newscientist.com/letter/mg16221887-600-reibadailty/).

7. Jason Santa Maria, "How We Read." *A List Apart*, August 5, 2014 (https://alistapart.com/article/how-we-read).

8. Ibid.

9. Victor Shklovsky, "Art as Technique." *Russian Formalist Criticism: Four Essays* (2nd ed.). Translated and with an introduction by Lee T. Lemon and Marion J. Reis (Lincoln: University of Nebraska Press, 2012), 11.

10. Ibid.

11. Ibid.

12. Ibid.

13. Ibid.

14. Ibid., 12.

15. Peter Mendelsund, *What We See When We Read* (New York: Vintage, 2014), 322.

16. Ibid., 334–335.

17. Ibid., 302.

18. Ibid., 302–303.

19. Wolf, *Proust and the Squid,* 16.

20. Charles Dickens, *Our Mutual Friend* (1865). Ed. and Intro. Adrian Poole (New York: Penguin Books, 1997), 14.

21. Elaine Scarry, *Dreaming by the Book* (New York: Farrar Straus Giroux, 1999), 7.

22. Ibid., 15.

23. Ibid., 25.

24. Ibid., 16.

25. Ibid., 141.

26. Alain De Botton, *The Art of Travel* (New York: Vintage, 2002), 225–226.

27. Ibid., 222.

28. Patrick Colm Hogan, "Literary Universals." In *Introduction to Cognitive Cultural Studies*, ed. Lisa Zunshine (Baltimore: The Johns Hopkins University Press, 2010), 40.

29. Ibid., 56.

30. Ibid., 46.

31. Ibid.

32. Ibid., 57.

33. Wolf, *Proust and the Squid.* 39, 50.

34. Joseph Campbell, *The Hero with a Thousand Faces* (1949; Princeton: Princeton University Press, 1973), 3.

35. Transmitting meaning into the future can be a surprisingly complex problem. Consider the case of Yucca Mountain, Nevada, a proposed nuclear waste disposal site: since the meaning of signs and symbols can be lost over millennia even as radioactivity remains, how would we transmit to people 10,000 years from now that there is dangerous material in this spot, and even that the sign carrying that information is a warning deliberately placed there for their use? The field of "nuclear semiotics" has arisen in response. One proposed solution is a "priesthood" of people who will transmit the knowledge from living mind to living mind into the future, riding the waves of inevitable cultural and linguistic change. See Orrin Pilkey and Linda Pilkey-Jarvis, *Useless Arithmetic: Why Environmental Scientists Can't Predict the Future* (New York: Columbia University Press, 2009).

36. Wolf, *Proust and the Squid,* 47–48.

37. Ibid., 48.

38. Manguel, *A History of Reading,* 27–28.

39. Ibid., 45.

40. Ibid., 44.

41. Ian Mortimer, *Millennium: From Religion to Revolution: How Civilization Has Changed over a Thousand Years* (New York: Pegasus Books, 2016), 344–345.

42. Orwell, *Essays,* 957.

43. Ibid., 964.

44. I have written about Shklovsky, Arendt, defamiliarization, and cliché at greater length in my book *The Hands-On Life: How to Wake Yourself Up and Save the World* (Wipf and Stock/Cascade, 2018.)

45. Orwell, *Essays,* 1082–1083.

46. I'm thinking of Saul Steinberg's "Untitled" from his book *All in Line* (1945), which appears on the cover of Adam Phillips's *In Writing: Essays on Literature* (London: Hamish Hamilton, 2017).

47. Ibid., 963.

48. Ibid., 965–966.

49. Hannah Arendt, *Eichmann in Jerusalem: A Report on the Banality of Evil* (1963; New York: Penguin, 2006), 49.

50. Of course, 'twas ever thus: see, for instance, Dwight Macdonald's takedown of the late 1950s "bestseller" landscape in "By Cozzens Possessed" (1958), reprinted in *Masscult and Midcult: Essays Against the American Grain* (New York: New York Review Books, 2011). A sample: "It is difficult for American reviewers to resist a long, ambitious novel; they are betrayed by the American admiration of size and scope, also by the American sense of good fellowship; they find it hard to say to the author, after all his work: 'Sorry, but it's terrible'" (130). See also Jonathan Mahler's article "James Patterson Inc." in the *New York Times,* January 20, 2010.

51. James Patterson, *Suzanne's Diary for Nicholas* (New York: Little Brown and Co., 2001), 3.
52. John Gardner, *The Art of Fiction: Notes on Craft for Young Writers* (1984; New York: Vintage, 1991), 31.
53. Frantz Fanon, *The Wretched of the Earth* (1961; New York: Grove Press, 2004), 131.
54. Wolf, *Proust and the Squid,* 102.
55. Ibid.
56. Ibid., 107.
57. Ibid., 103–104.
58. Wolf, *Proust and the Squid,* 129.
59. John Lanchester, "You Are the Product." *London Review of Books* 39:16 (August 17, 2017): 10.
60. Ibid.
61. Clips of Murrow on "See It Now" are available on YouTube; I recommend his short editorial on McCarthyism from March 1954, which begins and ends with quotations from Shakespeare's *Julius Caesar*: "we will not be driven by fear into an age of unreason," Murrow says. https://www.youtube.com/watch?v=vEvEmkMNYHY.
62. Tim Wu, *The Attention Merchants: The Epic Scramble to Get Inside Our Heads* (New York: Knopf, 2016), 142.
63. Ibid.
64. Ibid.
65. Ibid., 142–143.
66. Said during a reading at University Club of St. Paul, Minnesota, August 8, 2017.
67. See Matthew Crawford's discussion of the "monetization of attention" in his Introduction to *The World Beyond Your Head.*

# Chapter 3

1. Lamott, *Bird by Bird,* 21.
2. Ibid., 23.
3. I heard Hempel make this remark about her process at the Bread Loaf Writers Conference in 2010.
4. Ibid., 16.
5. Ibid., 17.
6. Ibid., 18.
7. O'Connor, *Mystery and Manners,* 67.

8. Charles McGrath, "Lorrie Moore's New Book Is a Reminder and a Departure." *New York Times*, February 17, 2014 (https://www.nytimes.com/2014/02/18/ books/lorrie-moores-new-book-is-a-reminder-and-a-departure.html).

9. Kevin Larimer, "The Emotional Realist Talks to Ghosts." *Poets & Writers*, March/April 2017: 40–41.

10. McDermott, "Only Connect," 436.

11. Ibid., 439.

12. Ibid.

13. Ibid., 442.

14. O'Connor, *Mystery and Manners,* 198.

15. Nick Flynn and Shirley McPhillips, *A Note Slipped Under the Door: Teaching from Poems We Love* (Portland, Maine: Stenhouse Publishers, 2000), 15.

16. Weldon, *Eldorado, Iowa* (unpublished manuscript), 1.

17. Lamott, *Bird by Bird,* 18.

18. Benjamin Percy, *Thrill Me: Essays on Fiction* (Minneapolis: Graywolf Press, 2016), 146.

19. Maxwell Perkins, *Editor to Author: The Letters of Maxwell E. Perkins*, ed. by John Hall Wheelock (New York: Scribner, 1987), 107.

20. Toni Morrison, *Beloved* (1987; New York: Vintage, 2004), 18–20.

21. Ibid., 86.

22. Anton Chekhov. *Letters in the Short Story, the Drama, and Other Literary Topics.* Sel. and ed. by Louis S. Friedland (New York: Dover Publications, 1966), 154.

23. Milan Kundera, *The Unbearable Lightness of Being* (1984; New York: HarperCollins, 2004), 251.

24. V. S. Pritchett, *Chekhov: A Spirit Set Free* (New York: Vintage, 1989), 84–85.

25. Chekhov, *Letters of Anton Chekhov,* 180.

26. Ibid.

27. Robert Graves, *Goodbye to All That* (1929; New York: Doubleday, 1957), 95–96.

28. Norman Lewis, *Naples' 44: An Intelligence Officer in the Italian Labyrinth* (1978; London: Eland Books, 2002), 24–25.

29. Harriet Jacobs [as Linda Brent]. *Incidents in the Life of a Slave Girl.* Edited and with an introduction by Nell Irvin Painter (1861; New York: Penguin Books, 2000), 135.

30. Ibid., 137.

31. Thoreau, *The Journal,* 608.

32. O'Connor, *Mystery and Manners*, 59.

33. Elizabeth Bowen, *The Last September* (1929; New York: Knopf, 1952), 7.

34. Elizabeth Bowen, *The Collected Stories of Elizabeth Bowen* (New York: Ecco Press, 1989), 231.
35. Ibid.
36. James Baldwin, *Collected Essays* (New York: Library of America, 1998), 63.
37. James Baldwin, *Early Novels and Stories* (New York: Library of America, 1998), 831.
38. Didion, *We Tell Ourselves Stories in Order to Live,* 173.
39. Joan Didion, *South and West: From a Notebook* (New York: Knopf, 2017), 119.
40. Didion, *We Tell Ourselves Stories in Order to Live,* 173.
41. Peter Matthiessen, *The Snow Leopard* (1978; New York: Penguin, 2008), 88.
42. Ibid., 169–170.
43. Howard Mittelmark and Sandra Newman, *How Not to Write a Novel: 200 Classic Mistakes and How to Avoid Them—A Misstep-by-Misstep Guide* (New York: HarperCollins, 2008), 57.
44. Flannery O'Connor, *The Habit of Being: Letters of Flannery O'Connor*, ed. Sally and Robert Fitzgerald (New York: Farrar Straus Giroux, 1979), 83.
45. Although Lynda Carter's official website indicates that her mother was Mexican-American.
46. Jules Renard, *Nature Tales* (1909; New York: New York Review Books, 2011), 88.
47. Ibid., 70.
48. Lesley Nneka Arimah, *What It Means When a Man Falls from the Sky* (New York: Riverhead Books, 2017), 93.
49. Ibid., 93–94.
50. Mohsin Hamid, *Exit West* (New York: Riverhead Books, 2017), 8–9.
51. Colson Whitehead, *The Underground Railroad* (New York: Doubleday, 2016), 69.
52. John Lanchester, "When Did You Get Hooked?" *London Review of Books* 35:7 (April 11, 2013): 20–22.
53. Margaret Atwood, "Voyage to the Otherworld: A New Eulogy for Ray Bradbury." *The Paris Review*, online, August 15, 2017 (https://www.theparisreview.org/blog/2017/08/15/voyage-to-the-otherworld-a-new-eulogy-for-ray-bradbury).
54. Percy, *Thrill Me,* 69.
55. Chekhov, *Letters,* 299.

# Chapter 4

1. George Saunders, "What Writers Really Do When They Write." *The Guardian*, March 4, 2017 (https://www.theguardian.com/books/2017/mar/04/what-writers-really-do-when-they-write).

2.  See Madeleine L'Engle, *Herself: Reflections on a Writing Life*, compiled by Carole Chase (Colorado Springs: Shaw Books, 2001).

3.  Laura Ingalls Wilder, *The Little House Books*. Ed. Caroline Fraser (New York: Library of America, 2012), 276.

4.  Ibid.

5.  Ibid., 278.

6.  Ibid., 341.

7.  Wikipedia entry for Olive Beaupré Miller.

8.  Olive Beaupre Miller, *My Book House: Volume 4: The Treasure Chest* (Chicago: The Bookhouse for Children Publishers, 1920), 223.

9.  Ibid., 235–236.

10. Elizabeth Bowen, *Collected Impressions* (New York: Knopf, 1950), 267–268.

11. Kory Stamper, *Word by Word: The Secret Life of Dictionaries* (New York: Penguin Random House, 2017), 15. Also described in Lewis Lapham's "The World in Time" podcast, episode 7, June 20, 2017.

12. Robert Macfarlane, *Landmarks* (London: Hamish Hamilton, 2015), 3.

13. Ibid.

14. See Amy Webb, "We Post Nothing About Our Daughter Online." *Slate*, September 4, 2013 (http://www.slate.com/articles/technology/data_mine_1/2013/09/facebook_privacy_and_kids_don_t_post_photos_of_your_kids_online.html).

15. Please see my discussion of this in my book. *The Hands-On Life: How to Wake Yourself Up and Save The World* (Wipf and Stock/Cascade, 2018).

16. Macfarlane, *Landmarks,* 22.

17. Conger Beasley Jr., "Cowbelly." In *Home Ground: Language for an American Landscape*, ed. Barry Lopez and Debra Gwartney (San Antonio: Trinity University Press, 2006), 89–90.

18. Thanks to *Home Ground,* we can remember that the place a spring comes up from the earth is called an *eye.*

19. Macfarlane, *Landmarks,* 23.

20. Ibid.

21. Ibid.

22. http://www.wnyc.org/story/on-the-media-2017-07-07

23. See also Amy Weldon, "Belle Dame Sans Merci: On Angela Carter." *Los Angeles Review of Books*, September 20, 2013 (https://lareviewofbooks.org/article/belle-dame-sans-merci-on-angela-carter/).

24. Angela Carter, *The Bloody Chamber* (1979; New York: Penguin, 1993), 89.

25. Claire Vaye Watkins, *Gold Fame Citrus* (New York: Riverhead Books, 2015), 17.

26. Charlotte Wood, *The Natural Way of Things* (New York: Europa Editions, 2016), 194–195.

27. Chekhov, *Letters,* 62.

28. Daphne Athas, *Gram-O-Rama: Breaking the Rules*. Edited and with a foreword by Marianne Gingher (Lincoln, NE: iUniverse, 2007), 6.

29. Jonathan Lethem, *Motherless Brooklyn* (New York: Vintage, 2000), 6.

30. Jon Day, *Cyclogeography: Journeys of a London Bicycle Courier* (London: Notting Hill, 2015), 6–7.

31. Jonathan Miles, "Lonesome Horses." *The New York Times*, August 18, 2002 (http://www.nytimes.com/2002/08/18/books/lonesome-horses.html).

32. Mittelmark and Newman, *How Not to Write a Novel*, 122–123.

33. James Wood, *How Fiction Works* (New York: Farrar Straus Giroux, 2008), 24.

34. Dante Alighieri, *Inferno*. Trans. John Ciardi (New York: Signet Classics, 2001), 59.

35. Ibid., 90.

36. Ibid., 252.

37. Rosemary Hill, "One's Self-Washed Drawers." *London Review of Books* 39:13 (June 29, 2017): 3–5.

38. Robert Hughes, *Rome: A Cultural, Visual, and Personal History* (New York: Alfred A. Knopf, 2011), 264–265.

39. Richard Jefferies, "The Acorn-Gatherer." In *The Oxford Book of Essays*, ed. John Gross (Oxford: Oxford University Press, 2002), 305.

40. Eudora Welty, *The Collected Stories of Eudora Welty* (New York: Harcourt Brace Jovanovich, 1980), 288.

41. Claudia Roth Pierpont, *Passionate Minds: Women Rewriting the World* (New York: Alfred A. Knopf, 2000), 166.

42. Welty, *Collected Stories*, 289.

43. Andrea Camilleri, *Rounding the Mark*. Trans. Stephen Sartarelli (New York: Penguin Books, 2006), 1.

44. Chinua Achebe, *Things Fall Apart* (1959; New York: Anchor Books, 1994), 171.

45. Hurston, *Folklore, Memoirs, and Other Writings*, 561.

46. Ibid., 743.

47. Wayne Flynt, *Keeping the Faith: Ordinary People, Extraordinary Lives* (Tuscaloosa: University of Alabama Press, 2011), 393.

48. Robert Darnton, "Remembering Bob Silvers." *New York Review of Books*, online, April 26, 2017 (http://www.nybooks.com/daily/2017/03/21/remembering-bob-silvers/#darnton).

49. Renata Adler, *Speedboat* (1976; New York: New York Review Books, 2013), 10.

50. Mittelmark and Newman, *How Not to Write a Novel*, 126–127.

51. Robert Cohen, "Going to the Tigers: Notes on Middle Style." *The Believer*, February 2010 (http://www.believermag.com/issues/201002/?read=article _cohen).

# Chapter 5

1. Liz Lerman and John Borstel, *Liz Lerman's Critical Response Process: A Method for Getting Useful Feedback on Anything You Make, from Dance to Dessert* (Takoma Park, MD: Liz Lerman Dance Exchange, 2003), 7.
2. Ibid., 19.
3. Ibid., 20.
4. Ibid.
5. Ibid., 22.
6. Ibid., 24–25.
7. Gerald Clarke, "P.G. Wodehouse: The Art of Fiction No. 60." *The Paris Review* 64 (Winter 1975) (https://www.theparisreview.org/interviews/3773/p-g-wodehouse-the-art-of-fiction-no-60-p-g-wodehouse).
8. Wood, *How Fiction Works*, 5.
9. Katherine Anne Porter, *The Old Order* (New York: Harcourt Brace Jovanovich, 1972), 70.
10. Wood, *How Fiction Works*, 11.
11. Amy Weldon, "A Miniature Handbook for New Woman Activists." In *Fracture: Essays, Poems, and Stories on Fracking in America* (North Liberty, IA: Ice Cube, 2016), 38–48.
12. Wilder, *Pioneer Girl*, 3.
13. Ibid.
14. Wood, *How Fiction Works*, 11.
15. Ibid.
16. Missy Elliot, "Go to the Floor." In *Under Construction* (The Goldmind, Inc/Elektra Records, 2002).

# Chapter 6

1. I told a shorter version of this story in *The Hands-On Life* as well.
2. Chung, "What We Teach When We Teach Writers."
3. If you're interested in this, check out BLOOM (http://bloom-site.com), a site devoted to celebrating writers who publish their first books after forty, and to which I have been pleased to contribute articles and interviews in the past.
4. Betsy Lerner, *The Forest for the Trees: An Editor's Advice to Writers* (New York: Riverhead Books, 2000), 149.

5.  Knowing its historical origins, I don't mind the label; see Richard Byrne's essay "A Nod to Ned Ludd." *The Baffler* No. 23, August 2013 (https://thebaffler.com/salvos/a-nod-to-ned-ludd.)

6.  Maria Konnikova, "The Struggles of a Psychologist Studying Self-Control." *The New Yorker,* online, October 9, 2014 (http://www.newyorker.com/science/maria-konnikova/struggles-psychologist-studying-self-control).

7.  Ibid.

8.  Wordsworth, *Lyrical Ballads,* 159–160.

9.  William Godwin, *Memoirs of the Author of a Vindication of the Rights of Woman.* Ed. Pamela Clemit and Gina Luria Walker (1798; Ontario: Broadview Press, 2001), 69.

10. Perkins, *Editor to Author,* 107–108.

11. Ibid.

12. Genevieve Smith, "Meghan Daum on Writing What Nobody Will Say." *The Cut,* November 21, 2014 (https://www.thecut.com/2014/11/meghan-daum-on-writing-what-nobody-will-say.html).

13. Lerner, *The Forest for the Trees,* 47.

14. Lin-Manuel Miranda, "Hamilton: An American Musical," 2015.

15. Chekhov, *Letters,* 270.

16. Strayed, Cheryl, "The Rumpus Advice Column #64: Tiny Beautiful Things." *The Rumpus,* February 10, 2011 (http://therumpus.net/2011/02/dear-sugar-the-rumpus-advice-column-64/).

# Recommended Reading

While this list can't be comprehensive, I hope it'll give you a place to start.

## On Writing, Reading, and Editing:

Athas, Daphne. *Gram-O-Rama: Breaking the Rules*. Lincoln, NE: iUniverse, 2007.

Baxter, Charles. *The Art of Subtext: Beyond Plot*. Minneapolis: Graywolf Press, 2007.
- This is part of Graywolf Press's excellent "The Art Of … " series, in which writers of fiction, creative nonfiction, and poetry discuss particular aspects of their genres. The titles are too numerous to list here but can be viewed at https://www.graywolfpress.org/books/nonfiction/on-writing.

Bell, Susan. *The Artful Edit*. New York: W. W. Norton and Co., 2007.

Hersey, John, ed. *The Writer's Craft*. New York: Alfred A. Knopf, 1974.

Lamott, Anne. *Bird by Bird: Some Instructions on Writing and Life*. New York: Pantheon, 1994.

Lerner, Betsy. *The Forest for the Trees: An Editor's Advice to Writers*. New York: Riverhead Books, 2000.

Lukeman, Noah. *The First Five Pages: A Writer's Guide to Staying Out of the Rejection Pile*. New York: Simon & Schuster, 2000.

Perkins, Maxwell. *Editor to Author: The Letters of Maxwell E. Perkins*. Edited by John Hall Wheelock. New York: Scribner, 1987.

Prose, Francine. *Reading Like a Writer: A Guide for People Who Love Books and for Those Who Want to Write Them*. New York: HarperPerennial, 2007.

Prunty, Wyatt, ed. *Sewanee Writers on Writing*. Baton Rouge: LSU Press, 2000.

Rilke, Rainer Maria. *Letters to a Young Poet*. Translated by M. D. Herter Norton. New York: W. W. Norton and Co., 1962.

*The Writer's Notebook: Craft Essays from Tin House*. Portland, OR: Tin House Books, 2009.

*The Writer's Notebook II: Craft Essays from Tin House*. Portland, OR: Tin House Books, 2010.

Yagoda, Ben. *The Sound on the Page: Great Writers Talk About Style and Voice in Writing*. New York: Harper Perennial, 2005.

# On Fiction:

Barrett, Andrea and Peter Turchi, eds. *A Kite in the Wind: Fiction Writers on Their Craft*. San Antonio, TX: Trinity UP, 2011.

Baxter, Charles. *Burning Down the House: Essays on Fiction*. Minneapolis: Graywolf Press, 1997.

Bernays, Anne and Pamela Painter, eds. *What If? Writing Exercises for Fiction Writers* (2nd edn.). New York: Pearson Longman, 2004.

Burroway, Janet, Elizabeth Stuckey-French, and Ned Stuckey-French. *Writing Fiction* (8th edn.). New York: Pearson Longman, 2011.

Gardner, John. *The Art of Fiction: Notes on Craft for Young Writers*. New York: Vintage Books, 1991 (1984).

Johnston, Bret Anthony, ed. *Naming the World and Other Exercises for the Creative Writer*. New York: Random House, 2007.

LeGuin, Ursula. *Steering the Craft: A 21st-Century Guide to Sailing the Sea of Story*. New York: Mariner Books, 2015.

McCann, Colum. *Letters to a Young Writer*. New York: Random House, 2017.

Mittelmark, Howard and Sandra Newman. *How Not to Write a Novel: 200 Classic Mistakes and How to Avoid Them—A Misstep-by-Misstep Guide*. New York: HarperCollins, 2008.

Percy, Benjamin. *Thrill Me: Essays on Fiction*. Minneapolis: Graywolf Press, 2016.

Wood, James. *How Fiction Works*. New York: Farrar Straus Giroux, 2008.

# On Nonfiction:

Forché, Carolyn and Philip Gerard, eds. *Writing Creative Nonfiction*. Cincinnati, OH: Story Press, 2001.

Gornick, Vivian. *The Situation and the Story: The Art of Personal Narrative*. New York: Farrar Straus Giroux, 2002.

Gutkind, Lee, ed. *Keep It Real: Everything You Need to Know About Researching and Writing Creative Nonfiction*. New York: W. W. Norton and Co., 2008.

Karr, Mary. *The Art of Memoir*. New York: HarperCollins, 2015.

Paola, Suzanne and Brenda Miller, eds. *Tell It Slant: Writing and Shaping Creative Nonfiction*. New York: McGraw Hill, 2004.

- Searching for this title will often yield multiple editions. I suggest choosing the edition with the orange cover and the ISBN number 978-0072512786, which includes an anthology; other editions don't.

Singer, Margot and Nicole Walker. *Bending Genre: Essays on Creative Nonfiction*. London: Bloomsbury, 2013.

Thomas, Abigail. *Thinking About Memoir*. Toronto: Sterling Publishing Co., 2008.

Zinsser, William. *Writing About Your Life*. New York: Marlowe and Co., 2004.

# On Poetry:

Addonizio, Kim. *Ordinary Genius: A Guide for the Poet Within*. New York: W. W. Norton and Co., 2009.

Behn, Robin and Chase Twichell, eds. *The Practice of Poetry: Writing Exercises from Poets Who Teach*. New York: HarperCollins, 1992.

Hugo, Richard. *The Triggering Town: Lectures and Essays on Poetry and Writing*. New York: W. W. Norton and Co., 1982.

Oliver, Mary. *A Poetry Handbook: A Prose Guide to Understanding and Writing Poetry*. New York: Harcourt Brace, 1994.

Stafford, William. *Writing the Australian Crawl: Views on the Writer's Vocation*. Ann Arbor: The University of Michigan Press, 1978.

Thiel, Diane. *Open Roads: Exercises in Writing Poetry*. New York: Pearson Longman, 2005.

Wiman, Christian. *Ambition and Survival: Becoming a Poet*. Port Townsend, WA: Copper Canyon Press, 2007.

# Anthologies:

## Annual Series:

Furman, Laura, ed. *The O. Henry Prize Stories 2017*. New York: Anchor Books, 2017.

- As of this writing, this is the most recent volume in the O. Henry Prize Stories series, which has been published annually since 1919. Like the *Best American* series (see below), the contents are chosen by the editors from among the stories published in a variety of journals and magazines that year.

Hempel, Amy and Kathy Pories, eds. *New Stories from the South: The Year's Best*. Chapel Hill: Algonquin Books, 2010.

- For years, I followed this series, published in an annual volume by Algonquin Books of Chapel Hill. Unfortunately, the 2010 volume cited above seems to be the last in the series – at least for now – but if you can find copies of the series volumes, they are still well worth reading.

Wolitzer, Meg and Heidi Pitlor, eds. *The Best American Short Stories 2017*. New York: Mariner Books, 2017.

- As of this writing, this is the most recent volume in the Best American Short Stories series, which has been published annually for more than two decades now. The *Best American* series also includes annual volumes dedicated to poetry, essays, travel writing, spiritual writing, mystery stories, sports writing, science and nature writing, science fiction and fantasy, and "nonrequired reading." Chosen by the editors from what's been published in literary journals and magazines that year, this will give you a great sense of what's happening now in your chosen genre, and if you are eager to send work out to journals, the lists of publications in the back of those books are a great place to start.

## General Short Fiction:

Angell, Roger. *Nothing but You: Love Stories from The New Yorker*. New York: Random House, 1997.

Ford, Richard, ed. *The Granta Book of the American Short Story*. London: Granta Books, 1993.

Ford, Richard, ed. *The New Granta Book of the American Short Story*. London: Granta Books, 2007.

Ford, Richard, ed. *The Granta Book of the American Long Story*. London: Granta Books, 1998.

Halpern, Daniel. *The Art of the Story: An International Anthology of Contemporary Short Stories*. New York: Penguin, 2000.

Jarrell, Randall, ed. *Randall Jarrell's Book of Stories* (1958). New York: New York Review Books, 2002.

- An "older" anthology reprinted by New York Review Books and worth mentioning because I haven't seen most of these reproduced anywhere else.

Marcus, Ben, ed. *The Anchor Book of New American Short Stories*. New York: Anchor Books, 2004.

Moore, Lorrie, ed. *100 Years of the Best American Short Stories*. New York: Houghton Mifflin, 2015.

*Short Stories from The New Yorker*. New York: Simon & Schuster, 1940.

- A great collection of pre-World War II stories, many not often anthologized elsewhere.

Updike, John. *The Best American Short Stories of the Century*. New York: Houghton Mifflin, 1999.

Woolf, Tobias, ed. *The Vintage Book of Contemporary American Short Stories*. New York: Vintage, 1994.

# General Nonfiction:

D'Agata, John, ed. *The Making of the American Essay*. Minneapolis: Graywolf Press, 2016.

D'Agata, John, ed. *The Lost Origins of the Essay*. Minneapolis: Graywolf Press, 2009.

D'Agata, John, ed. *The Next American Essay*. Minneapolis: Graywolf Press, 2003.

Lopate, Philip, ed. *The Art of the Personal Essay: An Anthology from the Classical Era to the Present*. New York: Doubleday/Anchor Books, 1994.

Oates, Joyce Carol, ed. *The Best American Essays of the Century*. New York: Houghton Mifflin, 2000.

Prentiss, Sean and Joe Wilkins. *The Far Edges of the Fourth Genre: An Anthology of Explorations in Creative Nonfiction*. East Lansing: Michigan State UP, 2014.

Prentiss, Sean and Joe Wilkins. *Environmental and Nature Writing: A Writer's Guide and Anthology*. London: Bloomsbury, 2017.

# General Poetry:

Collins, Billy. *Poetry 180*. New York: Random House, 2003.

Dumanis, Michael and Cate Marvin, eds. *Legitimate Dangers: American Poets of the New Century*. Louisville, KY: Sarabande Books, 2006.

Dungy, Camille, ed. *Black Nature: Four Centuries of African American Nature Poetry*. Athens: University of Georgia Press, 2009.

Dungy, Camille, Matt O'Donnell, and Jeffrey Thomson, eds. *From the Fishhouse: An Anthology of Poems that Sing, Rhyme, Resonate, Syncopate, Alliterate, and Just Plain Sound Great*. New York: Persea Books, 2009.

Fisher-Wirth, Ann and Laura-Gray Street, eds. *The Ecopoetry Anthology*. San Antonio: Trinity University Press, 2013.

Harmon, William. *The Top 500 Poems*. New York: Columbia University Press, 1992.

McClatchy, J. D., ed. *The Vintage Book of Contemporary American Poetry*. New York: Vintage, 1990.

Milosz, Czeslaw, ed. *A Book of Luminous Things: An International Anthology of Poetry*. New York: Mariner Books, 1998.

Strand, Mark and Eavan Boland, eds. *The Making of a Poem: A Norton Anthology of Poetic Forms*. New York: W. W. Norton and Co., 2000.

# Bibliography

Achebe, Chinua. *Things Fall Apart*. 1959. New York: Anchor Books, 1994.

Adler, Renata. *Speedboat*. 1976. New York: New York Review Books, 2013.

Alighieri, Dante. *Inferno*. Translated by John Ciardi. New York: Signet Classics, 2001.

Arendt, Hannah. *Eichmann in Jerusalem: A Report on the Banality of Evil*. 1963. New York: Penguin, 2006.

Arimah, Lesley Nneka. *What It Means When a Man Falls from the Sky*. New York: Riverhead Books, 2017.

Athas, Daphne. *Gram-O-Rama: Breaking the Rules*. Lincoln, NE: iUniverse, 2007.

Atwood, Margaret. "Voyage to the Otherworld: A New Eulogy for Ray Bradbury." *The Paris Review*, online, August 15, 2017: https://www.theparisreview.org/blog/2017/08/15/voyage-to-the-otherworld-a-new-eulogy-for-ray-bradbury.

Baldwin, James. *Collected Essays*. New York: Library of America, 1998.

Baldwin, James. *Early Novels and Stories*. New York: Library of America, 1998.

Balmuth, Miriam. "Female Education in 16th and 17th Century England: Influences, Attitudes, and Trends." *Canadian Woman Studies* 9:3 and 4 (1988): 17–20: cws.journals.yorku.ca/index.php/cws/article/viewFile/11719/10802.

Beasley, Conger, Jr. "Cowbelly." In *Home Ground: Language for an American Landscape*, edited by Barry Lopez and Debra Gwartney. San Antonio: Trinity University Press, 2006: 89–90.

Bell, Susan. *The Artful Edit*. New York: W. W. Norton and Co., 2007.

Boswell, James. *Boswell's Life of Johnson: Vol. I: The Life (1709–1765)*. Edited by George Birkbeck Hill. Oxford: The Clarendon Press, 1934.

Bowen, Elizabeth. *Collected Impressions*. New York: Knopf, 1950.

Bowen, Elizabeth. *The Collected Stories of Elizabeth Bowen*. New York: Ecco Press, 1989.

Bowen, Elizabeth. *The Last September*. 1929. New York: Knopf, 1952.

Brown, Larry. *On Fire: A Personal Account of Life and Death and Choices*. Chapel Hill, NC: Algonquin Books, 1994.

Camilleri, Andrea. *Rounding the Mark*. Translated by Stephen Sartarelli. New York: Penguin Books, 2006.

Campbell, Joseph. *The Hero with a Thousand Faces*. 1949. Princeton: Princeton University Press, 1973.

Carter, Angela. *The Bloody Chamber*. 1979. New York: Penguin, 1993.

Chekhov, Anton. *Letters of Anton Chekhov*. Translated by Michael Henry Heim and Simon Karlinsky. New York: Harper & Row, 1973.

Chekhov, Anton. *Letters in the Short Story, the Drama, and Other Literary Topics*. Selected and edited by Louis S. Friedland. New York: Dover Publications, 1966.

Chung, Sonya. "What We Teach When We Teach Writers: On the Quantifiable and the Uncertain." *The Millions*, October 29, 2010: http://www.themillions .com/2010/10/what-we-teach-when-we-teach-writers-on-the-quantifiable -and-the-uncertain.html.

Clarke, Gerald. "P.G. Wodehouse: The Art of Fiction No. 60." *The Paris Review* 64 (Winter 1975): https://www.theparisreview.org/interviews/3773/p-g -wodehouse-the-art-of-fiction-no-60-p-g-wodehouse.

Cohen, Robert. "Going to the Tigers: Notes on Middle Style." *The Believer*, February 2010: http://www.believermag.com/issues/201002/?read=article _cohen.

Crawford, Matthew. *The World Beyond Your Head: On Becoming an Individual in an Age of Distraction*. New York: Farrar Straus Giroux, 2015.

Darnton, Robert. "Remembering Bob Silvers." *New York Review of Books*, April 26, 2017: http://www.nybooks.com/daily/2017/03/21/remembering-bob -silvers/#darnton.

Day, Jon. *Cyclogeography: Journeys of a London Bicycle Courier*. London: Notting Hill, 2015.

DeBotton, Alain. *The Art of Travel*. New York: Vintage, 2002.

Dickens, Charles. *Our Mutual Friend*. 1865. Edited and introduced by Adrian Poole. New York: Penguin Books, 1997.

Didion, Joan. *South and West: From a Notebook*. New York: Knopf, 2017.

Didion, Joan. *We Tell Ourselves Stories in Order to Live: Collected Nonfiction*. New York: A.A. Knopf/Everyman's Library, 2006.

Emerson, Ralph Waldo. *Selected Journals 1841–1877*. New York: Library of America, 2010.

Fanon, Frantz. *The Wretched of the Earth*. 1961. New York: Grove Press, 2004.

Flynn, Nick and Shirley McPhillips. *A Note Slipped Under the Door: Teaching from Poems We Love*. Portland, Maine: Stenhouse Publishers, 2000.

Flynt, Wayne. *Keeping the Faith: Ordinary People, Extraordinary Lives*. Tuscaloosa: University of Alabama Press, 2011.

Gardner, John. *The Art of Fiction: Notes on Craft for Young Writers*. 1984. New York: Vintage, 1991.

Godwin, William. 1798. *Memoirs of the Author of a Vindication of the Rights of Woman*. Edited by Pamela Clemit and Gina Luria Walker. Ontario: Broadview Press, 2001.

Graves, Robert. *Goodbye to All That*. 1929. New York: Doubleday, 1957.

Griffiths, Jay. "Artifice vs. Pastoral." *Orion*, March/April 2009: 20–27.

Hamid, Mohsin. *Exit West*. New York: Riverhead Books, 2017.

Hill, Rosemary. "One's Self-Washed Drawers." *London Review of Books* 39:13 (June 29, 2017): 3–5.

Hogan, Patrick Colm. "Literary Universals." In *Introduction to Cognitive Cultural Studies*, edited by Lisa Zunshine. Baltimore: The Johns Hopkins University Press, 2010: 37–60.

Howe, Marie. *The Kingdom of Ordinary Time*. New York: W. W. Norton & Co., 2008: 62.

Hughes, Robert. *Rome: A Cultural, Visual, and Personal History*. New York: Alfred A. Knopf, 2011.

Hurston, Zora Neale. *Folklore, Memoirs, and Other Writings*. New York: Library of America, 1995: 559–769.

Hurston, Zora Neale. *Their Eyes Were Watching God*. 1937. New York: HarperCollins, 2013.

Jacobs, Harriet [as Linda Brent]. *Incidents in the Life of a Slave Girl*. 1861. Edited and with an introduction by Nell Irvin Painter. New York: Penguin Books, 2000.

Jefferies, Richard. "The Acorn-Gatherer." 1884. In *The Oxford Book of Essays*, edited by John Gross. Oxford: Oxford University Press, 2002: 305–308.

Kimball, Kristin. *The Dirty Life: A Memoir of Farming, Food, and Love*. New York: Scribner, 2010.

Kingsnorth, Paul. *Confessions of a Recovering Environmentalist and Other Essays*. Minneapolis: Graywolf Press, 2017.

Konnikova, Maria. "The Struggles of a Psychologist Studying Self-Control." *The New Yorker*, online, October 9, 2014: http://www.newyorker.com/science/maria-konnikova/struggles-psychologist-studying-self-control.

Kundera, Milan. *The Unbearable Lightness of Being*. 1984. Translated by Michael Henry Heim. New York: HarperCollins, 2004.

Lamott, Anne. *Bird by Bird: Some Instructions on Writing and Life*. New York: Pantheon, 1994.

Lanchester, John. "When Did You Get Hooked?" *London Review of Books* 35:7 (April 11, 2013): 20–22.

Lanchester, John. "You Are the Product." *London Review of Books* 39:16 (August 17, 2017): 3–10.

Larimer, Kevin. "The Emotional Realist Talks to Ghosts." *Poets & Writers*, March/April 2017: 38–45.

Lerman, Liz and John Borstel. *Liz Lerman's Critical Response Process: A Method for Getting Useful Feedback on Anything You Make, from Dance to Dessert*. Takoma Park, MD: Liz Lerman Dance Exchange, 2003.

Lerner, Betsy. *The Forest for the Trees: An Editor's Advice to Writers*. New York: Riverhead Books, 2000.

Lethem, Jonathan. *Motherless Brooklyn*. New York: Vintage, 2000.

Lewis, Norman. *Naples '44: An Intelligence Officer in the Italian Labyrinth*. 1978. London: Eland Books, 2002.

Lytal, Tammy and Richard R. Russell. "Some of Us Do It Anyway: An Interview with Harry Crews." In *Getting Naked with Harry Crews: Interviews*, edited by Erik Bledsoe. Gainesville: University Press of Florida, 1999: 273–290.

Macdonald, Dwight. *Masscult and Midcult: Essays Against the American Grain*. New York: New York Review Books, 2011.

Macdonald, Helen. *H Is for Hawk*. New York: Grove Atlantic, 2014.

Macfarlane, Robert. *Landmarks*. London: Hamish Hamilton, 2015.

Manguel, Alberto. *A History of Reading*. New York: Viking, 1996.

Matthiessen, Peter. *The Snow Leopard*. 1978. New York: Penguin, 2008.

McCarthy, Mary. "A Guide to Exiles, Expatriates, and Internal Emigres." *New York Review of Books,* March 9, 1972: http://www.nybooks.com/articles/1972/03/09/a-guide-to-exiles-expatriates-and-internal-emigres/.

McDermott, Alice. "Only Connect." *The Sewanee Review* 125:2 (Spring 2017): 420–443.

McDonell, Terry. *The Accidental Life: An Editor's Notes on Writing and Writers*. New York: Vintage, 2017.

McGrath, Charles. "Lorrie Moore's New Book Is a Reminder and a Departure." *New York Times,* February 17, 2014: https://www.nytimes.com/2014/02/18/books/lorrie-moores-new-book-is-a-reminder-and-a-departure.html.

Mendelsund, Peter. *What We See When We Read*. New York: Vintage, 2014.

Miles, Jonathan. "Lonesome Horses." *The New York Times,* August 18, 2002: http://www.nytimes.com/2002/08/18/books/lonesome-horses.html.

Miller, Olive Beaupré. *My Book House: Volume 4: The Treasure Chest*. Chicago: The Bookhouse for Children Publishers, 1920.

Mittelmark, Howard and Sandra Newman. *How Not to Write a Novel: 200 Classic Mistakes and How to Avoid Them—A Misstep-by-Misstep Guide*. New York: HarperCollins, 2008.

Morrison, Toni. *Beloved*. 1987. New York: Vintage, 2004.

Mortimer, Ian. *Millennium: From Religion to Revolution: How Civilization Has Changed over a Thousand Years*. New York: Pegasus Books, 2016.

O'Connor, Flannery. *The Habit of Being: Letters of Flannery O'Connor*. Edited by Sally and Robert Fitzgerald. New York: Farrar Straus Giroux, 1979.

O'Connor, Flannery. *Mystery and Manners: Occasional Prose*. Selected and edited by Sally and Robert Fitzgerald. New York: Farrar Straus Giroux, 1969.

Orlean, Susan. "The Walking Alive." *The New Yorker,* May 20, 2013: http://www.newyorker.com/magazine/2013/05/20/the-walking-alive.

Orwell, George. *Essays*. Selected and introduced by John Carey. New York: Knopf/Everyman's Library, 2002.

Panter-Downes, Mollie. *London War Notes*. London: Persephone Books, 2014.

Patterson, James. *Suzanne's Diary for Nicholas*. New York: Little, Brown and Co., 2001.

Percy, Benjamin. *Thrill Me: Essays on Fiction*. Minneapolis: Graywolf Press, 2016.

Perec, Georges. *An Attempt at Exhausting a Place in Paris*. Translated by Marc Lowenthal. Cambridge, MA: Wakefield Press, 2010.

Perkins, Maxwell. *Editor to Author: The Letters of Maxwell E. Perkins*. Edited by John Hall Wheelock. New York: Scribner, 1987.

Pierpont, Claudia Roth. *Passionate Minds: Women Rewriting the World*. New York: Alfred A. Knopf, 2000.

Pilkey, Orrin and Linda Pilkey-Jarvis. *Useless Arithmetic: Why Environmental Scientists Can't Predict the Future*. New York: Columbia University Press, 2009.

Porter, Katherine Anne. *The Old Order*. New York: Harcourt Brace Jovanovich, 1972.

Pritchett, V. S. *Chekhov: A Spirit Set Free*. New York: Vintage, 1989.

Rawlinson, Graham. "Rebadailty." *New Scientist*, May 29, 1999: https://www .newscientist.com/letter/mg16221887-600-reibadailty/.

Renard, Jules. *Nature Tales*. Translated by Douglas Parmée. New York: New York Review Books, 2011.

Rich, Adrienne. *On Lies, Secrets, and Silence: Selected Prose 1966–1978*. New York: W. W. Norton and Co., 1979.

Santa Maria, Jason. "How We Read." *A List Apart*, August 5, 2014: https:// alistapart.com/article/how-we-read.

Saunders, George. "What Writers Really Do When They Write." *The Guardian*, March 4, 2017: https://www.theguardian.com/books/2017/mar/04/what -writers-really-do-when-they-write.

Scarry, Elaine. *Dreaming by the Book*. New York: Farrar Straus Giroux, 1999.

Shklovsky, Victor. "Art as Technique." In *Russian Formalist Criticism: Four Essays* (2nd edn.). Translated and with an introduction by Lee T. Lemon and Marion J. Reis. Lincoln: University of Nebraska Press, 2012: 3–24.

Smith, Genevieve. "Meghan Daum on Writing What Nobody Will Say." *The Cut*, November 21, 2014: https://www.thecut.com/2014/11/meghan-daum -on-writing-what-nobody-will-say.html.

Stamper, Kory. *Word by Word: The Secret Life of Dictionaries*. New York: Penguin Random House, 2017.

Strayed, Cheryl. "The Rumpus Advice Column #64: Tiny Beautiful Things." *The Rumpus*, February 10, 2011: http://therumpus.net/2011/02/dear-sugar -the-rumpus-advice-column-64/.

Thoreau, Henry David. *The Journal 1837–1861*. Edited by Damion Searles. New York: New York Review Books, 2009.

Thoreau, Henry David. *Selections from the Journals*. Edited by Walter Harding. New York: Dover Publications, 1995.

Thoreau, Henry David. *A Week on the Concord and Merrimack Rivers; Walden; or Life in the Woods; The Maine Woods, Cape Cod*. New York: Library of America, 1985.

Tolkein, J. R. R. *The Hobbit*. 1937. New York: Houghton Mifflin Harcourt, 2012.

Tyson, Neil deGrasse. *Astrophysics for People in a Hurry*. New York: W. W. Norton and Co., 2017.

Watkins, Claire Vaye. *Gold Fame Citrus*. New York: Riverhead Books, 2015.

Webb, Amy. "We Post Nothing About Our Daughter Online." *Slate*, September 4, 2013: http://www.slate.com/articles/technology/data_mine_1/2013/09/facebook_privacy_and_kids_don_t_post_photos_of_your_kids_online.html.

Weldon, Amy. "Belle Dame Sans Merci: On Angela Carter." *Los Angeles Review of Books*, September 20, 2013: https://lareviewofbooks.org/article/belle-dame-sans-merci-on-angela-carter/.

Weldon, Amy. *Eldorado, Iowa*. Unpublished manuscript: 2012.

Weldon, Amy. *The Hands-On Life: How to Wake Yourself Up and Save the World*. Eugene, OR: Wipf and Stock/Cascade Books, 2018.

Weldon, Amy. "A Miniature Handbook for New Woman Activists." In *Fracture: Essays, Poems, and Stories on Fracking in America*, edited by Taylor Brorby and Stefanie Brook Trout. North Liberty, IA: Ice Cube Press, 2016: 38–48.

Welty, Eudora. *The Collected Stories of Eudora Welty*. New York: Harcourt Brace Jovanovich, 1980.

Whitehead, Colson. *The Underground Railroad*. New York: Doubleday, 2016.

Wikipedia. "Olive Beaupré Miller." N.p., n.d: https://en.wikipedia.org/wiki/Olive_Beaupr%C3%A9_Miller.

Wilder, Laura Ingalls. *Little House on the Prairie* (1935). *The Little House Books*. Edited by Caroline Fraser. New York: Library of America, 2012: 269–409.

Wilder, Laura Ingalls. *Pioneer Girl: The Annotated Autobiography*. Edited by Pamela Smith Hill. Pierre: South Dakota Historical Society Press, 2014.

Williams, Terry Tempest. *When Women Were Birds: Fifty-Four Variations on Voice*. New York: Sarah Crichton Books, 2012.

Wolf, Maryanne. *Proust and the Squid: The Story and Science of the Reading Brain*. New York: Harper Perennial, 2007.

Wood, Charlotte. *The Natural Way of Things*. New York: Europa Editions, 2016.

Wood, James. *How Fiction Works*. New York: Farrar Straus Giroux, 2008.

Woolf, Virginia. *A Room of One's Own*. 1929. New York: Harcourt Brace Jovanovich.

Wordsworth, William. *The Oxford Authors: William Wordsworth: A Critical Edition of the Major Works*. Edited by Stephen Gill. Oxford: Oxford University Press, 1984.

Wordsworth, William. *The Prelude: 1799, 1805, 1850*. Edited by Jonathan Wordsworth, M. H. Abrams, and Stephen Gill. New York: W. W. Norton and Co., 1979.

Wordsworth, William and Samuel Taylor Coleridge. *Lyrical Ballads*. 1798. Edited by W. J. B. Owen. Oxford: Oxford University Press, 1969.

Wu, Tim. *The Attention Merchants: The Epic Scramble to Get Inside Our Heads*. New York: Knopf, 2016.

Young, Dean. *The Art of Recklessness: Poetry as Assertive Force and Contradiction*. Minneapolis: Graywolf Press, 2010.

# Index